DO NOT REMOVE
CARDS FROM POCKET

11 - 20 - 85

THE ARTHUR YOUNG
INTERNATIONAL BUSINESS GUIDE

THE ARTHUR YOUNG INTERNATIONAL BUSINESS GUIDE

CHARLES F. VALENTINE

Arthur Young International Management Consulting Group
Washington, D.C.

WILEY

JOHN WILEY & SONS

New York • Chichester • Brisbane • Toronto • Singapore

Library of Congress Cataloging in Publication Data:

Valentine, Charles F.
    The Arthur Young international business guide/Charles F.
Valentine.
    p. cm.
    Bibliography: p.
    1. International business enterprises—Management.
2. International business enterprises—Management—Case
studies.   I. Arthur Young & Company.   II. Title.
HD62.4.V35   1988   658.18—dc19   88-10144
ISBN 0-471-60270-1

Printed in the United States of America

10 9 8 7 6 5 4 3 2 1

CONTENTS

PREFACE

"Black Monday"—October 19, 1987—not only obliterated at least half a trillion dollars in stockholders' wealth but also undermined widespread confidence in the U.S. economy. The reasons for the crash in confidence are as complex as those for the market crash. Economists agree, however, that one primary reason for the loss of investor confidence has been this country's vast foreign trade deficit. During the past ten years, the United States has generally imported far more goods than we have exported, with consequent damage to our economic well-being.

The Arthur Young International Business Guide does not intend to address the overall issue of U.S. foreign trade deficits; still less will it try to solve the problem. Rather, this book concerns itself with the underlying issues. Specifically,

- a small minority of U.S. companies export their products and services, and
- many more companies could succeed overseas if they would only try.

For the past fourteen years, I have advised American businesses on their efforts to do business in the lucrative and constantly growing global marketplace. My clients have entered markets throughout the Caribbean, Latin America, the Middle East, and Asia, often with great success. Generally speaking, I've found that many U.S. companies are in a better position to beat their competitors overseas than management believes possible; however, I've also watched a lamentable number of companies go international for the wrong reasons, without much forethought and sometimes without any preparation whatever. The results are predictably dismal. If only American executives would think more carefully about the new situations they encounter overseas, they might experience less disappointment—and make more money—in countries where consumers are in fact more than eager to buy American-made goods and services.

My intention in writing *The Arthur Young International Business Guide* is to provide an introductory guide to going international for small and medium-sized companies new to exports and the global marketplace. The process is complex. No single book can describe every step and substep in detail appropriate to every single company. Yet this book offers a systematic approach that, if followed closely, can assist your company in meeting the challenge of an international venture. Doing business abroad, despite its complexities, is neither as difficult nor as dangerous as many American corporate officers believe it to be.

The United States now faces a new economic reality. As American business people, we have a choice. We can limit ourselves to our large but mature domestic market, a market in which foreign competitors often beat us on our own turf. Or we can reach out to the huge, growing, often lucrative global marketplace where, if properly prepared, we can play the game and win. Our choice will determine our fate—certainly our fate as business people, and perhaps our fate as a nation as well.

A NOTE REGARDING THE CASE STUDIES

All case studies in this book describe actual incidents that have occurred in actual U.S. companies entering the global marketplace. In some cases, I have referred to the companies by name. In others, however, I have changed the names of the companies or their representatives. But the cases themselves exemplify real business issues and how real companies have dealt with them.

CHARLES F. VALENTINE

Washington, D.C.
June 1988

ACKNOWLEDGMENTS

Like all complex endeavors, the process of writing *The Arthur Young International Business Guide* has benefited from the ideas, insights, and experience of many people. Although the following acknowledgments can't provide sufficient recognition to everyone who has made a contribution, I want at least to thank all those who have helped me in significant ways.

First and foremost, I want to thank my family for their patience and support during all our many years of travel, and for their valuable input into this book. I could not have reached the final goal without their help. Most of all, I want to thank my wife, Jean, who suggested the idea for the book in the first place.

I also owe deep gratitude to my colleagues at Arthur Young. Their expertise has added much to this book; their critical comments, too, have provided valuable insights throughout the tasks of writing and editing. In particular, I would like to thank Ed Bartholomew, Mort Meyerson, Ginger Lew, and John Secondari for their energetic work in clarifying issues in the text and for their support and enthusiasm for the project from start to finish. I also greatly appreciate Dave Tierno's and Ed Bartholomew's reviewing the final manuscript on behalf of Arthur Young's Management Committee.

In addition, I wish to thank the following people (in alphabetical order) for contributions of advice in their areas of expertise: Mike Davidson, corporate strategic management; Sharif Hussein, business interactions in the Middle East; Charles A. McCue, customs issues; Harvey B. Mogenson, issues of corporate tax; Thomas J. O'Brien, selection, placement, and training of expatriate staff; Dimitri A. Plionis, economic analysis, export and investment promotion, and other topics; William H. Pugh, Japan; K. Dunlop Scott, mergers and acquisitions; John Sequeira, Indonesia and Europe; and Charles H. Smith, III, foreign investment and technology transfer. This book has benefited immeasurably from their information and wisdom.

I also want to thank Chieko Fujii, Daniel Lounberg, and Peter Taylor for their help in providing information on a multitude of research issues; and I appreciate Kathy Dalton's help in proofreading the final manuscript.

Many corporate officers have also made important contributions, both in their specific advice on going international and in their comments on the manuscript. I wish I could thank them all by name, for I appreciate their many kinds of help. Special thanks go to Norman St. Clair, who contributed tips for doing business overseas, and to Frank Kelly of Gerber Products Company, who provided excellent case studies and reflections on a wide variety of issues.

Jeff Brown, my editor at John Wiley & Sons, has been the ideal editor: constantly supportive yet ready with specific suggestions, comments, and ideas that have improved the manuscript in many ways. Maryan Malone, managing editor, has been thoughtful and efficient in seeing this book through the production process. And Lorraine Anderson made many insightful changes when she copyedited the manuscript. I am grateful to them for their help.

Finally, I wish to thank Ed Myers for his editorial advice and for his assistance in refining the book.

C. F. V.

INTRODUCTION

Consider for a moment this single fact: *Only 25,000 American companies sell their products and services abroad.*

Now reflect just briefly on the implications of this statistic. Since approximately 16.5 million firms exist in the United States, the percentage that exports is a remarkably small fraction of the total number. What about the millions of other companies? Are their products and services totally unappealing to customers in other countries? Highly improbable. Is marketing American services and goods overseas too much trouble to be worthwhile? Unlikely in an age when easy travel and instantaneous communications make the whole planet (in media theorist Marshall McLuhan's famous phrase) a global village. So why do only a small minority of American firms bother doing business abroad? Why, in fact, do only 250 U.S. companies account for 70 to 80 percent of our exports?

Before we answer these questions, consider a second statistic: *The U.S. trade deficit was $171.2 billion in 1987.*

Most American business people are aware of this dismal situation, and many express justified concern about its effects on the country's economic future. In his best-selling book *Iacocca* (Bantam, 1984), for instance, Chairman Lee Iacocca of Chrysler Corporation sounded the alarm: "Right now, we're in the midst of another major war with Japan. This time it's not a shooting war. . . . The current conflict is a trade war. But because our government refuses to see this war for what it really is, we're well on the road to defeat.

"Make no mistake: our economic struggle with the Japanese is critical to our future. We're up against a formidable competitor and . . . we'd be lucky to stay even with them" (p. 331).

However, blaming Japan misses the real point. The United States faces more than just one commercial adversary. "Japan, Inc." is only the most formidable of our competitors, and Japan-bashing is not the solution to our economic woes. Other nations pose dangers to American economic well-being as well. Germany, France, Italy, and other European countries are effective in their marketing efforts throughout the world. South Korea, Taiwan, and Singapore are entering global markets with consistent success. Brazil and Argentina are active and aggressive. The People's Republic of China—until recently a sleeping giant with little commercial muscle—now shows signs of rousing into a powerful long-term competitor. In short, Americans who sound the alarm against Japan are keeping their eyes on only one front.

The real tragedy is that these two problems—minimal American commercial activity abroad and U.S. trade deficits—are closely related. Worse yet, they are mostly our own fault. Although regulations, tariffs, and currency fluctuations unquestionably enter into the overall picture, the weak American role in global trade cannot be blamed solely on other countries' activities. Mark H. McCormack, in *What They Don't Teach You at Harvard Business School* (Bantam, 1984), describes how we run the risk of losing the battle by default: "You can count on your fingers the American companies which are maximizing their full potential in international markets.

"Of all the world's companies, American-run businesses are by far the most arrogant and chauvinistic. Most of their international divisions haven't taken the time to break down language and cultural barriers, preferring to declare them impenetrable" (p. 83).

If McCormack's statements are true—and the evidence continues to accumulate in his favor—then American businesses are choosing to pass up opportunities of truly historic proportions. To be sure, doing business abroad is complex. It presents difficulties that often differ from those that companies have learned to address in the domestic arena. However, American firms that refuse to consider the possibility of international ventures are ignoring three fundamental facts:

- The international marketplace is vast.
- Many nations are succeeding in markets where Americans once excelled.
- Financially sound companies stand to gain much from well-chosen, well-planned international ventures.

By ignoring these facts, American companies not only forfeit lucrative overseas markets but also thwart their domestic efforts. Foreign firms have not restricted themselves to local markets; on the contrary, companies of many nations regard the United States as their most profitable territory. U.S. firms, too, must widen their scope of activities to survive and prosper. The new business reality of the 1980s and 1990s is that international trade, far from being a luxury available to only a few firms, is crucial for most American companies *simply to compete effectively at home.*

Will U.S. companies take advantage of the opportunities awaiting them in the global marketplace? Or will they decide that the challenge is too great, thereby relinquishing sales and profits to other countries?

Iacocca describes the possible consequences of the situation: "I don't know when we're going to wake up, but I hope it's soon. Otherwise, within a few years our economic arsenal is going to consist of little more than drive-in banks, hamburger joints, and video-game arcades" (p. 339).

A NEW MAP TO THE NEW BUSINESS LANDSCAPE

The purpose of *The Arthur Young International Business Guide* is not to rectify the current U.S. trade deficit and its attendant economic ills. These problems are obviously beyond the scope of a single book. Moreover, the general issues of international trade are not the present focus. The overall trade situation *is* significant to us here, however, because of what it implies about how Americans do business overseas, or more often how we *don't* do business overseas. Because for the most part, American companies don't bother to compete outside the domestic marketplace.

This brings us full circle to the earlier statistic that only 25,000 American firms export their products or services. What accounts for such a low proportion of U.S. companies in the international marketplace?

The reason is *not* a lack of interest. Thousands of American business executives want to do business abroad. (In 1986 alone, for example, the U.S. Department of Commerce received 170,000 requests from American companies for information on how to export their products and services.) Most American business people have grasped the promise of international trade:

- *Many domestic markets have reached maturity.* If American companies are to expand, they must look overseas.
- *The United States accounts for only 4 percent of the world's population.* The other 96 percent of the world's people form a vast market as yet untapped by U.S. firms.
- *Foreign consumers are often ready—even eager—to buy American-made goods.* The label "Made in the U.S.A." gives many products special appeal overseas.

Yet despite their awareness of how promising overseas trade is, many executives hesitate to proceed with international ventures. Doing business abroad sometimes seems too complex, too confusing, too risky. Despite all the information available, few sources of facts and advice address the full range of the American business person's needs during the course of going international. The sporadic, often confusing array of data addressing issues of international trade often has tended to make the option of doing business abroad seem excessively risky. Many executives therefore hedge their bets and stick to domestic ventures.

As a result, the ultimate reason for America's poor showing in the world marketplace is that most corporate officers have not understood the specific tasks necessary for success overseas. American business people have lacked a map to guide them through the international business landscape.

The Arthur Young International Business Guide now provides that map.

THE FOUR STEPS

This book offers a systematic approach to determining whether your small or medium-sized company should consider undertaking an international venture, and—in case the answer is yes—the book also provides an overview of the tasks necessary for planning and executing the venture itself. The Arthur Young approach consists of four steps:

1. Testing the waters
2. Learning the language
3. Mapping out a strategy
4. Beating the competition at its own game

After an initial chapter that provides a brief sketch of the global marketplace, each of the four steps of this approach is explained in detail.

Step 1: Testing the Waters

The first step is to test the waters—that is, to evaluate your company's financial and organizational readiness for international ventures. Step 1 explains how to

- determine your company's state of readiness,
- acquire preliminary background information about foreign markets,
- establish possible target markets,
- identify potential windows of opportunity,
- confirm market readiness by seeking an "instant gratification" sale,
- acquire financial assistance for further research, and
- develop an initial focus.

Step 2: Learning the Language

International trade uses a language of current international conditions and business practices that differs from the language most Americans understand. Since foreign business competitors will be anticipating your company's arrival in their territory, you must learn their rules to have any chance for success.

Step 2 therefore provides information on how to

- develop an international perspective,
- identify and overcome obstacles,
- conduct market research,
- analyze risks,
- evaluate corporate tax issues, and
- explore available government funding programs and alternative schemes for financing.

Step 3: Mapping Out a Strategy

The key to entering foreign markets is an intelligent, well-considered strategy that addresses market analysis, risk analysis, legal and financial considerations, and timing. Step 3 provides the information you need to develop a market entry strategy for your international venture.

Initial discussions answer these questions:

- What is strategy?
- What are the differences between strategy and strategic management?
- Why is strategy necessary?
- What issues should a strategy address?
- What period of time should a strategy cover?
- Who should plan and implement a strategy?

After clarifying these issues, Step 3 provides a framework that can easily be adapted to your company's needs as you undertake the process of strategic management.

Step 4: Beating Them at Their Own Game

The final step of going international is to develop a capability for aggressive competition overseas. By selecting imaginative, adaptable expatriate staff members, training your personnel in cross-cultural issues, following several time-honored tips for success, and avoiding common pitfalls, your company can become self-sufficient in its international venture.

A final chapter provides case studies of three U.S. companies that have achieved excellence and profits overseas.

A compendium of appendixes offers a wide variety of technical information to assist you in locating resources, making decisions, and proceeding with your plans.

NEW CHALLENGES, NEW REWARDS

The challenges are clear: new ways of thinking about markets and territories, new ways of strategizing about your company's future.

The rewards are great: increased profits, wider name recognition, and the potential for corporate growth.

Ultimately, the rewards make the challenges worthwhile. The global marketplace—complex, diverse, and constantly changing—is still unexplored terrain for most American businesses.

Your company *can* succeed in doing business abroad.

PART 1

THE GLOBAL MARKETPLACE—
WHY AND WHEN TO REACH IT

International business is older than the ancient Phoenician traders and the trans-Asian caravans, yet only during the past century has the world become truly a global marketplace. The development of modern transportation and telecommunications technology has allowed business people in almost every nation on earth to sell their products and services to customers virtually everywhere else.

THE DECLINE AND FALL OF THE AMERICAN EMPIRE?

For most of the past four decades, the United States held a position of preeminence—if not outright dominance—in the global marketplace. American industrial productivity became the envy of the world; American distribution networks spread into almost every country; American marketing techniques achieved unprecedented effectiveness. The United States not only won the Second World War, but also established what, at least in commercial terms, proved to be the American Empire.

But now America's leadership has eroded. Several countries outstrip the United States in productivity; foreign goods often cost less than ours; other nations' marketing campaigns increasingly succeed at wooing American and foreign consumers alike. The most dramatic result of this erosion is that the U.S. trade deficit continues to grow. An equally disheartening consequence of this situation is more specific: individual American companies keep losing sales to foreign competitors, with harmful side effects both for corporate health and for the well-being of individual employees.

What accounts for this country's decline in commercial leadership? What has brought about the loss of American dominance in international trade?

Four commonly offered explanations for this situation are *increased materials costs, increased labor costs, trade protectionism,* and *the overvaluation of certain currencies.* Many raw materials have become steadily more expensive since the World War II era, with further increases likely as supplier nations grow more sophisticated and organized in dealing with their customers. Meanwhile, labor costs within the United States have risen as well, so that many American firms compete at a disadvantage with companies in foreign countries where wage scales are far lower. Laws and regulations in other countries have created worries about trade protectionism, and consequently about American companies' access to foreign markets. Finally, the periodic overvaluation of the U.S. dollar has made some American goods more expensive than comparable foreign products.

These factors unquestionably contribute to the problems of lost sales and trade imbalances. However, a couple of other factors over which we have more control also make a difference—factors that are uncomfortable to face but important to accept if American companies are to regain a position of strength in the global marketplace. These factors are *cultural presumptions* and *hasty or inadequate business strategies.*

Cultural Presumptions

Beliefs, customs, traditions, and ways of doing business all vary from one country to another, and even within individual countries. No one from one culture can know all the subtleties of another. Still, the reason many U.S. businesses fail overseas is that management refuses to grasp even the *possibility* of cultural differences. Too many American business people presume that the whole world does business our way. Worse, they say as much. How often have you heard Americans speak of other nationalities in words like these?

"Back home, we wouldn't waste so much time."

Or: "I can't understand how these people get anything done at all."

Or: "What this place needs is some good old American know-how."

Case Study

Three executives from an American farm machinery corporation flew to Tokyo with hopes of selling tractors to Japanese buyers. The Americans—none of whom had traveled to Japan before—then arranged a meeting with the representatives of a large soybean company.

As far as the tractor company executives could determine, their presentation went well. The Japanese listened politely to the English sales pitch and to the subsequent translation. After an initial statement of the price of the tractors, however, the Japanese just sat there. One of the Americans therefore held forth a while longer, elaborating on points he had already made. The Japanese listened but once again said nothing. As the silence became more and more disquieting, the senior American executive proposed a lower price for his company's products. Even so, the Japanese made no response. Ultimately the Americans lowered their price far lower than they had ever intended, never realizing that the Japanese executives had fallen silent not so much to show displeasure or disinterest, but simply to consider the initial proposal—all in keeping with standard Japanese practice.

People in other cultures use time, space, and language so differently from us that we often totally misread their intentions. For instance, Americans often feel uncomfortable with silence. We want a conversation to keep moving. On the other hand, the Japanese and many other nationalities prefer a less "crowded" style of verbal interaction. The American negotiators in the preceding case study assumed that their Japanese counterparts were ignoring them or brushing them off; they failed to understand that the Japanese preferred not to respond at once and needed time to ponder the situation.

The issue isn't merely linguistic. Food, clothing, and personal customs also can create vast obstacles for international business travelers to surmount or avoid. Almost everyone who has worked abroad can tell stories about mishaps and embarrassments while on assignment. The point isn't to avoid every conceivable misunderstanding or misstep. Rather, the point is to prepare yourself and your company for dealing with the new cultural rules overseas. To be unprepared is to damage your efforts—and, in some cases, to doom them altogether.

Hasty or Inadequate Business Strategies

Perhaps the most common factor contributing to lost international sales is faulty strategy. Businesses that routinely plan their domestic ventures with careful, thoughtful, long-term research and strategizing often throw caution to the wind when moving into the global marketplace. Some managers even prefer "winging it" to any kind of planning at all.

Instead of doing market research and planning a sound strategy, many American companies prefer a "U.S. Marines" approach to international ventures. Invade the foreign land! Establish a beachhead! Take the country by storm! Unfortunately, the usual result of this attitude is that companies fail miserably in their first foreign endeavor and resolve thereafter not to pursue international operations at all. "Oh, we tried going abroad once and lost our shirts," management says, "so we stick to selling where we understand the rules." The irony is that with proper forethought, research, and planning, you *can* come to understand the rules overseas. You can even use these rules to your own advantage.

Case Study

Bill Hastings, the assistant director of marketing for a small American manufacturing company, visited Bangkok to investigate the possibility of distributing the company's products in Southeast Asia. Bill traveled with Cheryl Acosta, field director for the company's international operations. Neither of them had had any prior experience in Asia. Bill, in fact, had never traveled outside the United States. Both executives felt mildly apprehensive about being neophytes in the field, but they felt great excitement, too, as if they were the first explorers in an uncharted area. (Neither acknowledged that their counterparts in other companies probably had had years of international experience and had developed a mastery of Southeast Asian business practices.)

Bill and Cheryl attempted to complete a twelve-country marketing study in six weeks. Bill figured that once he obtained the facts and made a quick decision on how to proceed, sales would start rolling in. But they found the environment baffling and made little headway. Frustrated, they impulsively recommended a plan to headquarters that ended in a fiasco one year later.

"I can't understand what happened," Bill reflected in the aftermath. "The same method worked just fine when we started operations in Los Angeles."

THE PROMISE OF DISTANT SHORES

The fact remains: foreign markets offer vast opportunities for American companies. The benefits in sales alone are difficult to overestimate. Other advantages include increased brand name recognition, potential product diversification, company expansion, and protection of domestic markets through more effective competition with foreign firms operating in the United States. Success in the international arena is a goal best achieved through careful planning. As such, it is a goal accessible even to small and medium-sized companies.

Any stable, healthy business should at least investigate the prospects of going international. The minimum requirements are the following:

- *An open mind.* Any international venture will bring you face to face with unfamiliar business practices; with different customs, beliefs, attitudes, expectations, and tastes; and with unaccustomed kinds of potential risk and benefit. To succeed overseas, you must set aside at least some of your assumptions about what makes sense and how to get things done.

- *Careful planning.* Commerce abroad differs from commerce at home, but the difference doesn't mean that the global marketplace is a free-for-all. Just as entering a new domestic market requires research, goal setting, and strategy, entering a foreign market requires careful planning. In a field where competitors are abundant, shrewd, and experienced, "winging it" is an invitation for disaster.

- *Aggressive, strenuous action.* When great geographical distances, cultural differences, and logistical complexities come into play, business people must act with foresight, clarity of mind, and energy. The effort involved is often considerable, but so are the potential payoffs.

Before sketching when and why companies should consider undertaking an international venture, we should have a look at the global marketplace today. An overview of world trade will provide a context for understanding what American businesses encounter when they go overseas.

Fifty or a hundred years ago, international commerce functioned in a relatively simple way. The less-developed countries sold raw materials to the industrialized nations; the industrialized nations sold finished products to each other and to the less-developed countries. Although this description oversimplifies the situation to some degree, it portrays the basic condition of the world economy before the Second World War.

Since then, however, the picture has changed. Raw materials and finished goods no longer flow in the relatively simple patterns of the prewar era. Economies are now intricately interdependent.

We Own Them, They Own Us

American corporations have established foreign subsidiaries throughout the history of this country's participation in international trade. General Motors, General Electric, IBM, E. I. du Pont de Nemours, and Exxon are only a few of the biggest firms whose network of companies extends literally around the world; thousands of smaller corporations have more modest multinational operations.

Meanwhile, the United States remains a magnet for foreign capital. In 1985 alone, some $130 billion poured into the United States from overseas. *Forbes* magazine recently summarized the situation as follows: "If Americans sometimes lack faith in their own economy, it is quite clear that many well-heeled foreigners have a good deal of faith in it" (July 28, 1986, p. 200). As a result, many companies regarded by domestic consumers as American firms are in fact partially or totally foreign-owned. For instance, Generale Occidentale SA, a French corporation, owns Grand Union supermarkets. Henkel KGaA of Germany owns 23 percent of Clorox. Bank of Tokyo Ltd. owns 77 percent of California First Bank. The Dutch corporation Unilever owns Lever Brothers and Thomas J. Lipton.

A New Economic Order

Obviously, the game has changed. American companies no longer dominate the international marketplace simply by virtue of being American. Firms based in other countries can match and frequently exceed U.S. firms' performance. Foreign companies have invaded markets—including markets within the United States—that were once almost exclusively the province of American corporations. The situation has no chance of returning to the "good old days." On the contrary, the situation is growing more and more complex.

Who are the players in this drama, and what are the implications for U.S. business?

Japan. The country that draws the most attention these days— and that inspires the most awe, fear, and anger—is, of course, Japan. With a 1985 GNP of U.S. $1.3 trillion and a 1986 trade surplus of $82.473 billion, Japan is the third most productive nation on earth.

Japan's rebirth out of the postwar ashes is one of the great success stories of modern industrialization.

During recent decades, the United States has found its former nemesis and current political ally more of a challenge than most observers once expected. America's trade deficit with Japan reached $51.401 billion during 1986, with the imbalance likely to grow annually for the foreseeable future. In response, prominent American spokespeople in both the public and private sectors have started calling for trade sanctions against Japan. These spokespeople assert that Japanese businesses have taken advantage of American labor costs, trade policies, and currency exchange rates to further their own goals unfairly. Yet it's surely significant that Japan maintains a surplus with most of its trading partners. (See Table 1 for statistics.) European nations whose exports and imports result in a trade deficit with Japan include the United Kingdom, France, West Germany, Italy, and the Netherlands. Japan also maintains a surplus in trade with South Korea, Taiwan, China, Thailand, Singapore, and Hong Kong. Clearly, if the Japanese are taking unfair advantage of the United States, they are somehow doing so as well with most other industrialized nations.

Table 1. Countries/regions with which Japan has a trade surplus (1986 figures, in U.S. $ millions)

Country/Region	Japanese Trade Surplus
Developed countries, total	68,917
United Kingdom	3,073
France	1,297
West Germany	6,180
Italy	228
Netherlands	2,684
USSR	1,178
North America (excluding Mexico)	52,032
United States	51,401
Developing countries, total	7,993

Source: "Statistical Profile, Part II: International Transactions of Japan in 1986," the Japan Economic Institute.

The likelier—though more painful—explanation is that Japan has developed more skillful and imaginative marketing and distribution practices than those used by other nations. The Japanese are simply excelling at the international game that other nations started.

The European Community.   Meanwhile, the European Community (EC) remains one of the United States' most important trading partners and one of its most powerful competitors. Founded in 1958 to promote economic integration and collaboration within Western Europe, the EC now consists of twelve member-nations: Belgium, Denmark, France, Greece, Ireland, Italy, Luxembourg, the Netherlands, Portugal, Spain, the United Kingdom, and West Germany. The EC nations had a combined GDP of $3,448.9 billion in 1986. Specific members of the EC vary in their productivity and marketing sophistication; consequently, trade surpluses and deficits vary from country to country.

EC firms provide U.S. companies with some of their most energetic competition. Phillips, Telefunken, Blaupunkt, and Denon produce electronics components that American consumers covet as much as they do Japanese components. Appliance manufacturers such as Krups and Braun are now virtually household names in the United States. And European clothing companies—among which Gucci, Yves St. Laurent, Benetton, and Giorgio Armani are only four of the most prominent—now draw customers worldwide. In short, the EC countries, though varied in their business practices and industrial productivity, challenge the United States as much as Japan does.

The Newly Industrialized Countries.   Japan and Europe are only part of the picture. Just as the United States once felt confident of its commercial supremacy only to face the challenge of Japanese and European competitors, now all the developed nations face new pressure from the newly industrialized countries (NICs). Taiwan, South Korea, and Singapore have now attained sufficient industrial prowess to compete in the global marketplace. Brazil—the fifth largest nation in land area and the sixth largest in population—has made striking advances in recent decades. Malaysia, though currently undergoing economic difficulties, may present a challenge as well.

The People's Republic of China. Meanwhile, the People's Republic of China (PRC) is the sleeping giant of international trade. With a population of over one billion and with vast natural resources (including coal and oil reserves, minerals, waterpower, and arable land), the PRC will some day present all other nations with a formidable trading competitor.

Future Contenders. Thailand, the Philippines, and Indonesia, though currently not cause for great concern among the industrialized nations, may become more economically active in the future. Variables influencing their development will include the state of the global economy, the cost of oil and other resources, political stability, and currency fluctuations.

New Challenges, New Opportunities

The United States, Europe, and even Japan can no longer assume a right to commercial supremacy by default. Other countries will join the ranks of the industrialized nations. Some of these nations will achieve leadership in trade through good strategy, hard work, and persistence. Whether the United States maintains its tradition of excellence in both industry and trade depends largely on how well and how imaginatively American companies take up the challenge before them.

To summarize: the global marketplace offers both great challenges and great opportunities. Competitors are numerous and often sophisticated, yet the potential benefits of international ventures often outweigh the risks.

Having briefly sketched the global marketplace, we now address the question of when a company should consider an international venture. What factors make doing business abroad worthwhile? And when does a company have insufficient reason to proceed overseas?

THE WRONG REASONS FOR GOING INTERNATIONAL

Going international can have many benefits, but far too many companies make this potentially good move for bad—or, more often, insufficient—reasons. Many executives misunderstand the real promise of international ventures. Instead of analyzing the advantages and disadvantages of specific options in carefully chosen markets, they press ahead impulsively, often basing their reasons on misconceptions about doing business overseas. The result is often disappointment, or even financial disaster.

The commonly held but wrong or insufficient reasons for undertaking international ventures are the following:

- To manufacture or assemble goods under tax-free conditions
- To take advantage of cheap labor
- To serve a previously existing clientele
- To acquire an attractive, tax-deductible corporate vacation spot

Let's look at why—in the absence of other, sounder reasons—these are faulty or insufficient grounds for going international.

Wrong Reason 1: Tax-Free Status

To attract foreign investment, many nations offer a "tax holiday" to certain companies, most often those that are either capital- or labor-intensive. A tax holiday generally lasts from five to twenty-five years. Tax holidays tend to increase in length the farther a company moves from urban centers that have adequate infrastructure and skilled labor. So far so good.

The problem is that tax-free status often blinds American business people to all other considerations. Executives look at their profit-and-loss statement at headquarters; they cringe at the sight of what U.S. taxes take out of their bottom line; they fall for the easy temptation of tax-free status overseas. "If we didn't have to pay taxes," they rejoice, "just think of our profits!"

Unfortunately, most people forget the drawbacks.

- *The farther from an overseas urban center (and hence from adequate infrastructure and skilled labor) a company establishes itself, the harder doing business is.* In remote areas of many countries, electrical power fails frequently; telephone communications are sporadic; bad weather can delay delivery of raw materials, and shipping costs can be exorbitant.

- *The time the company takes to fill an order can increase significantly as a consequence of manufacturing problems and unreliable transportation.* For many of the reasons just listed, delays and expense in acquiring raw materials and shipping finished products may exceed your wildest nightmares.

- *Finding even unskilled labor can prove difficult.* The more remote the location, the less likely it is that local workers will have had any experience—or will even have interest—in working in a factory environment.

- *All overseas ventures—even when tax-free—necessitate additional accounting and reporting procedures.* The cost of accountancy and legal advice may ultimately exceed the value of an enterprise if tax-free status is the only benefit.

Because of these drawbacks, many companies that move overseas never benefit from their tax-free status. The tax-free status itself is not the problem. Tax-free status is, however, small consolation when a company finds itself losing money in a remote part of the world.

Some executives attempt to circumvent the risky aspects of this situation by limiting their venture to assembly operations overseas. They transfer finished components at a low transfer price to an overseas location, thus showing a loss in the United States and avoiding U.S. taxes; then they assemble the products and transfer them back at an unreasonably high transfer price, once again showing no profit in the United States. This method allows the foreign operations to show maximum profits that are tax-free. However, the arrangement violates IRS regulations and frequently results in a net loss anyway.

If your reason for going international is chiefly to reap tax benefits, you should consider seeking a similar advantage in the United States. Many areas of the country offer tax incentives. By taking advantage of them here, you will enjoy a similar benefit without such a high degree of risk. Moreover, both acquiring raw materials and shipping finished products will cost you less.

Wrong Reason 2: Cheap Labor

With certain exceptions (such as Korea and Hong Kong), you should carefully and skeptically investigate countries notable for cheap labor. A production worker who costs twelve dollars per hour in the United States may cost only one dollar per hour elsewhere in the world. However, one well-trained, experienced American worker may produce more than several workers overseas. In addition, some countries have government regulations that virtually require management to hire a large number of workers to do the job that one worker could have handled in the United States. In China, for example, the government used to provide a foreign company with a factory and a full team of employees. The output of that factory, however, may resemble what you could have attained with a smaller staff of American workers. Other countries, such as Singapore, dictate benefits and wages, thus raising personnel costs.

Productivity statistics that are tempting are also often deceptive. Government ministry figures are especially suspect. Even those supplied by international companies deserve close scrutiny. How have these agencies and companies acquired their data? What are their sources of information? Few (if any) companies publishing such statistics run operations either for manufacturing or for assembly in the countries under study. Often their reports are derived from government surveys. The result, unfortunately, tends to be data with little or no foundation in reality.

Wrong Reason 3: Serving Existing Clientele

Some American businesses unexpectedly begin to acquire clients in a particular country or region. These clients may come about as a consequence of foreign business people visiting the United States, or from advertisements in trade publications that have caught someone's attention overseas. In other instances, a U.S. customer establishes operations overseas and turns to his American supplier to continue meeting his needs. One way or another, these unexpected foreign orders provide a pleasant surprise. A potentially dangerous result, however, is that management may conclude that a market exists for their products overseas when in fact no such distinct market exists.

This situation often leads to sloppy thinking—and, worse yet, to sloppy decision making. The illusion of an easy initial success can tempt management to proceed as if every subsequent choice will be successful as well.

Wrong Reason 4: Acquiring a Vacation Spot

As unlikely as it sounds, some companies undertake international ventures chiefly to acquire a tax-deductible corporate vacation spot. The usual sequence of events is that someone from top management visits a foreign country on business and, finding the locale attractive, inexpensive, and relaxing, suggests to fellow executives that they start a small operation there. "The beaches are nice, the shrimp are cheap," he tells them, "and—who knows?—we might even turn a profit some day." His colleagues make their own visits and concur. The company opens a facility that, if nothing else, provides the excuse for tax-deductible junkets. Unfortunately, the ill-planned enterprise flops after a year, costing the firm several million dollars.

Absurd? Of course. But all too common.

Case Study

One CEO visited North Africa and fell in love with Morocco. Imagining frequent trips to this desert kingdom, he established a Marrakesh subsidiary for his firm, which manufactures kitchen cabinets. Unfortunately, he neglected to notice that most Moroccans don't have indoor kitchens, much less kitchen cabinets. The branch operation was a total fiasco. The lure of exotic climes had distorted this executive's previously sound business judgment.

To summarize: international ventures often prove worthwhile, but companies sometimes undertake them for the wrong reasons. Tax-free status, cheap labor, preexisting clientele, and suitability as a vacation spot are insufficient justification for going international in the absence of other, better reasons.

However, good reasons *do* exist.

THE RIGHT REASONS FOR GOING INTERNATIONAL

Five sound reasons justify undertaking an international venture. These reasons are the following:

- Your company is approaching maturity in the United States, and you have the strength and resources to go overseas.

- Your current trade with overseas customers suggests a potential market and a competitive edge.

- Analysis of your competitors' activities abroad indicates a potential market, or their activities in the domestic arena indicate that you should go overseas to compete effectively.

- Demand for your product in the United States is exceptional, and you believe you have a unique product with universal appeal.

- Demand for look-alike products is high, or your product is sufficiently superior to the competition that it would have international appeal (or would tend to generate look-alikes).

Right Reason 1: Company Maturity

Entering the international marketplace requires time, money, and resources. Unless you have a good track record at home and a history of stable performance, an overseas venture may strain your resources and complicate problems for your domestic operations. You should be sure that your company is meeting the demand for its products and services in the domestic market before branching out into the foreign arena.

Some business people overestimate their company's readiness for going international. A firm that has been in business two or three years may have a record of good growth that tempts management to start looking overseas. But companies in early stages of development rarely have the managerial talent to cope with their growth problems. Such companies have generally not even begun to reach their potential in the U.S. market. Further, companies of this sort often lack the financial resources necessary for start-up operations overseas, for adequate advertising campaigns in an unfamiliar culture, and for extensive marketing. Under these circumstances, underestimating the initial problems of a new international business venture is easy—and dangerous.

If your company has a longer history of good performance, however, and if you have fulfilled your potential in the domestic market, then moving into the global arena may well make sense.

Step 1, "Testing the Waters," will explain how to assess your company's prospects and how to select a target market.

Right Reason 2: Current Overseas Trade

Earlier, we discussed how a preexisting clientele *in and of itself* is generally insufficient reason for going international. If a company's U.S. customers shift some of their operations overseas, doing business with them may give an impression—a false one—of a foreign market for the firm's products. On the other hand, a significant number of orders from one or more countries does warrant further investigation. Orders from customers with no U.S.-based operations suggest a potential market and point to a market niche that closer suppliers are not filling.

If you find yourself in this situation, you should consider visiting your overseas customers to discuss why they are buying your products. Such a visit can be enlightening, and can indicate that you have a sound basis for an international venture. You may find that your customers have not found a competitive product; in that case, you are at a competitive advantage either because of your product's price or its quality. On the other hand, you may discover that the situation is in fact less promising than you first hoped. You're certainly better off experiencing an early, small disappointment than a larger, more expensive one. In any case, the only way to determine the nature of the situation is to meet with your customers and find out why they buy your products.

Right Reason 3: Market Potential

Doing simple market research or reviewing your competitors' financial statements can give you an idea of the market other firms are servicing abroad. You should look farther than your U.S. competition alone, however. For example, if your business is manufacturing appliances, you should acquire financial and market data on Phillips, Telefunken, and other European competitors, as well as on Japanese firms. Similarly, if you are dealing in retail goods, consider visiting at least a few stores overseas. Viewing the products for sale and noting their origins can provide considerable information about the potential in these markets; talking with distributors and potential customers will give you an even more detailed impression.

Another situation that may justify going international is one in which your foreign competitors have invaded your domestic territory. With the global nature of the contemporary marketplace, you cannot count on corporate survival on the basis of U.S. sales alone. Some of your most energetic local competition may be based halfway around the world. If you find that your company is losing sales to overseas rivals, you may have to confront them thousands of miles away simply to retain your home turf.

Step 1, "Testing the Waters," and Step 2, "Learning the Language," analyze these circumstances and suggest ways to proceed.

Right Reason 4: Exceptional Demand for Your Product

Some products catch the whole world's fancy. The companies producing them almost can't go wrong in their marketing plans. American blue jeans are a classic example. From South America to Europe to Asia to the Soviet Union, people love to wear blue jeans. Of course, companies in many countries produce these garments—often violating copyrights and trademark laws—but the authentic item holds a special appeal. A single pair of real Levi's or Lee's jeans sells for hundreds of dollars on the Soviet black market. Similarly, American pop music sells wildly around the world. Even in some of the most anti-American cultures, the same people who protest against the United States simultaneously covet and acquire American-made goods. The upshot of this situation is that some products seem fail-safe overseas.

Assessing *which* products fall into this category is, of course, difficult, and the risks are great. A product with widespread appeal, however, may justify the risk. If the McDonald's Corporation had based a decision about going international solely on reasons 2 and 3 (current trade with overseas customers and analysis of competitors' activities), the company probably never would have taken the Big Mac and Egg McMuffin overseas. Neither reason applied to McDonald's. Before the company's inroads, little or no competition existed in its field. Yet the company's international operations have succeeded literally everywhere. The McDonald's outlet on Orchard Road in Singapore, for example, has the highest customer traffic of any in the world. Someone within the McDonald's organization had the foresight to believe that the company's products would have international appeal.

Right Reason 5: Demand for Look-alike Products

Do your products have the sort of appeal that will eventually tempt someone to copy them? Clothing, appliances, luxury food items, and other high-status products often fall into this category. The fact is, if you don't take such products overseas, someone somewhere will copy them and reap the profits. American businesses lose millions of dollars annually to look-alikes and pirated products marketed under their brand names. The businesses that suffer are most often mature companies with established international brand recognition but without appropriate or adequate international operations.

In certain parts of Southeast Asia, for instance, you can buy imitation Rolex and Cartier watches for a small fraction of their cost in the United States. Similarly, Apple and IBM computer look-alikes have been sold extensively during recent years. Likewise, copies of designer clothes are sold well below the cost of the originals.

Here, as with the kinds of market research already mentioned, you need to proceed in part through "gut feel." However, you can get a sense of the situation by visiting the various countries around the world that might provide customers for your products. Step 1, "Testing the Waters," also suggests ways to analyze potential risks and benefits.

WHY BOTHER?

The preceding discussions of the global marketplace, the complexities facing American businesses, and the wrong and right reasons for going international may have left you wondering why your company should bother in the first place. Isn't the task too difficult? Isn't it too risky?

The answer, as already noted, depends mostly on factors specific to each company. However, the general situation is so significant that you should take special care not to miss the forest for the trees.

- *The U.S. economy is limited in size and growth rate.* Several factors influence the situation. The U.S. population is fairly stable; American consumers' spending power has increased only slowly over the past decade; many products have reached maturity in their domestic life cycle.

- *The world's population is shifting.* Currently, the population of the earth has reached approximately five billion people. By far the greatest growth is occurring in the Southern Hemisphere. By the year 2000, a small minority of human beings will live in Europe and North America.

- *Per capita income is rising in some regions.* Until recently, most countries outside the Northern Hemisphere had only small population segments with any appreciable buying power. Now many nations have become industrialized. Even some previously depressed economies (such as those of India and the People's Republic of China) show signs of remarkable development.

- *Recent changes (like improved infrastructure and communications) are affecting the distribution of goods.* Obtaining raw materials, shipping finished products, and exchanging data are now easier than ever throughout the world and possible for the first time in some areas.

- *Nations have become economically intertwined.* Companies across the world may present as much challenge to American firms as local competitors; there is no commercial safety in geographical distance.

- *Other nations challenge America's economic well-being.* The United States has half willingly, half unwittingly relinquished its economic primacy in the world market. The consequences of ignoring global competition will affect the quality of life in this country for decades to come.

- *Done right, international ventures are fun, challenging, profitable, and rewarding.* The potential benefits—personal and corporate, tangible and intangible—usually outweigh the potential risks.

No single section in a single book can do justice to the size and complexity of the global marketplace today. This overview has served chiefly to sketch the most striking features of international trade and to suggest that many American managers' dreams and night-mares about doing business abroad are equally illusory.

The global marketplace is not a private club that Americans lack the confidence to join. Neither is it a race or competition that Americans can win simply by virtue of being Americans. Like any commercial turf, the global marketplace is both a geographical place— more accurately, a multitude of places—and an intricate web of regulations, financial conditions, supplies, demands, cultural expectations, and ways of doing business. Success in international trade requires nearly the same combination of skills, experience, open-mindedness, timing, and gut-level business intuition that success in domestic trade requires. The specific circumstances you will encounter in the international marketplace differ from those in the domestic sphere. Hence, what you must do to succeed differs as well.

Part 2 of this book spells out the steps necessary to compete effectively as you start doing business abroad.

PART 2

THE ARTHUR YOUNG FOUR-STEP APPROACH TO GOING INTERNATIONAL

STEP 1 _____

TESTING THE WATERS

Testing the waters is the process by which your company initially determines its cultural, financial, and organizational readiness for doing business abroad. It is also a process of evaluating the suitability of your company's products for overseas sale, license, or manufacture. In its later stages, testing the waters is a means of identifying the best potential markets to enter and the best methods for succeeding in those markets. In short, this first step is *cursory* research performed on your home turf. It is the international business equivalent of getting your feet wet.

Testing the waters is a serious, significant step in the process of going international, and should be approached thoughtfully and executed carefully; however, because the tasks involved here are relatively theoretical and inexpensive, this step is safe even for companies whose executives want only to explore the possibilities of doing business abroad.

GETTING STARTED—COMMITMENT AND PREPARATION

Two conditions must exist before your company undertakes any international venture: commitment and preparation.

Commitment means that you acknowledge the two fundamental aspects of the situation discussed in Part 1:

- The benefits of entering international markets may contribute significantly to the bottom line.
- The task itself—that is, doing business in the global marketplace—involves business practices substantially different from those customary within the United States.

Accepted together, these two aspects of commitment mean that your company is willing to devote *significant* amounts of *time*, *personnel*, and *money* to master the challenges of doing business abroad. International ventures cannot succeed when undertaken as impulsive, improvised, short-term endeavors. You can't just dabble at going international. On the contrary, commitment to overseas business presupposes patience, tenacity, and strategic imagination.

Preparation is therefore the second necessary aspect of the initial stage of doing business abroad. Preparation means planning the ideal course of action for an international venture, and subsequently following that plan.

If, after reviewing the general reasons for doing business abroad, you believe that your company can achieve both the commitment and the preparation necessary for success in the global marketplace, then you are ready to test the waters.

To guide you through this process, this step explains the following tasks:

- Determining your company's state of readiness
- Acquiring preliminary, basic background information on international trade and various markets
- Establishing possible target markets
- Identifying possible windows of opportunity
- Confirming market readiness by making an "instant gratification" sale
- Acquiring financial assistance for further research
- Developing an initial focus

There is one other consideration, however, before we explore these stages of the process.

For most companies, these seven tasks are best accomplished in sequence. Finishing each task assists in beginning the next. Yet some companies may wish to rearrange the sequence, or even to skip tasks altogether. Perhaps your company is in this category. If so, then you may already have acquired enough background information; you may already know your company's state of readiness; or you may already perceive a window of opportunity. Depending on your company's intentions, structure, and goals, you may therefore end up testing the waters in a somewhat different fashion from that outlined here. If so, fine. This section—like all others in the book—is a compendium of guidelines and suggestions, not an inflexible blueprint to follow line by line. However, *it is crucial that your company accomplish each task in some way at one point or another.*

DETERMINING YOUR COMPANY'S STATE OF READINESS

First, you should make an initial assessment of whether your company is able to benefit from doing business abroad. Whether you should proceed with an international venture is largely a function of whether the firm has sufficient financial, production, and personnel resources to make doing business abroad worthwhile.

An Evaluation Checklist

The following checklist is a simple, preliminary device for assessing readiness. How many of the ten factors listed are present in your situation? Go through the list, indicating yes or no to each factor.

Factor	Present in your situation?	
	Yes	No
1. Interest from company CEO	( )	( )
2. Sales greater than $5 million per year	( )	( )
3. Appropriate growth rate	( )	( )
4. Good capital position	( )	( )
5. Evident foreign competition in U.S.	( )	( )
6. Overseas demand indicated	( )	( )
7. Adequate or excess plant capacity	( )	( )
8. Personnel with overseas sales experience	( )	( )
9. Technological advantage	( )	( )
10. Evident window of opportunity	( )	( )
TOTALS:	___	___

After checking the appropriate response to each factor, total the number of "yes" and "no" answers. Seven out of ten "yes" answers indicates that your company is a prime candidate for going international. More than seven suggests especially great promise overseas; fewer than seven suggests a lower likelihood of success in the global marketplace.

Two caveats, however.

First, this checklist provides only a rough guide for judging the advisability of an international venture. A more accurate assessment requires a more thorough investigation. The rest of this subsection will outline the most critical factors in such an assessment.

Second, the answer to question 1 *must* be affirmative if your company is to have any chance of success overseas. The firm simply cannot succeed in doing business abroad without the commitment of adequate time, money, and managerial resources; and such commitment is impossible if the CEO is negative or indifferent toward the whole endeavor. A "no" answer on this issue essentially dooms the venture from the start.

On the other hand, if the CEO's support is strong, and if six other factors on the checklist look favorable, then you have good reason to proceed with a more detailed evaluation.

Taking the Measure

To determine your company's actual state of readiness, you should consider the following issues:

Present Operational Capability. First, examine the company's operational methods and attitudes as they relate to the following questions:

- Are companywide operational procedures able to support an overseas venture?
- Does the firm have sufficient and appropriately trained personnel capable of dealing with international business issues and a variety of cultural expectations? Alternatively, if such personnel are not on board, can the firm afford to hire them?
- Is management sufficiently flexible in its attitudes and methods to adapt to the various requirements of doing business abroad?
- Will the company culture permit the changes necessary for entering the international marketplace?

Current Financial Leverage. No matter how small, international ventures tend to be expensive. Your company must be prepared to invest heavily in a venture for it to succeed. Consequently, you should consider the following questions and how they apply to your firm:

- Will the company's current financial relationships (for example, with bankers) support this endeavor?
- How much flexibility does the company have in its finances? (A heavily leveraged firm is unlikely to succeed overseas.)
- What sorts of funding can the company acquire?

- Is the firm financially able to carry significant amounts of inventory before sales? To maintain extended payment schedules? To sell on consignment or on letters of credit?
- If necessary, can the company afford to open some form of facility overseas, with appropriate funding for staff and operational costs?

Existing Plant Capacity.   Because of both the risks and the potential rewards of international ventures, initial expansions of plant capacity may be necessary. Ideally, your company should have some degree of excess capacity; otherwise, the firm should be financially strong enough to expand quickly from the outset.

Consider the following questions in light of your own company's situation:

- *At what capacity is your plant currently operating?* The ideal range is about 75 to 80 percent. A higher level of capacity than that suggests a narrower margin of safety if the company were to expand into the global marketplace.
- *If your current excess capacity is small enough that you would have to expand your plant to sell products overseas, is there a specific opportunity that would justify that capital investment?* In some instances, an unusual technological breakthrough or change in currency exchange rates will make the gamble worthwhile. (A later section of Step 1 will discuss windows of opportunity.)
- *What is the proportion of fixed costs to variable costs in producing your company's products?* The higher the proportion of fixed costs, the more advantageous an international venture may become, since increasing your output will result in economies of scale and consequent reductions of per-unit cost.

Present Products and Product Line.   You should examine your company's products—both individually and as a product line—to determine their suitability for overseas sale. Consider the following questions:

- *How appealing will consumers in other countries find your products?* Advice from a consultant with firsthand experience in potential target markets is crucial in this regard.

- *What hidden issues may exist in your products?* Might members of your target markets object to some aspect of your product for religious, aesthetic, or other cultural reasons? Here, too, the impressions of an experienced advisor can be invaluable.

- *Is your whole product line suitable, or perhaps just one or two products?* If the whole line appeals to foreign consumers, so much the better; but even a single product with widespread appeal can justify taking your business overseas.

A useful resource in addressing these issues is the Department of Commerce pilot program called the Comparison Shopping Service. Designed to provide information about markets and products in various countries, this program can assist you in clarifying the suitability of your company's products and product lines for overseas sales. For information, write to Comparison Shopping Service, United States and Foreign Commercial Service (US&FCS), International Trade Administration, Department of Commerce, Washington, D.C. 20230.

Current Market Penetration.   Finally, you should examine your company's current market share within both the domestic and international arenas, by asking these questions:

- *What is your current domestic market share?* Will you be able to acquire further points of market share without excessive cost? Or have you already reached a point of diminishing returns?

- *If your product is already mature within the domestic market, what is its potential overseas?* The product may have tremendous potential in other countries even if sales have flagged in the U.S./Canadian market. For example, the National Cash Register Company reconditions and sells obsolete mechanical cash registers in Third World countries.

- *If you are still growing in the domestic market, will overseas sales help to keep your overall production costs down?*

Reaching a Conclusion to Proceed or Not

How you analyze the answers to these questions will depend, of course, on your company's overall goals and objectives, on its corporate culture, and on its budget. However, a couple of generalizations about the five organizational readiness issues just raised are appropriate.

The following three issues are of paramount importance:

- *Operational capability.* Your operational capability *must* be supportive of initial overseas ventures.
- *Financial leverage.* Your company *must* have sufficient financial flexibility and leverage.
- *Plant capacity.* Your plant *must* have enough excess capacity to handle the new venture *or* you must be financially capable of expanding rapidly.

The following two issues are less crucial and more flexible:

- *Product line.* You may have a product line that is totally acceptable overseas; alternatively, only a single product, or several, may be acceptable, but may be sufficiently promising to justify going abroad.
- *Market penetration.* You can take your products overseas at various stages of product maturity. The late stages of the domestic product life cycle may, in fact, be one of the most promising times. On the other hand, your company's continuing growth in the domestic market at a time of concurrent overseas opportunities development can also justify an international venture. Many American software companies, for instance, sell programs whose popularity has peaked in the United States. (Examples are Lotus 1-2-3 and Multiplan.)

In any case, determining your company's state of readiness brings you to the first in a series of go/no-go decisions. Perhaps your company lacks the financial leverage, the personnel, or the time to undertake an international venture. If so, taking further steps will be unproductive, even counterproductive. On the other hand, your company may possess the resources necessary for doing business abroad. If so, then you should proceed to the next task in testing the waters.

ACQUIRING PRELIMINARY
BACKGROUND INFORMATION

Now you should obtain abundant background information about the region or regions under consideration for an international venture, about the characteristic business practices, and about the most promising markets.

This advice may seem to belabor the obvious. How could you enter a market without information about its size, consumer needs, potential advantages, potential risks, and peculiarities? Unfortunately, untold numbers of American business people leap headlong into the global marketplace with scanty, vague, dated, or simply erroneous information. A remarkable number have attempted to start business ventures with no background information at all. (See Case Study, page 40.)

From a business standpoint, limited or inaccurate information can be suicidal. Not all Americans overseas end up staring their lack of data so plainly in the face as Sam Parry did, but analogous situations are appallingly common. Ignorance of host-country politics is only one kind of fiasco possible overseas. Ignorance of local tastes, customs, and taboos has also wrought havoc on otherwise well-planned business ventures; representatives of U.S. firms have all too often attempted the equivalent of selling bikinis to Eskimos or ham to Israelis.

What makes these problems all the more unfortunate is that excellent information is readily available from numerous sources. A wide variety of institutions—both public and private—can help you acquire data on countries, markets, or products, and thereby help you explore your options in the global marketplace. Once again, the keys to success are commitment and preparation. You should commit your company to adequate research before making any actual moves, and you should then prepare to use the new information in a systematic, effective way.

Generally speaking, there is no reason to rush the process of going international. Steady, concerted efforts make more sense than a crash program. Thoroughness will serve you better than haste. Accordingly, you should take the time necessary to explore the global marketplace first in a general manner, then in detail, and always with a look to the long term.

Case Study

Sam Parry was the assistant director of a corporate team investigating the prospects of a manufacturing venture in a small Caribbean country. After six weeks in the field, the team received a request from the government to address the head of state and his cabinet about their proposal. The team spent several days preparing a presentation. At the last minute, however, the project director was called away; she assigned Sam to address the assembled leaders in her place.

Sam had spent enough time helping to prepare the presentation that he felt comfortable with it. He even practiced his introduction to the prime minister—the honorable Mr. Tollis—and to the prime minister's cabinet. Finally, the day arrived for the address. Sam and the team were received at the governmental palace.

Once settled into the prime minister's meeting room, Sam opened the presentation. "Honorable Mr. Tollis," he began, "and esteemed members of the cabinet . . . "

Abruptly, the prime minister interrupted Sam. "Won't you please start over?" he asked with a peeved smile.

Sam was taken aback. He hadn't expected his hosts to be so formal. They always seemed so casual in their open-necked short-sleeved shirts while Sam and his team sweated away in their suits. But Sam soon regained his composure. "Most honorable Mr. Tollis and highly esteemed members of the cabinet . . . "

"Be so kind as to begin again," said the prime minister, now visibly annoyed.

"Most esteemed and honorable Mr. Tollis—"

"Perhaps you should start yet again."

Shaken, Sam glanced desperately at his team, then at the government officials surrounding him. The ceiling fans rattled lightly overhead.

One of the cabinet ministers sitting nearby took pity on Sam. Leaning over, the elderly gentleman whispered, "Excuse me, but Mr. Tollis was deposed six months ago. You are now addressing the honorable Mr. Herbert."

General Research

Before taking any other steps, you (or someone within your company) should do some general research. This kind of research is the most basic sort—essentially a process of acquiring information off the shelf. Because the sources are readily available, general research is inexpensive and quick—a good way to survey the world business scene as painlessly as possible.

International Publications.   One particularly cheap, accessible source of information already lies at your fingertips: international business publications. Just as U.S. business magazines and newspapers are invaluable in following developments in the domestic marketplace, so, too, are the international equivalents useful and often crucial in keeping track of changes and opportunities abroad. Such publications can provide, if nothing else, a general background to the business climate throughout the world.

Any American business person even remotely considering an international venture should habitually read the standard publications. The *Asian Wall Street Journal,* the *International Herald Tribune,* the *Economist,* and *International Business* are reliable up-to-the-minute sources of information on both general and specific business issues worldwide.

Regional Magazines and Newspapers.   Regional magazines and newspapers will also help you develop a sense of specific markets. Examples are *Euromoney, Financial Times,* the *Far Eastern Economic Review, Financial Weekly,* and the *Investors Chronicle.* As well as providing data about the conditions and issues characteristic of particular regions, these publications also supply information about your competitors' activities, since many of them carry news about the opening of new facilities.

Incidentally, many of these publications are available through computer databases as well as in libraries. A computer search on particular topics—your company's product, for example, or the state of the economy in certain regions—can provide a detailed portrait for a limited expenditure of time and money.

Government and Corporate Literature

Both public and private organizations can provide extensive information to companies intent on learning more about the global marketplace. Data often include statistics for products or product groups comparable to your own goods or services.

U.S. Department of Commerce.   Among other reports, newsletters, and reference manuals, the U.S. Department of Commerce publishes the following:

- *Annual Worldwide Industry Reviews*—reports combining country-by-country market assessments, data on export trends, and a five-year statistical table of U.S. exports for particular industries.
- *Country Market Surveys*—short summaries of international market research highlighting market size, trends, and prospects.
- *Country Trade Statistics*—four key tables indicating the demand for U.S. products.
- *Foreign Commerce Handbook*—sources of assistance to U.S. exporters.
- *International Market Information*—special bulletins indicating market situations and new opportunities.
- *Product/Country Market Profiles*—tailor-made, single-product/multi-country or single-country/multiproduct reports.

For information and prices on these and a wide variety of other Department of Commerce publications, write to Export Promotion Services, U.S. Department of Commerce, P.O. Box 14207, Washington, D.C. 20044. (See Appendix G for a listing of other publications from the Department of Commerce and other U.S. government agencies. In addition, Appendix B provides a directory of federal agencies, most of which issue publications on various aspects of international trade.)

American Business Conference.   The American Business Conference (ABC) is an organization whose mission is to foster the growth and development of U.S. businesses worldwide. The ABC publishes information about overseas investment, lobbying activities, and member-companies' circumstances in specific countries. In addition, the ABC sponsors informational breakfasts concerning business opportunities in foreign countries. Headquarters for the ABC is located in Washington, D.C.

Individual Nations' Embassies and Consulates. Most countries maintain a trade promotion office in their embassies. To obtain information about current opportunities, policies, or other subjects, contact the trade attaché at the embassy of the particular country under consideration. (See Appendix E for a list of offices to contact at embassies and consulates.)

Certified Public Accounting Firms. All major American accounting firms publish informational guides based on data from their foreign affiliates or operations in specific countries or regions. Many accounting firms have been highly successful in providing services to overseas clients; hence, their information about specific foreign markets is often extensive. Information of this sort can help you avoid asking questions or doing research on topics for which abundant data already exist.

Banks. Commercial and merchant banks compile statistics on overseas trade. Some banks also publish newsletters or brochures about business opportunities in specific countries and regions.

Consultants and Advisors

In addition to doing your own research, you can obtain information about international trade through consultants and advisors who specialize in providing assistance on this subject. Two options in this regard are

- hiring someone with international experience to serve as your in-house advisor, and
- seeking part-time assistance from an international business consultant.

Despite the expense involved, either of these options will probably save you money in the long run. Some circumstances—such as an early decision to commit your company to export trade or offshore manufacture—may even justify hiring a full-time employee to head your international operations from the start, since an arrangement of this sort will allow you to obtain crucial input during the early stages of investigation and strategic planning.

A sense of hesitation toward the whole endeavor of international trade, however, may just as strongly justify hiring a consultant. The cost will be far lower than the expenses incurred through an ill-considered or badly planned venture; likewise, the money spent on advisory services may ultimately seem insignificant compared to the profits gained through a successfully planned and executed international campaign.

Where can you find these consultants and advisors? You can locate suitable consultants through an executive search firm or head-hunting organization; through any of the large international consulting firms; through the major accounting firms; and through other companies with interest and experience in international trade.

ESTABLISHING POSSIBLE TARGET MARKETS

Once you have acquired some initial information, you should use it to establish a list of promising target markets. Specifically, you should analyze your research data using any of several methods, and develop a sense of which countries or regions most closely suit your purposes. Before discussing one of those methods, however, we should note a mistake that's all too common at this stage of the process.

Many American companies attempt too much in their first international ventures. Having previously held off from doing business abroad, their officers now attempt to make up for lost time. But excessive ambition in the global marketplace is as risky as excessive timidity. The initial goal is *not* to take the entire planet by storm. Just as fighting a war on several fronts at once is difficult, if not impossible, going international in more than one region or country at a time is dangerous and unlikely to succeed.

For this reason, you should *narrow the field.* To avoid the risk of doing too much too soon, you should focus on a particular region, country, or area most suitable for your products, services, or overall strengths as a company.

One of the best ways to narrow the field is the "rifle approach" to research. This method resembles the use of a rifle's spotting scopes for target shooting. To shoot accurately, you first locate the target by means of your own vision. Next, you sight the target through a low-power scope. Finally, you zero in on the bull's-eye through a high-power scope. This step-by-step process allows greater accuracy than is possible by scanning a wide area with an inappropriately powerful scope at the outset. Translated into business terms, this method proceeds as follows:

1. First, consider a region as a whole.

2. Next, narrow the focus to two or three countries.

3. Finally, zero in on a specific country or market.

Using an Evaluation Matrix

For purposes of narrowing your company's focus in the international marketplace, the evaluation matrix shown in Figure 1 works like a rifle's low- and high-power scopes in target shooting. Using this matrix will allow you to identify goals, eliminate risks, and pinpoint potential opportunities more objectively and efficiently than you would by following hunches and whims alone.

The evaluation matrix works as follows: On the horizontal axis, you list the countries and regions that interest you—for example, China, Southeast Asia, Europe, Latin America, the Caribbean. On the vertical axis, you list the attributes that could affect your decision regarding which regions or countries to investigate. You can specify the attributes in whatever way you deem appropriate, based on your initial research.

You should examine two kinds of attributes:

1. Those relating to the general business, economic, and political climates.

2. Those specific to your industry or product.

FIGURE 1 The foreign market evaluation matrix

COUNTRIES OR REGIONS

ATTRIBUTES	WEIGHTING FACTOR	COUNTRY A		B		C		D		E		ETC.	
		RS	WS	RS	WS	RS	WS	RS	WS	RS	WS	RS	WS
GENERAL													
1. Political Stability		RS	WS	RS	WS	RS	WS	RS	WS	RS	WS	RS	WS
2. Economic Stability		RS	WS	RS	WS	RS	WS	RS	WS	RS	WS	RS	WS
3. Currency Strength		RS	WS	RS	WS	RS	WS	RS	WS	RS	WS	RS	WS
4. Currency Mobility		RS	WS	RS	WS	RS	WS	RS	WS	RS	WS	RS	WS
5. Tax Incentives		RS	WS	RS	WS	RS	WS	RS	WS	RS	WS	RS	WS
6. Other Incentives		RS	WS	RS	WS	RS	WS	RS	WS	RS	WS	RS	WS
7. Quality of Infrastructure		RS	WS	RS	WS	RS	WS	RS	WS	RS	WS	RS	WS
8. Ability to Serve as Marketing Hub		RS	WS	RS	WS	RS	WS	RS	WS	RS	WS	RS	WS
9. Etc.		RS	WS	RS	WS	RS	WS	RS	WS	RS	WS	RS	WS

COUNTRY / REGION TOTALS (SUM OF WS)

COUNTRIES OR REGIONS

ATTRIBUTES	WEIGHTING FACTOR	COUNTRY A		B		C		D		E		ETC.	
		RS	WS	RS	WS	RS	WS	RS	WS	RS	WS	RS	WS
SPECIFIC													
1. Income per Capita		RS	WS	RS	WS	RS	WS	RS	WS	RS	WS	RS	WS
2. Competition		RS	WS	RS	WS	RS	WS	RS	WS	RS	WS	RS	WS
3. Sales		RS	WS	RS	WS	RS	WS	RS	WS	RS	WS	RS	WS
4. Specific Laws		RS	WS	RS	WS	RS	WS	RS	WS	RS	WS	RS	WS
5. Cost of Labor		RS	WS	RS	WS	RS	WS	RS	WS	RS	WS	RS	WS
6. Labor Productivity		RS	WS	RS	WS	RS	WS	RS	WS	RS	WS	RS	WS
7. Taxes of Expatriates		RS	WS	RS	WS	RS	WS	RS	WS	RS	WS	RS	WS
8. Cost of Raw Materials		RS	WS	RS	WS	RS	WS	RS	WS	RS	WS	RS	WS
9. Shipping Costs, Raw Material, Finished Goods		RS	WS	RS	WS	RS	WS	RS	WS	RS	WS	RS	WS
10. Etc.		RS	WS	RS	WS	RS	WS	RS	WS	RS	WS	RS	WS

COUNTRY / REGION TOTALS (SUM OF WS)

GRAND TOTALS

RS = Raw Score
WS = Weighted Score

47

You should consider at least the following five fundamental business and political attributes. How you eventually weight them depends on the nature of the activity your company plans within a given region or country.

Political Stability.   The stability and durability of a host country's political system obviously affect your long-term potential for profit. The most attractive setting may become the site of a corporate disaster if governmental crises undermine the nation's economic base, or if a new regime takes an overtly antibusiness stance. These are the most relevant questions to ask:

- How sympathetic to business is the host-country government?
- How smoothly has power passed from one governmental administration or regime to the next in recent years?
- What threats (for example, conflict with other nations, class or racial conflict, or insurgency) might endanger the government?

Currency Stability.   Similarly, stability of the local currency is important. Two factors are most significant.

First, *how stable is the unit of currency itself*? What is this unit's recent history? What factors have affected it? What does the currency's forward market indicate about future stability?

Second, *what international currency is the local unit linked to*? The answer to this question is as crucial as the answers to the previous questions, for it determines not just how you price your product on the international market, but also how you maintain your accounts.

Quality of Infrastructure.   No matter how stable a country's government and currency are, successful business operations depend on a high-quality infrastructure. In particular, you should examine the nature and quality of the following:

- Factories and other industrial plants
- Access to and quality of ports and port facilities
- Roads and highways
- Rail service

- Local transportation system
- Telecommunications (including telephone, telex, and FAX services)
- International and domestic airline service
- Regional and local airports
- Housing (both for expatriate staff and local labor force)

Laws, Regulations, Taxes.   To provide a useful business setting, a host country must have a pragmatic set of overall laws, regulations, and taxes. In particular, these must be conducive to a free-market or capitalistic laissez-faire system. Some countries have established laws and regulations so restrictive as to discourage any investment there. Others have less problematic laws and regulations that nonetheless complicate business practices. Given the burdensome consequences of operating in some of these environments, you should investigate all ramifications of legal and tax issues as early as possible.

Specific issues to investigate include the following:

- Overall regulations for doing business
- Ownership regulations
- Regulations on expatriates
- Regulations on structure and composition of management
- Taxes
- Tax incentives
- Regulations on transfer of technology
- Patent and copyright issues

Ability to Serve as a Marketing Hub.   A secondary but sometimes worthwhile factor to consider is the host country's usefulness as a staging area for business ventures in contiguous regions or countries. Your initial location can allow access to neighboring areas.

From a classic marketing point of view, the procedure is no different from trying to market in the United States. A company starts in one region, then branches out. Entering a particular site overseas is expensive. Rather than establishing a base in each of several countries, your company may do well to consider settling into one of the hub countries—either a financial or manufacturing center or both. These centers generally have regional distribution companies that can help you enter area markets as well.

The hub approach is a highly cost-effective way to spread your business throughout the world. However, the selection of the hub is important. Typical hub choices include the following:

- *Europe*: London, Zurich, Germany, or the Benelux countries
- *Asia*: Singapore and Hong Kong
- *South America*: Buenos Aires, Rio de Janeiro, and São Paulo

Other Facets to Consider.   The general facets just listed are the most crucial to consider in a region; they should unquestionably be part of your matrix. In addition, one or more of the following facets may be appropriate to consider if they seem relevant, given your company's or industry's performance and goals:

- Population with a per capita income over a targeted amount
- Existence and strength of competition
- Current gross country purchases of products similar to yours
- Taxes on expatriates
- Labor costs
- Labor productivity
- Cost of raw materials originating locally
- Local participation requirements
- Shipping costs for both raw materials and finished goods

Again, the appropriate list of attributes to consider depends on the factors affecting sales performance and cost of your product.

How to Use the Matrix

Having identified relevant attributes, you can proceed to use the matrix. For each attribute in each country, you should specify a raw score. Rate each item from 1 to 10, with 1 being poor and 10 being excellent. (The rating can derive either from your basic research or from information that your consultant has supplied.)

You should then weight each attribute according to its significance to your company's product and operations. For each attribute, specify a number from 1 to 10 in the weighting factor column. For example, if your company is considering a major capital investment, then political stability warrants a weighting factor of 10. Similarly, the weighting factor for economic stability will vary in accordance with how much this attribute affects your product. A rating of 10 indicates that the effect is high; a rating of 1 indicates that the effect is minimal.

Once you have finished providing the weighting factors, multiply the weighting factor times the raw score (RS) for each attribute for each country. The result of this multiplication is the weighted score (WS). You should focus on this weighted score for further analysis. Finally, total all weighted scores by country or region to obtain a prioritized list of potential markets. The example matrix shown in Figure 2 indicates that for the product under consideration, Europe is the most desirable market.

You can use this matrix both to assess opportunities and to establish target markets. You should, in fact, use this evaluation matrix as part of an iterative process. That is, you can use it periodically to continue narrowing your list of potential locations for overseas operations. For example, if the initial review indicates that the top priority market for your products is Europe, then you should use the same matrix *employing the same criteria* to identify the specific country within Europe most suitable for operations. Likewise, you could use the matrix to identify a particular city within a particular European nation.

(Note: Once you establish a set of criteria in the matrix, you should not change it—with the exception of additions—as the narrowing-down process continues. Deletions of criteria will skew your results and distort your data.)

IDENTIFYING WINDOWS OF OPPORTUNITY

Completing the preceding tasks will have provided a general sense of your most promising target markets and the most suitable products for those markets. Your data may also have given you a sense

FIGURE 2 Typical foreign market evaluation matrix results

COUNTRIES OR REGIONS

ATTRIBUTES	WEIGHTING FACTOR	CHINA RS	CHINA WS	SOUTHEAST ASIA RS	SOUTHEAST ASIA WS	EUROPE RS	EUROPE WS	LATIN AMERICA RS	LATIN AMERICA WS	THE CARIBBEAN RS	THE CARIBBEAN WS	ETC. RS	ETC. WS
GENERAL													
1. Political Stability	8	8	64	8	64	10	80	3	24	7	56		
2. Economic Stability	8	2	16	8	64	8	64	3	24	3	24		
3. Currency Strength	5	1	5	7	35	8	40	3	15	5	25		
4. Currency Mobility	10	0	0	10	100	7	70	2	20	10	100		
5. Tax Incentives	10	5	50	8	80	5	50	7	70	7	70		
6. Other Incentives	2	5	10	5	10	8	16	5	10	5	10		
7. Quality of Infrastructure	9	2	18	8	72	10	90	5	45	5	45		
8. Ability to Serve as Marketing Hub	10	0	0	9	90	9	90	5	50	5	50		
		RS	WS	RS	WS	RS	WS	RS	WS		WS	RS	WS

COUNTRY/REGION TOTALS (SUM OF WS)	163	515	500	258	380

RS = Raw Score
WS = Weighted Score

COUNTRIES OR REGIONS

ATTRIBUTES	WEIGHTING FACTOR	CHINA		SOUTHEAST ASIA		EUROPE		LATIN AMERICA		THE CARIBBEAN		ETC.	
		RS	WS	RS	WS	RS	WS	RS	WS	RS	WS	RS	WS
SPECIFIC													
1. Income per Capita	7	2	14	4	28	9	63	4	28	3	21		
2. Competition	4	1	4	5	20	8	32	6	24	3	12		
3. Sales	8	1	8	5	40	9	72	4	32	2	16		
4. Specific Laws	9	1	9	5	45	9	81	4	36	3	27		
5. Cost of Labor	1	1	1	5	5	8	8	5	5	4	4		
6. Labor Productivity	2	3	6	6	12	8	16	4	8	3	6		
7. Taxes of Expatriates	5	7	35	7	35	9	45	6	30	6	30		
8. Cost of Raw Materials	4	2	8	2	8	8	32	4	16	7	28		
9. Shipping Costs, Raw Material, Finished Goods	3	8	24	4	12	8	24	5	15	8	24		
		RS	WS	RS	WS	RS	WS	RS	WS	RS	WS	RS	WS

COUNTRY / REGION TOTALS (SUM OF WS)	109	205	373	194	168
GRAND TOTALS	272	720	873	452	548

of particular niches that your products might fill. Step 3, "Mapping Out a Strategy," will show you how to take your findings and build on them, ultimately developing a strategy suitable for entering a particular market overseas.

Something to consider before proceeding, however, is the prospect of identifying a window of opportunity. A window of opportunity generally results from one of the following:

- A temporary relaxation of one or more constraints normally obstructing vigorous commerce, often a change in currency values or a relaxation of government regulations or obstacles
- A sudden technological breakthrough
- An evolutionary change in customer needs
- An increase in market sophistication

Almost by definition, *windows of opportunity appear suddenly, often without any warning at all.* One of their characteristics is that they tend to last only briefly. To succeed in taking advantage of a window of opportunity, a company must therefore act quickly, exploiting the situation as fully as possible. Hesitant, ill-considered action may mean that the firm loses the chance altogether. And while the risks are high and the venture may seem likely to fail, the potential rewards of exploiting a window of opportunity are often great. (A company culture that is risk-averse, however, may argue against taking chances with windows of opportunity.) We'll consider each of the four factors that create a window of opportunity.

Relaxation of Constraints

A relaxation of constraints is the type of window of opportunity that is perhaps the most difficult to predict. However, when one occurs, it can provide unusual advantages to a company intent on doing business overseas.

Essentially, what happens is that economic or political constraints of one sort or another suddenly ease, thus creating new opportunities and facilitating more vigorous commerce. The most common event is a change in currency values. Because currency exchange rates have such a pronounced effect on pricing of exported and

Case Study

A large American manufacturer of processed foods attempted for many years to market its product line in Europe, but the unusually strong U.S. dollar limited the company's chances of attracting European consumers. The Europeans simply maintained their loyalty to local and EC brands.

Then, in mid-1986, the U.S. dollar started to decline in value. Given the new exchange rates, the company's products suddenly became competitive. The firm's international division made a big push to introduce its products—a push that succeeded in establishing the company as a major competitor in the market, and that now appears to have won the company a much larger market share than it had.

imported goods, some otherwise promising American products simply end up too expensive to sell well overseas when the U.S. dollar is strong. For similar reasons, foreign products may appeal to American consumers over comparable domestic brands at such times. Yet fluctuations of currency values can provide windows of opportunity to companies able to take advantage of them.

Technological Breakthroughs

Technological windows of opportunity are somewhat easier to predict than the economic variety, though they, too, tend to last only temporarily. In a sense, the issue is simple: if your company has developed a new technology, you may have opened a window of opportunity. Entering the marketplace at a time when you are the technological innovator may establish you as the market leader. Technological windows of opportunity do not necessarily involve high technology, though they often do. Some products that seem basic—even homely—can take advantage of windows of opportunity created by a lack of comparable products overseas. (Case Studies appear on page 56.)

In short, taking advantage of technological windows of opportunity does not necessarily require the resources of Bell Laboratories

Case Study

In 1976, Digital Equipment Corporation introduced the first mini-computer on the market. DEC initially acquired a 100 percent share of the minicomputer market by default; then other firms developed comparable products. With increasing competition, DEC's market share declined to its current 20 percent. However, DEC remains an acknowledged leader in this technical area and continues to retain its competitive edge.

Case Study

Dale Kirby, a cooper (barrel maker) in Higbee, Missouri, learned in 1985 that executives from the Nikka Whisky Distilling Company of Japan might be interested in purchasing barrels from his shop. After negotiating a contract, Kirby began producing barrels for Nikka. In 1986, production for the Japanese totaled 1,300 barrels and $100,000 in sales. Kirby had found a window of opportunity not because his product was high-tech, but precisely because it was *low*-tech—involving traditional skills of a sort the Japanese found valuable.

or IBM. All you need is a product or service that no one else previously has been able to provide.

Changing Customer Needs

When legal, cultural, or aesthetic situations change within a particular market, new customer needs can create yet another type of window of opportunity. (See the Gerber Case Study opposite.)

Increased Market Sophistication

Changing levels of market sophistication provide the final type of window of opportunity. This type of window is more predictable

Case Study

Gerber Products Company has undertaken extensive market research in India. Despite India's predominantly poor population, the country has a prosperous middle class and a small but wealthy upper class that Gerber considers a promising market.

Until recently, most Indians have been unlikely to show any interest in Western-style baby foods. Lately, though, the convenience of such products, plus their status appeal, has heightened consumers' curiosity and openness. Initial focus groups show that baby foods have high potential for success in certain areas of the subcontinent.

Case Study

Sony determined the advantages of and possible customer demand for the compact disc player. After deciding that growing sophistication among audiophiles would justify the expense of developing the necessary technology, Sony created a whole new technology to supplant the cassette player.

In this instance, Sony saw a need for digital audio products, then created the technology to match a higher degree of consumer sophistication. The company created its own window of opportunity.

than the others, and a company capable of sensing the new sophistication can, given sufficient technical and marketing creativity, design a response to it.

To conclude: the nature of all windows of opportunity is that they are unpredictable, relatively rare, and potentially risky to exploit. If recognized soon enough and acted upon decisively, however, they can give a company both an initial head start and a long-term competitive advantage.

MAKING AN "INSTANT GRATIFICATION" SALE

Your company has now reached a crucial but potentially rewarding juncture. You have determined the company's state of readiness. You have acquired background information. You have performed sufficient market research. You have identified windows of opportunity. So far so good: you have tested the waters and you like what you find.

Despite all the good information and favorable signs, however, you note with growing concern that everything you have accomplished to date is theoretical. The initial research, the data on company capacity, the preliminary market research, and the other information you have acquired are all on paper. How will your company truly perform in the international marketplace? Perhaps the company will do well, but can you be certain? You would feel more secure if you could simply get a better sense of the situation before committing the company to such a major project.

In fact, you *can* test the situation in a more real way. For this stage in the process of going international is a perfect time to make an "instant gratification" sale—a relatively modest sale capable of demonstrating whether your product *does* appeal to customers overseas, whether it is competitive, and whether the process of doing business abroad will be worthwhile. This kind of sale will also indicate if the product requires any changes. The purpose of an instant gratification sale is not to start full-fledged operations. Rather, the sale serves to test the waters in the most tangible, real-world way. By using one of several short-term means of marketing overseas—a trade mission, brokered deal, or consignment sale—you can discover if the task of doing business abroad truly appeals to you and serves your company's best interests.

A sale of this sort serves five purposes beyond the obvious benefit of profits earned:

- The sale can pay for part or all of your market research expenses to date.
- The sale can confirm, refute, or clarify assumptions about the target market based on research thus far.
- The sale can indicate unexpected windows of opportunity.

- The sale can provide solid evidence that your product appeals to customers beyond previous market boundaries (or, if its appeal is mixed, the sale can indicate what changes will make it more acceptable).

- Last but perhaps most important, the sale can give you a sense of satisfaction and accomplishment in actually starting to succeed in the global marketplace.

How do you make this kind of sale? The most common way is through an export trading company. These companies serve as brokers between American manufacturers and overseas distributors. By using an export trading company, you can arrange a test sale of your product without establishing a long-term presence in the target market. The export trading company acquires your stock and sells it at a 5- to 10-percent commission; you then receive payment in U.S. cash. Properly negotiated, the deal allows you to test your competitiveness abroad with minimal risk.

One caveat, however. Export trading companies often insist on exclusive rights extending far beyond the initial arrangement. Such rights may include the right to represent your firm not only in one country, but in all, or the right to represent you long-term. Although export trading companies are often useful, *you should exercise extreme care in negotiations with them.* You should set the shortest possible time limit on the period of representation. If possible, you should make the initial sale a one-shot deal.

For companies that prefer not to deal with export trading companies, another source of instant gratification sales is the trade mission. The U.S. government sponsors and organizes trade missions to foreign countries, thereby providing contacts, publicity, and travel arrangements to participating firms. Although the ultimate success of a particular company's participation depends mostly on its products and marketing expertise, trade missions are a relatively inexpensive means of making initial sales. At times they can prove almost bewilderingly successful.

In short, an instant gratification sale can be bankable proof that your hunches and ideas about going international are as good as you thought they were from the start. Such a sale is one of the best possible ways to test your competitiveness overseas.

Case Study

The United States and Foreign Commercial Service (US&FCS) of the Department of Commerce sponsored a week-long trade show in Paris focusing on American-made apparel. Taking a show of this sort to the fashion capital of the world might seem a hopeless quest; however, the show had a special emphasis—western attire. The participants brought cowboy boots, hats, and other articles of western-style apparel rarely seen in France outside of movie theaters.

Within three days, all the participants had sold out. One manufacturer ended up selling a year's production in that brief time span.

FINDING FINANCIAL ASSISTANCE
FOR FURTHER RESEARCH

Much to the surprise of most American corporate officers, the U.S. government will help companies conduct research into potential overseas trade. Your company may qualify for a cash grant to investigate international markets and your product's suitability for them.

Once you have developed a list of target countries, you should consider applying for one or more of these grants to fund further research. Several different federal government programs can finance marketing research or a detailed feasibility study. Some of the most promising possibilities include the following:

- *Export Import Bank (Eximbank)*, 811 Vermont Avenue, N.W., Washington, D.C. 20571. Eximbank provides funding to businesses interested in doing business abroad. Programs include the Working Capital Guarantee Program, the Foreign Credit Insurance Association, commercial bank guarantees, and the Small Business Credit Program.

- *Overseas Private Investment Corporation (OPIC)*, 1615 M Street, N.W., Suite 400, Washington, D.C. 20527. In addition to financing insurance programs for investors in foreign projects, OPIC offers specialized insurance and financing services for U.S. service contractors and exporters operating in developing countries.

- *U.S. Department of Commerce, Trade and Development Programs (TDPs)*, Washington, D.C. 20523. The various Department of Commerce TDPs offer funding for businesses wanting to undertake feasibility studies on international ventures.
- *U.S. Department of Commerce, United States and Foreign Commercial Service (US&FCS)*, P.O. Box 14207, Washington, D.C. 20044. The US&FCS sponsors trade shows, trade missions, and a variety of informational services on commercial aspects of going international.

Other agencies include the Minority Business Development Agency and the International Division, both part of the U.S. Department of Commerce; the U.S. Department of Agriculture Foreign Agricultural Service; the Small Business Administration; the U.S. Agency for International Development; and the Private Export Funding Corporation. In addition, some state and local governments provide grants for similar kinds of research. For a listing of all relevant federal agencies and a selection of state agencies, with a matrix for matching needs and programs, see Appendixes B and D. (Step 2, "Learning the Language," includes a detailed discussion of federal financial assistance measures, among them funds for purposes other than initial research.)

DEVELOPING A FOCUS

Now suppose you have determined your company's readiness; you have conducted sufficient research to see how your product will appeal to certain markets; you have identified several windows of opportunity; and you have made an initial overseas sale. What you should do next is to develop the right focus.

Developing a focus is the process of taking all the information acquired thus far and confirming your goals and objectives as they relate to the prospective international venture. Although corporate officers can accomplish this task through a variety of methods, the most common and systematic way involves reviewing and perhaps adjusting the company's business plan to accommodate an international venture. (A useful resource in this regard is *The Arthur Young Business Plan Guide* [New York: John Wiley & Sons, 1987].)

To some extent, business plans for international ventures do not differ substantially from their domestic equivalents. The components are similar: identification of a product, identification of a market, plans for a structure (that is, division, subsidiary, and so forth), and development of a budget. Although a formal business plan is ideal, a more informal plan may serve the purpose. Above all else, you should confirm that your company's intentions in the global marketplace complement and support existing domestic goals and objectives. After all, your purpose in going international is not just to start a new endeavor, but to strengthen and augment the firm's activities in the domestic market—in short, to position the company's products better at home as well.

The old maxim holds true here as elsewhere: the best defense is a good offense. Strengthening domestic markets requires expanding into new territory. For example, if a manufacturer of a certain device enters new markets, the increased production for satisfying the new customers' demands will almost certainly reduce the overall per-unit production costs. This will in turn produce two consequences. First, the lower production cost will provide greater flexibility in sales price, thus possibly increasing market share. Second, expansion into new markets presents increased strategic flexibility in implementing tactical market thrusts. The end result will be strengthened company position through increased flexibility for maneuvering in the various markets.

On the other hand, if you determine that your international endeavors will conflict with domestic operations or jeopardize the company's financial stability, then doing business abroad may not be advisable.

This situation leads to the second go/no-go decision in the process of going international.

- *Go*: You have developed a short list of target markets for your products. You now feel even more interested in doing business abroad than you felt before. You want to proceed, narrowing and clarifying your options.

- *No-go*: The result of your initial research is negative. Going international does not appeal to you as much as you first thought.

My experience leads me to believe that executives in most companies have an accurate impression at this stage of whether they should proceed with the four-step process. Generally, the outlook is pretty clear one way or the other.

However, sometimes it's too close to call. If you find yourself in this situation, how can you make a decision? One way is use a checklist similar to the one that started off this section as a means of clarifying the relevant issues one by one.

Factor	Present in Your Situation?	
	Yes	No
1. CEO willing to commit to going international	( )	( )
2. Assessment shows good capital position	( )	( )
3. Background research shows demand overseas	( )	( )
4. Matrix indicates worthwhile target markets	( )	( )
5. Window of opportunity is evident	( )	( )
6. Products/product line appear suitable	( )	( )
7. Plant capacity is adequate or excessive	( )	( )
8. Personnel have overseas sales experience	( )	( )
9. Government funding available for research	( )	( )
10. "Instant gratification" sale made	( )	( )
TOTALS:	___	___

As with the previous checklist, seven out of ten "yes" answers points to a go decision, while fewer than seven "yes" answers suggests that your decision perhaps should be no-go. But if it's a close call, you might consider weighting your answers. Using the following checklist, answer each question yes or no. Give each "yes" answer and each "no" answer a raw score (RS) of 1. Then put a 0 in the space for the alternate answer to each "yes" or "no." (That

Factor	Present? Yes (1)	No (1)	×	Weighting Factor (1–10)	=	Weighted Total Yes vs. No	
1. CEO willing to commit to going international	( )	( )		—		—	—
2. Assessment shows good capital position	( )	( )		—		—	—
3. Background research shows demand overseas	( )	( )		—		—	—
4. Matrix indicates worthwhile target markets	( )	( )		—		—	—
5. Window of opportunity is evident	( )	( )		—		—	—
6. Products/product line appear suitable	( )	( )		—		—	—
7. Plant capacity is adequate or excessive	( )	( )		—		—	—
8. Personnel have overseas sales experience	( )	( )		—		—	—
9. Government funding available for research	( )	( )		—		—	—
10. "Instant gratification" sale made	( )	( )		—		—	—
GRAND TOTALS:						— vs. —

is, if your answer to a particular question is yes, put a 1 in the "yes" space and a 0 in the "no" space.) Then allot each question a weighting factor from 1 to 10, with 1 being least significant and 10 being most significant. Multiply the raw score by the weighting factor to produce the weighted score (WS). Add the weighted scores for a grand total. These weighted scores will highlight the strengths and weaknesses in your company's situation as you consider going international.

Note that *you should use this more detailed method of analysis only if the overall outlook is not evident from the simpler checklist.* Don't look around for the trees if you're already standing in the middle of the forest.

Finally, remember that *the CEO's interest in continuing consideration of an international venture is (as before) still paramount.* All the weighted scores in the world won't help you succeed if your company's top officer regards doing business abroad as a waste of time or an excessive risk.

Whether your ultimate decision is go or no-go, you have based it on real data and on a series of analytical steps. Either way, you have decided what is best for your company. If you decide not to proceed, you have reached this conclusion with minimal risk and expense. If, on the other hand, you decide to continue with the process of going international, testing the waters is only a preliminary step. Its function has been to provide an overall cost-effective means to assess your potential success in the global marketplace. Now, provided that your decision is go, you should investigate the situation in more detail and on-site.

And so we turn to the next step in the four-step process.

STEP 2

LEARNING THE LANGUAGE

American domestic business practices, as noted earlier, often differ from those common in other countries. Attitudes, customs, and expectations about doing business can vary widely from one region of the world to another. Americans who aspire to commercial success overseas should not assume that what makes sense here will always make sense elsewhere; on the contrary, competing effectively in the global marketplace means learning a new language of contemporary international business.

Words are certainly part of this language. Few businesses succeed in the global marketplace without someone in-house able to speak German, Thai, Japanese, or whatever the firm's foreign partners and customers happen to speak. But the issue transcends verbal communication. What we call language includes customer needs and preferences, ways of marketing products, legal issues, and bureaucratic procedures. In short, learning the language of international business involves accepting differences among cultures—in this case, differences that chiefly affect business transactions—and then transforming the differences from obstacles into advantages.

Learning the language does not necessarily mean *agreeing* with other countries' ways of doing business. Business practices, like other aspects of culture, have developed over the centuries as expressions of local needs, preferences, and ways of life. Many Americans consider foreign business practices strange, overly complex, or counterproductive. But culture is always relative. Business people from other countries have their own misgivings about equivalent procedures and attitudes in the United States. (In both cases we are *not* referring to unethical practices; rather, the issue is what people regard as the "sensible" or "efficient" way of getting things done.) This is the issue: if you intend to profit from the opportunities awaiting you abroad, then you must open your mind to new ideas and new ways of doing things. Business is always an art of compromise.

THE UGLY AMERICAN, INC.

Americans often have been accused of cultural insensitivity. The "Ugly American" is a worldwide stereotype. Unfortunately, the cliché contains more than just a kernel of truth. To make matters doubly unfortunate, American tourists are not the only culprits. American business people, too, have often been insensitive to many cultures throughout the world.

Too often, American executives and managers speak dismissively and uncomprehendingly of other cultures.

"We'd like to do business in Japan, but the Japanese just don't speak English well enough to make it feasible."

"They paid us ten million lire [or baht, or escudos, or whatever]. Now what's that in *real* money?"

"This country is so inefficient."

"This isn't how we do things back in the U.S."

Immediately following World War II, when the United States was the world's preeminent exporting country, Americans got away with these sorts of cultural chauvinism. The reason, however, was not that our overseas customers didn't mind what we said or how we acted; rather, the reason was that only the United States—of all the great industrial nations—had escaped wartime devastation. We Americans possessed the money, the work force, and the natural resources to dominate the marketplace almost regardless of our attitudes. But the situation has changed in the decades since then. The United States now has many competitors. Customers can—and do—pick and choose among available suppliers. The result is that businesses whose executives continue to express the old "Ugly American" attitude are now doomed to failure.

INTERNATIONAL "STREET SMARTS"

Luckily, there is an alternative to the old attitude.

The alternative is to attain a new sophistication in dealing with the global marketplace. To put it another way: the alternative is to get "street smart" on an international level.

International trade uses a specialized language of current conditions and business practices. Unfortunately, many foreign competitors already know this language. The good news is that you can learn the language, too, and it will serve you well in your effort to do business abroad.

Step 2 provides information designed to help you learn the language of international trade by means of the following tasks:

- Developing an international perspective
- Identifying and overcoming obstacles
- Conducting market research
- Analyzing risks
- Evaluating corporate tax issues
- Exploring available government funding programs and alternative schemes for financing

A brief word before proceeding, however.

Some of the issues discussed in this step will resemble those discussed in Step 1. Certain tasks necessary in learning the language overlap with those involved in testing the waters. The reason is that these two steps differ in degree rather than kind. Testing the waters involves preliminary, basic research; learning the language requires more detailed research. Both steps are necessary for most companies, but not for all. Moreover, some firms may wish to delete or modify certain tasks within either or both steps. The specific tasks that you undertake, and the depth in which you pursue them, will depend on your specific corporate circumstances.

For these reasons, some intentional redundancies exist among the preceding discussions and those that follow.

DEVELOPING AN INTERNATIONAL PERSPECTIVE

To put the matter bluntly: many U.S. business practices are not understood, appreciated, or even tolerated outside this country. American attitudes toward commitment, strategic planning, employer-employee relations, financial and business planning, and even time itself are, generally speaking, not held in high regard outside North America. For this reason, you must develop a background of business knowledge and a repertoire of business skills appropriate to the global marketplace—in short, you must develop an international business perspective.

Elements of this perspective include

- committing the company to long-term objectives,
- recognizing the cultural challenges,
- pledging personnel and capital resources, and
- developing patience.

Committing the Company to Long-term Objectives

American businesses do not generally focus on long-term planning. During the past thirty years, executives in the United States have tended to stress short-term return on investment, with a consequent emphasis on the quarterly period as *the* unit of planning. Many U.S. companies consider long-term planning to mean planning ahead a year or two—at most, three to five years. European and Asian firms, by contrast, stress a long-term orientation, generally perceived as planning ahead at least ten years. (Grand strategies can extend to fifteen or twenty years or even longer.)

Admittedly, these differences in time sense are partly a matter of opinion. They are a cultural variable. Yet the differences have consequences, and the consequences often work to the disadvantage of American firms.

Case Study

Jake Herbert, the director of a team attempting to sell construction equipment to a Saudi Arabian petroleum company, allotted a year to establish his company as a presence in the region. Little came of initial efforts, however. Saudi businessmen often kept Jake waiting; discussions seemed to meander and stray from substantive matters; making even the most basic arrangements took months.

Frustrated, Jake found that he had made little headway even after half the allotted year. Bureaucratic issues were only one of the problems. If anything, the leisurely pace of Saudi negotiations took even more of a toll. Jake eventually concluded that the Saudis had no real interest in reaching a deal. He recommended to his superiors that the company drop Saudi Arabia as a potential market.

Jake ignored two critical aspects of doing business abroad. First, people in other cultures often proceed less directly—and in some cases more slowly—than do Americans. What Jake mistook for Saudi indifference toward his company was in fact the indirect, often cautious pattern of negotiation characteristic throughout the Middle East. Second, people in other cultures use time as a way of testing a potential business partner's intentions. The Arabs, for instance, often want to do business with Americans but distrust our haste and impulsiveness. (Arabs speak with special derision about American "cowboys"—businessmen who gallop into town as if in a Western movie, only to rush out again at day's end.) Jake jeopardized his own potential success because he failed to perceive the obstacles that his own impatience created.

The fact remains: if you are tempted to emphasize only the immediate future in your attempts to do business overseas, the outcome will likely be dismal. Foreign competitors will simply outlast you. Their successes will not necessarily indicate that their products are better than yours or that their marketing methods are superior. But their sense of time will give them a critical advantage. Outside the United States, few cultures (if any) view time as we do, as a very scarce, quantifiable substance. Most other cultures have a different sense of time—a sense that nothing is really new, and that anything that claims to be new deserves careful scrutiny and forethought. The result of such differences is plain enough. Unless you are willing to plan farther ahead than a few years, you should probably refrain altogether from international ventures. Your competition, after all, will be busy planning ten, fifteen, or even twenty years down the road.

Recognizing the Cultural Challenges

You should recognize certain other general cultural challenges aside from time sense and deal with them as systematically as possible. One of the most basic challenges of doing business abroad is understanding and respecting the varied ways in which other people live their lives. What makes perfect sense to us strikes others as pointless, silly, or absurd. We in turn often regard foreign customs with bafflement or disdain. We tend to mock, belittle, or ignore what we do not understand. As much as adjusting to another culture offers the potential for insights into human variety and flexibility, cultural differences are nonetheless a common source of friction between people of differing backgrounds. The pressures of business dealings do nothing to make matters simpler.

Four examples:

- A Chinese may not look you straight in the eye during conversation or negotiation. This is not a sign of weakness, timidity, or fear, but rather of politeness; the Chinese consider eye-to-eye gazing intrusive.
- A Saudi will take offense if you cross your legs in his presence. Like many other Middle Eastern peoples, the Arabs regard the

soles of the feet as unclean; even the sight of them is considered offensive.

- A Japanese may agree with your statements or answer affirmatively to your questions without meaning to indicate actual approval or intention to follow through. His or her assenting to your words is intended simply to save face for you, and to indicate understanding.
- An Indian or a Greek shaking his or her head left to right does not mean no, but rather yes.

Understandably, effective interaction with business people overseas requires both respect for cultural differences and specific knowledge of customs in particular regions or countries. General sensitivity is usually a question of attitude. Specific knowledge of customs requires either firsthand experience of the other culture, reliable advice, or training through cross-cultural seminars or other programs. Since culture affects business practices, communication styles, and values, cultural understanding smoothes the path of interpersonal relations and also simplifies the task of making business decisions. The time and money you invest in this regard will pay off in the long run. Shortcuts generally lead straight toward a fiasco.

Besides customs, another challenge involves differences in consumers' tastes and attitudes in other countries. Products currently considered unappealing here may have great appeal overseas. Likewise, products that seem surefire winners in the United States may not appeal to consumers elsewhere. What sells in Peoria may not sell in Hong Kong. (See page 74 for a Case Study.)

The issue here is not simply the products or services themselves. The challenge of going international also involves adjusting to different styles of marketing. How you package your product is one aspect of the task. Another is how you advertise. Still another is how you deal with distribution networks and competitors. Each case is different, but in all cases you face cultural biases. Accepting the existence of widely varied consumer wants and needs overseas is the first task in surmounting this challenge. The second task is careful market research—a task explored at length later in Step 2.

Case Study

A widely franchised health club opened a facility in Singapore. With its young, urban population and a widespread appreciation of Western culture, Singapore seemed a site destined for success. Moreover, the club's physical appearance and stock of equipment equaled or surpassed that of comparable facilities in the United States.

Yet the club couldn't sign up enough members. Despite the Singaporeans' interest in sports, the club attracted few of them and ended up catering to the relatively small expatriate community instead. Citizens of Singapore felt little enthusiasm for the American-style health club; they were more attracted either to Western competitive sports or to Chinese calisthenics and other traditional Asian forms of exercise.

Pledging Resources

Overseas ventures require a substantial commitment of resources. Few facts about international business are so obvious, yet the challenge of allocating funds alarms many executives. The predictable consequence is that many ventures never get off the ground.

American firms going abroad for the first time tend to underestimate the competence of the local work force. The result is an expensive overuse of American expatriates. You *do* need personnel from your own country—at least initially—because they know the business, the company, and its preferred ways of operating. However, placing Americans overseas is very expensive. The average foreign posting can cost three times the employee's domestic salary. For obvious reasons, your company should limit the number of expatriate positions to the minimum possible.

With regard to personnel, consider also the following factors:

- *The inadvisability of frequent rotation of personnel.* Because foreign assignments involve a long learning curve, most expatriate staff members don't reach peak efficiency until their third year. Frequent rotation of personnel may therefore jeopardize a foreign staff's potential in the host country. In contrast to most U.S. companies, European and Asian firms keep executives at their overseas posts at least five or ten years; twenty or twenty-five years is not unusual. Although such long-term assignments may not be realistic for American executives, short postings—a year or two—are often self-defeating.

- *The effects of company culture on expatriate personnel.* Most European companies offer international posts as a sign of faith in an executive's ascent up the corporate ladder. By contrast, American firms—with a few notable exceptions, such as banks and oil companies—sometimes have tended to see the international sector as a pasture for languishing executives. Fortunately, this attitude has begun to change. Attitudes within your company will clearly affect the number and caliber of personnel you can attract for increasingly important assignments overseas.

Ultimately, the issue is whether your company wants the long-term benefits of international trade enough to pledge shorter-term capital resources. Going international is always expensive. Half-hearted, ill-planned efforts will not pay off; in contrast, more thoughtful investments may well yield worthwhile results.

Developing Patience

Some host countries use tests of patience as a bellwether to determine the degree of foreign companies' real interest. If you are intent on doing business in a particular country, your plans may proceed smoothly and with due speed. On the other hand, you should always be prepared for the long haul.

Your company may not be as big as Rolls Royce, and you probably won't have to wait seventeen years to turn a profit overseas. But the story indicates that certain countries expect a long-term commitment from companies wanting to do business there. Are you willing to make that sort of commitment? Your foreign competitors are almost certainly ready for a long wait. To succeed, you must be ready to make similar concessions. In this respect, as in others, learning the language of international trade is really a matter of developing the competitive perspective.

Case Study

In 1963, Rolls Royce reached an agreement with the People's Republic of China to build a plant for manufacturing aircraft engines. Seventeen years passed without Rolls Royce turning a profit on their plant.

Then during the early 1980s, the Chinese government started ordering large numbers of jets—all without engines—from the Boeing Company. The Chinese wanted the planes without engines because they already have the Rolls Royce engine manufacturing plant in place. Current Chinese plans call for extensive modernization of both civilian and military aircraft fleets, with large numbers of engines necessary for both.

Since 1980, Rolls Royce has turned a profit on its Chinese engine manufacturing division.

IDENTIFYING AND OVERCOMING OBSTACLES

The next task in learning the language is to identify and overcome obstacles. Most of these obstacles are artificial, for the most part various sorts of restrictions on free trade.

Many governments give a high priority to developing their local economies and protecting their home markets. Their leaders believe that if a multinational company enters the country, the economy should benefit not just from increased employment, but from other aspects of the operation as well. For these reasons, most countries have established laws that they believe will foster local economic development. Whether they succeed in attaining this goal or not is debatable. In some cases, they do; in other cases, they do more harm than good to all parties concerned. But one way or another, these laws confront virtually any American company intending to go international.

Such laws and regulations vary from country to country. In general, however, there are two kinds: *explicit controls* and *indirect controls*.

Explicit Controls

The most common explicit controls are *tariffs, quantitative restrictions,* and *exchange controls.*

Tariffs. A tariff is a tax on an imported product. Tariffs serve two purposes: they raise government revenues and they shield a country's industries from foreign competition. With many countries attempting to develop their own industries, tariffs have become an increasingly common means of protecting local products. Malaysia, for example, requires a 200 percent surcharge on imported cars to protect sales of the Proton Saga, a Malaysian-made auto. Indonesia is developing a semiconductor industry, which it protects through heavy duties on certain electronic chips.

Currently, three major tariff nomenclature systems exist: the U.S. system, the Canadian system, and the basic system used everywhere else. The harmonized system, a system reconciling these three current systems, is under negotiation, with congressional approval likely in the near future.

Quantitative Restrictions. A wide variety of nontariff measures also restrict international trade. One of the most common of these measures is quantitative restrictions (QRs). Quantitative restrictions include bans on the import or export of certain products, as well as import/export quotas limiting other products. Although in fact prohibited by the General Agreement on Tariffs and Trade (GATT), certain QRs remain permissible—for instance, those needed to protect local industries from imports that would cause them serious economic damage.

Exchange Controls. One of the most difficult international business issues is exchange controls. A number of countries restrict or even ban the transfer of company profits to the parent company's nation. Greece, for example, requires government approval for all transfers of funds out of the country; the People's Republic of China prohibits transfers altogether. Other countries have established less drastic but nonetheless restrictive exchange controls. For instance, Brazil allows foreign companies to repatriate a percentage of profits tax-free, then taxes all further profit repatriation at a higher rate.

Currency does not become an issue when your company sets up a local operation with intent to use it as a self-financing operation. For one reason or another—perhaps for tax purposes—you may choose not to repatriate the profits at all. The profits show up on the books; at the same time, you maintain a self-sustaining operation inside that country. (A forthcoming section of this step explores issues of corporate tax planning overseas.)

Indirect Controls

In addition to explicit controls, you may have to contend with other, more indirect controls on international trade.

Content Requirements. Even countries that allow relatively unhindered exchange of goods may stipulate that a certain percentage of an exported product must be locally made. Others specify an assembly clause: that is, they require that products not locally made must be locally assembled.

Stipulations for Local Ownership. Some countries require local equity participation in a multinational operation. This requirement provides the government with a measure of control over foreign companies. The specific terms vary from country to country. Requirements may be either explicit or indirect. India, for example, requires that an Indian firm own 51 percent or more of any multinational company. In contrast, Brazil does not demand local ownership, but the government ties a company's tax rate directly to the percentage of ownership by a Brazilian national. If your Brazilian partner owns only 5 percent of your local operation, the consequent tax rate will be high. If your partner owns 25 percent, the tax rate will be lower. Other countries do not require local ownership at all.

Local participation is not always undesirable. Despite the obvious disadvantages, a local partner can provide advantages as well. A good local partner can provide you with knowledge about the local marketplace, with firsthand expertise about host-country customs and ways of doing business, and with entrées that might take you years to develop otherwise.

Whatever your company's product or service, and wherever you intend to do business abroad, exploring the nature and consequences of these various controls is a necessary first step in learning the language of international trade.

CONDUCTING MARKET RESEARCH

In Step 1, "Testing the Waters," we discussed preliminary research into international markets. Your company should now identify and define foreign markets in more detail. Just as expanding into new domestic territory requires sizing up various factors in the U.S. market, expansion overseas requires thorough, thoughtful market research.

The Need for Objectivity and Expertise

When investigating international markets, most companies should consider seeking assistance from a reputable market research firm or other suitable consultant. This generalization holds true even if the firm maintains its own research department. There are two important reasons for obtaining outside data under these circumstances:

- In most firms, company culture and politics will distort a study of overseas markets to some extent. This is likely even if top management makes an effort to stay open-minded about eventual decisions.

- Most companies—no matter how capable—do not have adequate on-site resources for conducting an effective market study in other cultures. Useful market research cannot be done at a distance; it must be done in the field by personnel with firsthand knowledge of that particular market or country.

Ignoring either of these two reasons may result in operational difficulties and loss of revenue at later stages of the international venture, since decisions on how to proceed will have been based on potentially flawed data. Moreover, market research must encompass wider aspects of the targeted countries than those characteristic of domestic research.

Case Study

Richard Sanderson targeted a prime Asian market for distribution of U.S.-made whiskey. Sanderson's market study indicated that the consumers would be willing to try American brands of liquor for two reasons. First, the taste of American whiskey resembled that of local brands. Second, the characteristically high prices of the local brands would motivate consumers to consider buying American whiskey. Sanderson therefore set up an import company and made arrangements with American whiskey companies to begin exports to this new market.

   Within a matter of months, Sanderson had acquired a significant market share. The local consumers did in fact like the taste of the American products. In addition, the American brands sold at a significantly lower price—at least 10 percent less—than domestic whiskeys. Sanderson had successfully challenged the local companies' market dominance.

   Eight months after starting operations, Richard Sanderson was arrested by the host country's authorities on immigration violations and was charged by their ministry of commerce with violation of import laws. The American embassy contested the charges, which by all appearances had been trumped up. Eventually, however, the host country closed down the import operation.

   In terms of the market itself, Richard Sanderson's assumptions were correct. The host country's consumers liked the taste of American whiskey, and price did indeed provide further motivation. Sanderson therefore had two good reasons for entering the market. However, he failed to explore how his competition would react to his arrival on the scene; he also neglected to assess their influence on the local government. The domestic whiskey producers and distributors were in collusion with host-country government agencies. Sanderson's neglect of these possible factors led to a costly fiasco.

Legal and Regulatory Issues

The preceding case study underscores an important point. In addition to exploring conventional economic aspects of the target market, you should also consider the legal, regulatory, and political dimensions as well. Specifically, you should investigate the following:

- *U.S. certification and export licensing regulations.* A variety of U.S. government agencies maintain specific regulations on imports and exports. If you fail to supply the necessary information, your company may be subject to fines or criminal penalties. For example, the U.S. government maintains strict guidelines for the export of computer technology. Even some seemingly innocent products must meet the applicable regulations. Export of the toy called Teddy Ruxpin—a talking bear whose speech is generated by a computer chip—involved approval of paperwork similar to that required for export of a small computer.

- *Host-country laws and regulations.* Each country has its own specification requirements, health and safety codes, labor requirements, labor laws, and tax laws. These requirements may or may not prove obstructive to your venture, but you must identify and clarify the issues before proceeding. Malaysia, for instance, held up the marketing of a U.S.-made diet cola for over a year because the country's food and drug administration maintains its own testing standards for synthetic sweeteners.

- *Trade obstacles.* Possible impediments in the form of tariffs, trade restrictions, and certification requirements may complicate your efforts at doing business in certain countries. Some obstacles are of minimal significance, but determining which of them actually affect you will require appropriate attention. For instance, Japan maintains such stringent controls on foreign-grown produce that U.S. firms exporting oranges to that country must deal with more than twenty separate regulations.

- *The nature of the host-country government.* Is the local government responsive in principal to free-market access and competition? If not, you should consider delaying when or modifying how you enter the market, or you should look elsewhere, even if all other factors check out. Unfortunately, some host-country agencies promise more than they ultimately deliver. Even the economic development boards in some countries will mislead potential foreign investors about the terms or conditions likely once a company sets up its operations. To assess the situation accurately, you should interview not only the officials in charge of local economic development, but also American and other foreign business people who have (or used to have) facilities in the area, to obtain the widest possible overview.

Other Commonly Ignored Market Research Issues

The regulatory and legal issues just discussed are too often ignored or given short shrift because they do not fall within the scope of traditional research. Other more traditional aspects of market research also escape the attention of some corporations. These issues deserve at least the attention normally given to standard topics of research within the domestic arena. Your study should explore these aspects of the situation:

- *The possibility of corruption among host-country competition.* What are the ties between companies? Do one or two companies dominate the market? If so, is there evidence of collusion between them? Is there collusion between these companies and the government? Is there evidence of close family ties between government officials and local business people? Even the most promising market can become a trap if local business practices are corrupt or closed to outsiders. Take as much time as necessary to explore local connections.

- *The nature of the local culture.* What are the tastes and preferences of the local populace? Are these consumers likely to appreciate American products? Or will they find them strange and unappealing? One of the biggest mistakes that Americans make is to assume that people in other nations go about their lives much as we do. Consequently, even the most detailed market studies often overlook the fundamental differences of lifestyle elsewhere in the world.

Case Study

The chairman of a large American soft drink company decided that the firm should target Indonesia for sales of its most popular beverage. With a population of nearly 180 million people, Indonesia is the fifth most populous country in the world. Management considered this huge potential market irresistible and worked out a bottling and distribution arrangement to serve the country. The company sold the soft drink syrup to a bottler, who then bottled the drink and distributed it.

Unfortunately, sales were terrible. The drink simply didn't sell. The marketing campaign flopped despite predominantly good initial research, including research into the local competition and government attitudes, because the chairman and his project directors forgot to consider two major factors. First, Indonesia does have 180 million inhabitants, but most of them live in rural areas still functioning within a preindustrial economy. Most Indonesians simply don't have much money. Second, many of them prefer sweet, coconut-based drinks; they are unaccustomed to American-style carbonated beverages. A market for American drinks does exist, but almost exclusively in the major cities. That market—consumers with Western tastes and sufficient disposable income to purchase foreign-style beverages—totals only about 8 million people.

In short, basing market projections on raw demographic numbers is a mistake. Moreover, even a potentially appropriate target population may have tastes that an urban American sitting in a corporate office cannot assess.

The most lamentable aspect of these situations is that many companies' field contacts perceive the potential problems and make a point of communicating their perceptions back to headquarters, but top management often overrides the field staff's recommendations in favor of their own biased assessments.

To put the matter bluntly,

- do not be lulled or lured by numbers;
- find good market researchers in the field, and let them study local consumers without interference from biased home-office expectations; and
- above all, listen to what your field researchers tell you.

Appropriate Market Research Techniques

Many standard techniques for market research are appropriate in the initial phases of testing the international waters. You can use a variety of research instruments and acquire roughly comparable data. What you should keep foremost in mind is the need to obtain the most accurate, complete picture possible of customer preferences in the target market, and to grasp this picture as fully as possible. As mentioned earlier, you will only get this accurate and complete picture if your research personnel—whether in-house or outside consultants—truly understand the market.

One risk to watch closely is the *effects of cultural bias on research instruments*. U.S. market research firms—regardless of their excellence within the domestic arena—may not fully grasp the subtleties of consumer issues in other countries. Using American-style research questionnaires may prove inappropriate and counterproductive. In some cultures, you cannot ask direct questions of your respondents at all; you must employ a more indirect method instead. (Many Asians, for example, would find direct questioning pushy and offensive.) In other cultures, questions that may seem worthwhile to an American market researcher may prove pointless, awkward, or insulting to respondents. (For instance, interviewing Latin American men about their preferences in household appliances would insult their masculinity, since many of them generally consider the kitchen to be exclusively a woman's domain.)

Respondents may also misperceive some questions that they do answer, thus providing inaccurate data. For example, because Italians dislike the number 7 (it has implications similar to the number 13 in Anglo-American culture), if you use a questionnaire with seven parts or seven questions, Italian respondents may respond hesitantly or not at all. The Chinese, in contrast, believe that the number 8 brings good fortune, so a questionnaire with eight sections may receive a favorable response.

Since few Americans, regardless of their cultural sensitivity, can second-guess all misunderstandings possible in another culture, your team should arrange some sort of *review process* before employing a research instrument in the field. Although such a review extends the duration of learning the language, the expenditure of time and effort is worthwhile. At a minimum, you should have your field contacts try out the questionnaire themselves. A test run among host-country consumers would be a wise investment as well. The same holds true for focus groups or other means of obtaining a firsthand sense of consumer responses (for example, taste testing where applicable). Otherwise you risk skewed data and, in the long run, damage to your whole enterprise.

A Suggested Sequence of Research Steps

If you decide that your company should proceed with independent market research, the process should include the following steps:

1. Defining the market
2. Evaluating market potential
3. Examining market niches
4. Identifying potential regional centers
5. Evaluating present products and product lines

1. Defining the Market. The global marketplace is so complex and competitive that you should strive to be as precise as possible in defining the market you seek overseas. This is especially important if your company is doing business abroad for the first time. You should answer two critical questions in this regard:

- What is your target market?
- What is your goal within that market?

For instance, you may have defined market expansion as your goal and Southeast Asia as the target market. Alternatively, your goal may be to introduce a new product, and your target market may be Europe, a market the company already serves. Whatever your choice, you should narrow the market to the greatest degree possible.

Consider your company's product. Where is it likely to appeal most to foreign consumers? Where could it be sold most successfully? How can you test the product's appeal before making more substantial commitments of time and money?

2. Evaluating Market Potential. Equally important are issues of market potential. How large is this market? What is the estimated per capita income of potential consumers? What is the history of consumer demand for similar products? What changes may be necessary in your product before it is appealing?

Case Study

McDonald's started its first franchise in Japan during the 1960s. Despite the Japanese penchant for fast food, the operation failed to catch on among local consumers for ten years.

Later, McDonald's started conducting extensive market surveys to determine the nature of Japanese tastes. What resulted was a realization that a market for American-style hamburgers did in fact exist, but that the product itself needed to be changed somewhat to accommodate local dietary preferences. The Japanese consumers wanted a sweeter bun, more pickles on the hamburger, and more salt and less fat in the meat. Once McDonald's made these adjustments, their fast food started appealing to the Japanese market. By the mid-1970s McDonald's hamburgers had become a big hit throughout Japan.

Elsewhere, McDonald's has made other adjustments to meet other consumer preferences. In France, for example, the company sells vintage wines as well as popular soft drinks. Customers at McDonald's in Germany can buy local beers. In Malaysia, the choice of milkshakes includes not only the familiar chocolate and vanilla, but also tropical flavors including *durian*—a malodorous fruit popular throughout Southeast Asia.

Another important issue to consider is the deceptive nature of some markets. For example, most American business people would consider India to be a poor market for baby food. The widespread poverty among residents of the subcontinent would surely rule out any possibility of success. Yet the Gerber Products Company has found that the upper 20 percent of India's urban population respond well to test marketing of baby food; the company is therefore considering a new Indian operation.

3. Examining Market Niches. Market niches are essentially current and future consumer demands. The demands may be technological, aesthetic, or financial; in any case, discovering an unmet demand can provide a niche that other companies have missed.

Case Study

General Electric originally developed the concept of the video cassette recorder, but Japanese electronics firms were the ones who grasped the real potential of the VCR.

The Japanese realized that a whole new market existed among busy professionals who wanted to watch certain programs but couldn't because of business and social engagements. Sony and other firms filled the niche by providing technology to satisfy these customers' needs. People now tape programs while away from home, then watch them when their schedules allow. In short, the concern for flexibility created a market niche that VCRs fill.

In dealing with the global marketplace, the most important factor is understanding local attitudes. Some aspect of consumers' needs has not been met, or has not been fully met; this gap provides a potential market niche.

4. Identifying Potential Regional Centers. Another step in market research should concentrate on investigating overseas markets as potential centers for regional operations. If several markets look promising but one of them allows easy access to contiguous countries, then the one capable of serving as a hub for the others is clearly the most promising. Targeting that market now may prevent the later expense of setting up several sites overseas.

5. Evaluating Present Products and Product Lines.   Finally, you should return to an issue first raised in Step 1: examining your company's products both individually and as product lines. The initial examination—brief and cursory—met the early needs of testing the waters. Now, however, you should determine specific ways in which your products are suitable or unsuitable.

Consider the following questions:

- Are your products in conformance with tastes, legal requirements, and cultural expectations overseas? Base your answer on previous research—both off-the-shelf and in the field—and, if necessary, on further market studies.

- Are some products suitable while others are not? Is the entire product line suitable? Is the product line perhaps not suitable at all? Here, too, you should perform further sample market testing if necessary.

- If modification is necessary to make a product or the product line suitable, then what are the changes? What level of change does each product require? Have you reviewed all applicable U.S. and host-country laws and regulations? (Some products require such extensive changes that the trouble of making them cannot be justified. For instance, Century Products, Inc., a manufacturer of car seats and other children's gear, found that modifying its seats to meet Sweden's idiosyncratic requirements wasn't worth the trouble. Other products involve virtually no change at all— modification of packaging, perhaps. In other cases, you may have to change the products themselves.)

- Are hidden issues present? Might your products offend overseas sensibilities, tastes, beliefs, or preferences, or violate taboos?

By the time you conclude this task, you should have a clear sense of which product or products you intend to take overseas, as well as a sense of which country or region is your prime target market. Are you sure, though? To double-check the decision your company is reaching, proceed to the next task.

ANALYZING RISKS

Throughout this book, we have stressed that doing business abroad involves several iterative processes. That is, you must repeat certain kinds of analysis or planning at different stages of going international. The iterative process just concluded is market research: first the cursory research of testing the waters; now the deeper, more detailed research of learning the language. Similarly, risk analysis—a part of the matrix used earlier—now requires another examination.

Factors to evaluate include the following:

- Political stability
- Currency strength and mobility
- Issues affecting financial operations
- Suitability of the infrastructure
- Capabilities of the work force

Political Stability

Your analysis of potential target markets should consider the various host countries' political stability. In these settings, can there be a successful transition of government without disruption of business? A positive answer does not necessarily presuppose a fully democratic system; some countries have orderly political transition without full-fledged democracy. The most critical factor under these circumstances is whether one leadership or regime can leave the scene and another replace it without resultant political chaos, and without seriously disrupting local business functions. For example, Thailand undergoes frequent military coups, but the political changes have scarcely affected the favorable Thai business climate and the country's steady rate of growth during the past several decades. Other countries, though more democratic in their political processes, have nonetheless ended up with administrations less responsive to multinational companies' needs. (Greece is one such country.)

Currency Strength and Mobility

In Step 1, we touched on issues of currency strength. Now we examine these topics more closely.

The earlier issues were

• How stable is the unit of currency itself? and
• What international currency is the local unit linked to?

Now you should consider how these issues can augment or diminish the risk your company faces overseas.

If your primary balance sheet and pricing strategy is based on U.S. dollars, for example, you will want to enter a country tied primarily to the U.S. currency. Hong Kong, Taiwan, and Singapore all tie their currencies to the U.S. dollar, since the United States is their major trading partner. Fluctuations in the U.S. dollar do not affect the prices of goods bought or sold between the United States and these three Asian countries. On the other hand, if you locate in Singapore but price your goods in yen, fluctuations of the Singapore dollar will make your prices fluctuate as well, causing major accounting headaches.

Note also that certain economic treaties provide stability to otherwise weak currencies. Some U.S. companies are able to operate effectively in European countries with relatively unstable currencies—for example, the Italian lira and the Spanish peso—because the European Currency Unit (the ECU) provides a framework for interchange with the EC. The so-called Snake, to which all EC currencies are tied, also provides some stability.

A final but critical consideration: currency mobility. Many governments restrict the amount of currency that a company can withdraw from the country. You should investigate in detail what percentage of your profits can be repatriated, and under what conditions. The most profitable enterprise in the world will prove pointless if your earnings cannot leave the host country. Greece, for instance, is a potentially profitable market; however, the Greek government limits repatriation of foreign companies' profits.

Issues Affecting Financial Operations

In addition to currency restrictions, other obstacles may affect financial operations. The most significant are the following:

- *Restrictions on local borrowing.* Some countries prohibit multinational companies from borrowing locally. Others require a local partner to take out the loan. Still others require that loans be made in local currency but repaid in a foreign unit of exchange. Determining the nature of such regulations is crucial, since local borrowing may solve some of the currency issues discussed earlier.
- *Restrictions on foreign accounts.* A number of nations restrict the amount of foreign currency that a company can control at any one time.

Suitability of the Infrastructure

You should focus with special care on the host country's infrastructure. The crucial factors are the same as in Step 1, but you should now base your assessment on as much firsthand information as possible, data that either company personnel or hired consultants have provided. The most critical factors remain the following:

- Factories and other industrial plants
- Access to and quality of ports and port facilities
- Roads and highways
- Rail service
- Local transportation system
- Telecommunications (including telephone, telex, and FAX services)
- International and domestic airline service
- Regional and local airports
- Housing (both for expatriate staff and local labor force)

Capabilities of the Work Force

Employment presents two kinds of issues overseas. The first concerns the local work force; the second concerns expatriate staff.

You should consider the following issues that affect the number of available local workers and their quality:

- *Training.* If the local work force in your host country is not trained to the level appropriate for your operations, then you must choose between finding another site or training local workers yourself. Such training programs require additional investment; however, the cost may end up far lower than the cost of bringing in expatriate staff.

- *Unions.* Some countries have more militant unions than others. Depending on the strength and political stance of local unions, an otherwise high-quality work force may prove unreliable.

- *Attitude toward employment.* In the United States, employers and employees tend to see each other in expedient terms. Workers take and quit jobs with varying degrees of commitment; similarly, management hires and fires workers more or less to suit its own needs. Other countries maintain a different attitude toward employment, however. In many cultures, the owners and managers of a business feel a deeper sense of duty toward their employees than Americans expect. The depth of this duty at times resembles that of a parent toward children. The *patrón* in Latin America and the *bapak* in Indonesia are only two expressions of this quasi-paternal relationship. American executives should investigate the local customs regarding their responsibilities toward a host-country work force.

As for the issues of hiring expatriate staff, these are so complex that we will address them in a later section. If you feel a need to investigate the question of expatriates now, read the section on this subject in Step 4, "Beating Them at Their Own Game."

EVALUATING CORPORATE TAX ISSUES

You should also evaluate the international tax issues affecting your overseas venture. Ideally, your company should plan its overall response to corporate taxation before proceeding with any other task in going international. The following discussion highlights the broad concepts of international corporate tax issues. *You should acquire detailed advice on both U.S. and foreign taxes before entering into any venture.*

The U.S. taxing authority taxes not only all income earned within the United States, but also income earned overseas and later repatriated to this country. Since other countries may tax income earned within their jurisdictions, American companies risk double taxation. Fortunately, the U.S. Internal Revenue Code recognizes this risk. To avoid the double taxation resulting from a foreign country's tax on the income earned there, the U.S. taxing authority grants a foreign tax credit to offset the U.S. tax on the foreign income. As you set up operations overseas, you should therefore strive for the maximum tax benefit allowable under the circumstances: deferral from U.S. taxation on the foreign-source income. Deferral is, in fact, the key U.S. tax planning concept affecting operations outside the United States.

For example, if your company earns income through a foreign subsidiary, and if that income is not subject to a high tax rate in the host country, your U.S. parent firm benefits only as long as— and to the extent that—those earnings are retained outside the United States. Under these conditions, the U.S. tax is deferred. Once the earnings are repatriated to the United States, however, your U.S. group is subject to taxation of the earnings at the U.S. rate, with foreign tax credit for foreign income taxes already paid. The amount of foreign tax credit is limited to the amount of U.S. tax liability with respect to the foreign income. For this reason, the final tax paid on repatriated foreign earnings will be either the U.S. rate or the already-paid foreign rate of tax, whichever is higher. If your company has several sources of foreign income, you may be able to plan the repatriation so that you apply the foreign tax credit limitation according to the "average" foreign taxes paid from several sources. With this type of cross-crediting of foreign taxes, you may be able to average down the foreign tax rate to at least the U.S. rate in order to maximize the benefit of the foreign tax credit system.

A variety of issues affect your use of tax deferral under these circumstances. Not all issues affect all companies; however, you should explore any and all such issues to establish which are relevant to your international operations.

Corporate Structure

Given current regulations, indefinite deferral of U.S. taxation on foreign earnings is the optimum benefit obtainable by an American corporation. The structure of foreign operations can affect the nature of deferral; therefore, you should examine the consequences of how you organize your company in a foreign country. Your two principal alternatives are doing business as a *branch* or as a *subsidiary*. In general, the decision to structure overseas operations as a branch or as a subsidiary turns chiefly on the following two questions:

- Do you anticipate that profits from foreign operations will be retained by that business, or will they be repatriated on a current basis to the United States?
- Do you anticipate losses during the start-up period?

Branch.   If you conduct business in a foreign country as a branch, then the profits of that branch are subject to immediate U.S. taxation. The U.S. taxing authority grants you a foreign tax credit in the current year for any foreign taxes already paid. The use of a branch structure does not provide a deferral of U.S. taxation on the branch income.

However, if your company pays a high rate of foreign tax on that branch income, there may be no current detriment in using a branch structure, since the company has not benefited from deferral of U.S. taxation in the first place. Structuring your foreign operations as a branch may provide another important benefit, especially in the early years: the branch may not be profitable initially, and that loss can be part of the U.S. tax return, available to offset the U.S. tax on other income on a current basis.

Subsidiary.   Alternatively, if you do not expect to repatriate profits on a current basis, or if you can benefit from deferral because the foreign tax rate is lower than the U.S. rate, then using a subsidiary can be an advantage. This is because your company will initially pay the foreign taxes on a current basis; only upon repatriating subsidiary profits to the United States will the U.S. tax differential become payable.

Host-Country Issues Affecting Branch or Subsidiary Structure.   Your decision to use a branch or a subsidiary structure must also take host-country tax issues into account. These are the most critical questions to address:

- Is the foreign tax rate different for a branch or a locally incorporated subsidiary?
- Is there an advantage with respect to the possible withholding tax on repatriation of profits from that foreign country?
- From a host-country viewpoint, is there a difference between how a branch and a subsidiary is financed? (Generally speaking, a U.S. corporation gains some advantage financing its foreign operations as fully as possible with debt rather than equity; debt often provides for an interest deduction in the local jurisdiction, and thus there is a resulting tax reduction.)

Tax Holidays

In structuring foreign operations, the rate of foreign taxation is also critical. You should structure the foreign business to reduce foreign taxes. To maximize the host-country tax benefits available, you should also understand and fully use any local "tax holidays." Many countries provide benefits that vary depending on whether the U.S. corporation has structured a branch or a subsidiary within the foreign jurisdiction. Tax holidays also affect the status of U.S. taxation. If a company intends to conduct business in a foreign country that offers a tax holiday—which will generally result in a lower rate of current foreign taxation—your company may benefit from structuring its foreign operations as a subsidiary. This will allow you a deferral of U.S. taxation, as previously mentioned.

Local tax incentives may provide the following benefits:

- *A current lower rate of tax on foreign earnings to the extent that they are not repatriated to the United States.* Lower-taxed foreign earnings may also enhance the use of foreign tax credits from high-tax countries when the low-tax profits are repatriated.
- *Other cost-reduction incentives,* such as job incentives providing either free or subsidized personnel training, or reductions in the payroll tax or other costs involved with employment in the host country.
- *Local loans* at preferential interest rates.

Methods of Conducting Business

In many countries, you may be able to conduct business in ways that minimize the amount of income subject to local taxation and thus the amount of actual foreign taxes paid. Factors to consider in this regard include the following:

- *Whether a local sales company is actually necessary*—that is, your corporation may be able to set up a non-locally incorporated entity to conduct sales within the host country, thereby avoiding local taxation altogether.

- *Whether the activities within the foreign country can be compartmentalized to reduce local taxation* through arrangements like consignment sales or cost-plus arrangements, both of which limit the amount of income subject to local tax.

Transfer of Technology

The U.S. Congress has recently become concerned with the outflow of American technology to facilities outside the United States. Accordingly, Congress has passed legislation—specifically, the Tax Reform Acts of 1984 and 1986—regulating the transfer of technology. If an American corporation or individual develops a certain technology, then the firm cannot transfer it to a foreign-related party (including its own foreign subsidiary) without subjecting that technology to full U.S. taxation. You should therefore pay close attention to how, and in what form, your parent company makes its technology available to any foreign subsidiary.

From a legal point of view, there are essentially three ways in which you can transfer technology to a foreign subsidiary.

- *You can sell the technology for a lump-sum payment to the foreign subsidiary.* This arrangement results in full, immediate taxation for the value of the technology transferred.

- *You can license the technology for a stream of future royalty payments.* Generally, a licensing arrangement of this sort is an advantage to the U.S. group, since it defers from current taxation the value of the intangible transferred, with taxation occurring in future years as the actual royalties are received. (A royalty arrangement may also be advantageous from a local tax jurisdiction point of view, since royalty payments to a U.S. parent company are often tax-deductible in the foreign country.)

- *You can often transfer technology to the foreign subsidiary as a contribution to the capital of the subsidiary.* That is, you can transfer the technology in exchange for shares or other equity interest in the foreign subsidiary. This alternative also results in U.S. taxation of the value of the intangible.

The Tax Reform Acts of 1984 and 1986 provide a comprehensive scheme for U.S. taxation of all three types of transfer. Each type involves advantages and disadvantages. Generally speaking, however, the best current alternative is either to sell or to license the technology directly to the foreign subsidiary. In each case, the U.S. taxing authority has the power to continuously review the value of the technology transferred, to ensure that the price paid (such as royalties) keeps pace with the value of the intangible transferred.

Two final points.

First, the term "transfer of technology" encompasses all kinds of intangibles, among them those currently recognized as protected intangibles (patents, trademarks, tradenames, and so on), as well as less easily identifiable intangibles, such as general know-how or processes that the U.S. company may make available to the foreign subsidiary.

Second, you should investigate not only the initial formation or transfer of the base technology to your foreign subsidiary, but also rules applicable to ongoing research or enhancement of technology.

Anti-Abuse Rules

Because the opportunity to defer taxation of foreign-earned income tempts some American corporations to shift income or operations overseas for this reason alone, the U.S. government has developed the most comprehensive anti-abuse rules of any industrialized country. These rules are contained in several areas of the tax law, the most famous being the so-called Subpart F rules. Subpart F rules affect current taxation of certain types of income earned by a foreign subsidiary and may cause current taxation of deferred foreign income if the funds are directly or indirectly made available to the U.S. group.

With respect to income, the Subpart F rules generally provide for immediate or current U.S. taxation of certain types of "tainted" income earned by a controlled foreign subsidiary. The types of tainted income that cause immediate taxation generally fall into two categories: passive income, and other kinds of business income.

Passive Income. The Subpart F rules consider all types of passive income earned by a foreign subsidiary—whether interest, dividends, rents, royalties, or gains from the sale of property—to be tainted income. When a foreign subsidiary has a significant amount of tainted income, the U.S. tax rules immediately consider the passive income distributed to the U.S. shareholder and thus subject to current taxation.

Passive Foreign Investment Companies. The rules relating to passive foreign investment companies (PFICs) can be significant to U.S.-based multinationals. In general, a PFIC is any foreign corporation that earns 75 percent or more of its income as passive income, or that holds 50 percent or more of its assets as passive assets. When a foreign company meets either of these criteria, its entire income is either currently taxed to the U.S. shareholder, or—if the U.S. tax continues to be deferred—an interest is applied to the deferred U.S. tax, thereby removing the economic benefit of the tax deferral. If the U.S. firm does proper tax planning to achieve the tax deferral for low-taxed foreign earnings, and if the foreign business is successful, the foreign corporation may quickly reach the point where it has significant passive assets and is subject to these PFIC rules.

Other Kinds of Business Income. The Subpart F rules also target income (such as sales, service, or insurance income) whose origins are business operations established overseas chiefly or exclusively to avoid U.S. taxation. For example, suppose that a U.S. company establishes a Hong Kong subsidiary to purchase inventory from the U.S. exporting company and to sell it to the ultimate third-party customer. The sale of that property takes place away from Hong Kong. Under these circumstances, the IRS will view the U.S. parent company as having no reason for conducting that business transaction through Hong Kong other than to avoid U.S. taxation. The income from that transaction will be taxable immediately to the U.S. shareholder.

The Subpart F rules are highly complex and restrictive. For this reason, you should analyze all expected business transactions to determine if these rules will affect the transactions.

Intercompany Pricing of Goods and Services

Most developed nations, including the United States, follow the concept that when two companies that are part of the same corporate group provide each other with services or sell each other goods, the price charged between the related companies should equal the price an unrelated party or person would be charged. For purposes of tax planning, you should review the independent intercompany pricing rules of each of the countries in which your business is conducted, to make sure that your overseas venture complies with this "arm's length" principle.

The first step in this regard is defensive. That is, you should comply with each country's rules so that the local taxing authorities do not consider your intercompany pricing as a means of reducing your taxable profit in their jurisdiction. This is a defensive strategy because if an intercompany price is established and one of the countries in which you do business does not accept that price, that country may attempt to increase its taxation. The result would be double taxation of your profit, since the two countries may be using a different base or a different price to determine the profit on an intercompany transaction.

From a tax planning point of view, determining the proper intercompany price may be part of a worldwide tax strategy for your business. There is often no precise intercompany price acceptable to the various foreign country governmental authorities; however, you can probably establish or determine the intercompany pricing within a range of acceptable prices. Your company can then use that range to establish an optimal worldwide strategy. For example, you may be able to use intercompany pricing as a means of minimizing taxation (or of minimizing income and therefore taxation) in a country where tax rates are high, while at the same time earning more profit in another country with lower tax rates. For this reason, you should review and analyze the activities performed by various foreign subsidiaries to determine what the optimal pricing structure should be. This will allow you to maximize worldwide tax planning by earning profits where they are most advantageous.

A cautionary note: intercompany pricing as a tax-saving strategy should not be used to an extreme. Also, keep in mind that most countries adopt the strategy of requiring an independent or arm's-length price; only within the range of acceptable prices can such a strategy be used.

Joint Ventures

If you conduct foreign business through a joint venture arrangement, this results in certain unique and often conflicting U.S. tax planning requirements.

The Subpart F anti-abuse rules generally apply when the U.S. ownership of the foreign business is greater than 50 percent. Many of the anti-abuse rules may not apply where the U.S. party is not a majority owner. However, one of the difficulties of conducting business through a joint venture is the transfer of technology to a joint venture entity. As mentioned earlier, the transfer of technology or intangibles involves strict U.S. tax rules and may subject the U.S. company to current taxation on the disposition of the technology.

This often leads to a conflict of interest with the other partner in the joint venture. While from the U.S. viewpoint it may be preferable to license rather than to contribute the technology in question, this arrangement alters the economics of the proposed venture. The result may not be an acceptable alternative to the other partner.

Exports of U.S. Products

The United States government has attempted to promote the export of American-made products by providing tax incentives relating to export profits. Specifically, the U.S. tax rules have a special provision for the use of foreign sales companies. A foreign sales company is a foreign corporation that acts as the selling agent for an American manufacturer or exporter. American exporters are allowed or encouraged by the tax rules to provide or shift some of the profit from the export to the foreign sales company; subsequently, through a series of specially provided intercompany pricing rules, the U.S. regulations exempt a portion of the foreign sales company income from U.S. tax, even upon repatriation.

The result of using a foreign sales company is that the U.S. exporter can in effect earn and exempt from U.S. tax a portion of the export sales profits. In general, this type of export benefit results in an approximately 4–5 percent reduction in the federal income tax rate applicable to the export.

Foreign sales companies offer an important means of reducing the U.S. tax on export profit. Although this arrangement entails creating and maintaining an additional foreign company, the U.S. government has attempted to simplify for American exporters the task of complying with the foreign sales company rules so they can obtain the resulting benefits.

Service Companies

Unlike most countries, the United States taxes its citizens on their worldwide income regardless of where they reside. However, the U.S. government provides certain tax incentives to American citizens employed outside the United States.

Specific incentives available to U.S. expatriates are the following:

- *An exclusion from taxation for up to $70,000 of foreign-earned income per year,* if that income is already taxed in the country where it is earned. This is an advantage to an American citizen if the local tax rate is lower than the U.S. taxes otherwise payable on those earnings.

- *Foreign tax credits in lieu of the foreign-earned income exclusion.* In this situation, the employee is not achieving a real tax savings, but rather merely avoiding double taxation while paying at least the U.S. tax rates.

Because the American expatriate is subject to worldwide taxation when working outside the United States, most U.S. corporations provide their employees with some form of tax equalization or tax protection. These programs generally take the form of an agreement between the employer and the employee that if the employee incurs a greater amount of foreign tax due to his or her foreign assignment, then the U.S. company will subsidize or reimburse the employee for the excess foreign taxes payable. In situations where the employee incurs a greater foreign tax liability than his U.S. tax liability, the tax protection or equalization policy effectively results in an increase in employment costs to the American company. These circumstances mean that when your company analyzes projected costs and expenses related to transferring a U.S. employee to a foreign subsidiary, you should consider the difference in tax rates payable by the U.S. employee (as well as possible compensations) as possible costs.

LOCATING GOVERNMENT FUNDING PROGRAMS AND ALTERNATIVE FINANCING

The final task of learning the language is once again a subject touched on earlier: government funding. Like the other iterative aspects of going international, this return to an earlier subject can work to your advantage, for many federal, state, and local government programs exist to provide assistance at this stage of the process.

Specialized Funding for Exports

The U.S. government and many state governments have established programs to assist American companies to export their products and services. Most of these programs—both federal- and state-sponsored—work under the auspices of commercial banks. Consequently, commercial banks themselves can be a source of excellent information on available government funding.

The Export-Import Bank of the United States (Eximbank) offers three programs to assist companies with exports.

- The *Working Capital Guarantee Program,* which can guarantee loans for working capital before actual sales. Although the company takes out the loan with a commercial lender, Eximbank guarantees repayment of 90 percent of the principal, thus leaving the lender with only a 10 percent risk on the loan.

- Eximbank's *Commercial Bank Guarantees Program* offers guarantees against nonpayment of foreign purchases on medium-term (181 days to five years) export loans by U.S. companies. Loans can be used to finance capital and quasi-capital goods and services.
- *Small Business Credit Program.* Since exporters face the risk that their cost of money will rise before a loan is repaid, Eximbank also provides a program to insure small businesses' loans against this eventuality.

For further information on these and other programs, contact the Export Import Bank at 811 Vermont Avenue, N.W., Washington, D.C. 20571. You can also obtain Eximbank publications, including *Eximbank Information Kit,* from the same address. Another useful source of information is the U.S. Department of Commerce publication *A Guide to Financing Exports,* which you can obtain from United States and Foreign Commercial Service (US&FCS) district offices.

Sponsorship and Assistance for Trade Missions

You can undertake trade missions—planned visits to potential buyers or clients overseas—either on your own or as part of an organized group. If you prefer to travel with a group, participation in a Department of Commerce–sponsored mission may serve your purposes. The Department sponsors three types of missions:

- *U.S. specialized trade missions.* Department personnel plan, organize, and lead these missions after selecting a product line and an itinerary that offer the best potential for export sales. Commercial officers make hour-by-hour individual appointments tailored to the specific needs of each participating firm. Mission members pay their own expenses and a share of the mission's operating costs.
- *State and industry–organized government-approved (S&IOGA) trade missions.* State development agencies, trade associations, chambers of commerce, and other export-oriented groups plan and organize S&IOGA trade missions. The Department of Commerce offers guidance and assistance from planning stages to completion of the mission.

- *U.S. seminar missions.* Like trade missions, seminar missions promote the sale of U.S. goods and services abroad; in addition, they assist companies in finding agents and other foreign representatives. These seminar missions are especially appropriate for facilitating the sale of sophisticated products and technology.

Contact the Office of Marketing Programs, Room 2116, Export Promotion Services, US&FCS, U.S. Department of Commerce, Washington, D.C. 20230, for further information on trade missions.

Other Kinds of Trade Assistance

In addition, several agencies provide financial assistance to U.S. companies. The most notable are the following:

Small Business Administration. The Small Business Administration (SBA) has established several programs to aid American exporters. Such programs include an arrangement with Eximbank that permits certain applicants to borrow up to $1 million through a commercial bank, which submits the application to an SBA field office. The SBA's Export Revolving Line of Credit (ERLC) loan program, meanwhile, permits any number of withdrawals and repayments within the designated dollar limit (certain other conditions apply). Note: to qualify for these programs, a business must meet size and other criteria. For further information on these and other SBA programs, contact the nearest SBA field office, or contact the Small Business Admistration, Office of International Trade, 144 L Street, N.W., Washington, D.C. 20416.

U.S. Department of Agriculture. Within the U.S. Department of Agriculture, the Foreign Agricultural Service (FAS) provides financial support to U.S. firms wishing to export agricultural products through the Food for Peace program and the Commodity Credit Corporation. The Food for Peace program authorizes U.S. government financing to companies selling agricultural commodities to friendly countries on concessional credit terms. The Commodity Credit Corporation grants U.S. exporters short-term commercial export financing under the Export Credit Guarantee Program and the Blended Credit Program. For further information on these programs, contact the General Sales Manager, Export Credits, Foreign Agricultural Service, 14th Street and Independence Avenue, S.W., Washington, D.C. 20250.

State and Local Programs.   Almost every state government has established an export financing program to assist potential exporters. Some states allow one of their agencies to deliver Eximbank funds, while others offer state-funded loan guarantees. If your company wishes to consider state programs, refer to Appendix D, "Sources of State Assistance," for further information.

Investment Protection

Because foreign investment in certain countries involves more financial risk than in others, the U.S. government has established an agency to facilitate U.S. private investment in less-developed nations. This independent, financially self-supporting corporation is the Overseas Private Investment Corporation (OPIC). The purpose of OPIC is to provide investment protection of several kinds:

- Political risk insurance for contractors and exporters, protecting them against the arbitrary and unfair drawing of letters of credit that some countries require
- Insurance against the risks of currency inconvertibility; confiscation of tangible assets and bank accounts; war, revolution, insurrection, and civil strife; and losses sustained under certain other conditions

For further information on these programs, contact OPIC at 1615 M Street, N.W., Suite 400, Washington, D.C. 20527.

In addition, Eximbank offers credit insurance through the Foreign Credit Insurance Association (FCIA), which covers 100 percent of a company's losses from political conflict (war, expropriation, currency inconvertibility, and so on) and up to 95 percent of commercial losses (nonpayment due to the buyer's insolvency or default). To learn more about FCIA programs, contact the Foreign Credit Insurance Association at Eximbank (address given on page 103).

To summarize, given this country's current trade deficits, the federal government and most states are increasingly eager to help U.S. companies with their efforts to go international. However, many executives feel hesitant to seek or use help from the government. The reasons vary, ranging from suspicion of the various agencies' intentions to contempt for their ability to accomplish anything in the Real World. Such attitudes are unfortunate. Ironically, some of the most skeptical business people are those who simultaneously deride the collaboration between foreign companies and their governments. Why shouldn't American companies similarly benefit from the U.S. government's interest in easing the process of doing business abroad? There's nothing wrong with obtaining well-selected assistance from the federal or a state government, especially since it can make a big difference to your company's success, both in the short and the long run.

TO GO OR NOT TO GO?

Having completed all the tasks that make up learning the language, you have now reached one of the most critical decision points in the course of going international. You have developed an international perspective. You have identified and overcome obstacles. You have conducted market research. You have analyzed risks. You have evaluated corporate tax issues. And you have explored available government funding programs and alternative schemes for financing. Now what?

Unfortunately, this is one of those points where each person or board faces the decision alone. To go or not to go?

This juncture is an appropriate place for further use of the matrix (Figure 1) described in Step 1. As suggested at that time, you can modify the matrix at each step of going international to narrow the focus of your attentions. If you feel some uncertainty about which specific market to enter, for example, you might use the matrix to zero in on particular areas within a country, or even to target individual cities. On the other hand, if you feel misgivings about the regions you've selected thus far, you might back up and redo the matrix altogether, now specifying countries you have previously disregarded.

Overall, the writing on the wall ought to be fairly clear.

If the writing says no-go, then don't. Likewise, if the writing seems a bit fuzzy—or if the words don't seem to have shown up at all—then, generally speaking, the message is also no-go.

If, on the other hand, the writing says go, then it's time to address the issues of strategy and strategic management.

Which brings us to Step 3 in the four-step process.

STEP 3 _____

MAPPING OUT A STRATEGY

For many decades, the U.S. economy grew so quickly and steadily that many competitors could prosper at the same time. More recently, however, several factors—among them the complexity of the domestic marketplace, the scarcity of resources, the expense of money, and the end of constant growth—have changed the rules of the game. The international situation is even more complex: many nations now compete effectively with the United States. Few organizations can now take survival for granted.

One of the central issues for businesses has become confronting and addressing the challenge of competition. Top management must now focus even more than before on *mapping out a strategy for maximum competitive advantage.* Nowhere is this focus more important than in doing business abroad, where commercial practices and cultural factors are more complex than at home.

STRATEGY: YOUR PLAN FOR COMPETITIVE SUCCESS

Strategy is a plan for action to achieve certain goals within a competitive environment. Whether your goal is winning a football game, increasing market share, or conquering another country, strategy directs the means to the end. A team, a company, or an army might choose to take action without formulating a plan in advance, but even this choice—"winging it"—is a kind of strategy. It's simply an improvisory, spontaneous, confident (perhaps overconfident) strategy. Generally speaking, however, strategy involves conscious, concerted planning. For the most part, strategy requires careful planning focused on the specific goals an organization wants to reach and on overcoming the obstacles between that organization and its goals.

Mapping out a strategy is the logical third step in the four-step process of going international. Testing the waters has given you a general sense of the global marketplace and your company's place within it. Learning the language has provided a more specific impression of how and where your company might succeed overseas. Now the time has come for mapping out a strategy to enter a foreign market. In this step, you can develop a detailed, systematic program for taking your products or services to consumers in another country.

This step—like others in this book—may seem self-evident. What could be more obvious than the need for a strategy in going international? Yet here, too—as with the other steps—a surprising number of companies proceed without well-formulated plans. All too many corporate officers fall prey to the temptation to "wing it." Because other countries seem remote and unfamiliar, it's easy to imagine that improvisation is the only possible way. Many other business people go ahead and develop a strategy but then fail to implement it properly. A third and regrettably common fate befalls overseas ventures when management plans a strategy, begins to implement it, but then loses its nerve or departs unthinkingly from the chosen goals and tactics along the way. The results are predictable: confusion in the field, poor corporate performance, and minimal or nonexistent profits. For these reasons, it is all the more important to plan carefully from the start to ensure successful strategic management.

A note on that last phrase, *strategic management*. In a business context, it's important to distinguish between strategic planning and strategic management. Strategic planning is a method of formulating a strategy that tends to be relatively static. The planners formulate a strategy, then pass it on to the personnel who implement it. By contrast, strategic management is a more dynamic method. Strategic management involves the organization in an ongoing process, and the personnel who formulate the strategy are the same as those who implement it. Strategic management provides a means of integrating organizational capabilities to ensure effective strategic thinking and day-to-day behavior throughout an organization. Strategic management rather than strategic planning is our focus in Step 3.

Careful strategic management is especially critical in the competitive global marketplace. Competitors are abundant; they are experienced and aggressive; they are committed to the long term. Nothing short of thorough, imaginative planning is likely to prevail. However, *the goal is not to devise a strategic plan so extensive that it becomes a burden.* Some corporations have tended to create strategies in such detail—often filling entire volumes—that they serve no practical purpose and ultimately end up ignored and unused. Rather, *the goal is to define the company's mission and how to achieve it, and then to plan a brief, convenient strategy that management will find useful and productive in the course of doing business abroad.*

WHY IS A STRATEGY NECESSARY?

Studies of military history indicate that as a battlefield becomes increasingly complex, strategy becomes more and more crucial. Engaging an enemy in battle and competing against business adversaries have some important similarities. Both require planning. Both involve complex logistics. Both demand imagination, foresight, and steady nerves. Both can result in the loss of territory and resources. Moreover, both can benefit from the insights of the classical military strategists. Perhaps most significantly—at least for the present discussion—both business and war can involve smaller forces defeating larger, better-equipped ones.

This case study illustrates why a strategy is necessary in going international: to plan for action that will achieve certain specified goals

Case Study

During the late 1960s, Japanese car manufacturers wanted to enter the U.S. market. They looked for a niche and found one at the low end of the market: students and other consumers who wanted no-frills transportation. The small-and-cheap car market, as it so happened, was a niche that did not interest the Detroit auto companies. (Even relatively small American-made cars—such as Ford's Falcon and Fairlane—were essentially family cars.) The only formidable presence in this market was Volkswagen. Even so, VW could not fill the wide-open small-car market fast enough. The Japanese companies responded by following a time-tested military strategy: taking uncontested ground first.

Datsun and Honda first began to introduce their cars into the United States around 1967. U.S. automakers paid little attention to the newcomers; they derided the Japanese cars as cheap models suitable only for a market that did not interest them in the first place. Essentially, the American automakers' attitude was to let Volkswagen fight it out with Datsun and Honda. Meanwhile, the Japanese focused on providing low-cost products, built up a following (and, more important still, built up a low-cost, high-quality manufacturing base), then gradually introduced larger, better, higher-priced models.

Now Toyota, Datsun, Honda, Mitsubishi, and all the other major Japanese manufacturers have established themselves as a permanent, formidable presence in the U.S. automobile market. These companies have moved beyond their initial niche to satisfy America's demands for a wide variety of high-quality cars. The Detroit automakers have had an increasingly difficult time competing effectively against them.

within the highly competitive global marketplace. The Japanese automakers used strategy to take market share from the American companies even though they were competing against unfavorable odds on foreign territory. By defining where their companies had been, where they were, and where they wanted to go, the Japanese developed a plan for systematically achieving not only their ultimate *corporate goals* (taking U.S. market share from the domestic auto-makers), but also for achieving the interim *means to the goals* (acquiring an initial niche, then expanding into other niches).

WHAT ISSUES SHOULD A STRATEGY ADDRESS?

While mapping out a strategy, your company should use the information acquired through testing the waters and learning the language to focus on and clarify the following issues:

- Corporate strengths and weaknesses, including products, organizational structure, financial capability, and operational capability
- Corporate goals
- Market trends and opportunities, both current and future
- Market segmentation, including most promising niches
- Competition

In general terms, a strategy should relate the corporation's identity, capabilities, and goals to the nature of the market. More specifically, a strategy provides a means for bringing corporate strengths and weaknesses into the most effective interplay with the competition.

WHAT PERIOD OF TIME SHOULD A STRATEGY COVER?

A good strategy is dynamic; that is, it is flexible enough that management can continually review, evaluate, and change elements of it even in the course of generally successful implementation. As with virtually all other aspects of going international, strategic management is an iterative process. You should not expect to formulate a strategy and then follow it without revision for the indefinite future; you will most likely adjust many aspects of the strategy as you go. Although international ventures invariably require a long-term commitment of time and resources, effective strategic management requires adaptability to future changes, problems, trends, and opportunities.

Generally speaking, no strategy is entirely sound for more than about three years. Circumstances can change drastically over that time span, making predictions risky and the success of recommendations uncertain. Most companies therefore tend to plan three years in advance, while sketching the general contours of later strategy to cover another two or three years. At the year-and-a-half point following initial implementation, management reviews the strategy and adjusts it as needed. Accurate prediction beyond that time horizon is generally difficult, and detailed planning is ineffective or even counterproductive.

There are, however, numerous exceptions to this rule. For instance, the nuclear power industry must plan the construction and operation of power plants to take several decades of work into account. The fashion industry and many high-tech industries such as the computer industry deal with far more unpredictable market demands and far shorter production schedules.

WHO SHOULD PLAN? WHO SHOULD IMPLEMENT?

Given the complexities of strategic management, you must give special attention to the following three conditions if your efforts are to succeed.

- Management must have a shared vision of the company's ultimate goals. Companies driven by a clear purpose and shared values are far more likely to succeed than those with uncertain purposes and conflicting values.
- Management must have a common understanding of the company's resources (material, financial, personnel); of its competitive environment (market, competitors, products, critical success factors); and of relevant strategic principles involved.
- Management must have an across-the-board acceptance of the direction and urgency of implementing a chosen strategy as the planning process reaches its final stages.

Note that all three of these conditions relate to in-house commitment to the strategy. To put the issue most succinctly, the doers must be the planners. That is, all senior-level personnel should be involved in some or all phases of the strategic management process, and these same people should be responsible for implementing the strategy they decide upon. (The actual degree of their involvement will, of course, depend in part upon the size of the company.)

All too often, top executives delegate implementation to staff members within the management team. The result is that the people who are most thoroughly involved in implementing a plan have little or no investment in its success. Operations managers can—and often do—simply wash their hands of the strategy if difficulties arise. By contrast, if the persons responsible for implementation are those who devised the strategy in the first place, they have bought into the whole scenario more than if they simply inherited a set of advisories from a group of planners.

ONE APPROACH: STRATEGY WORKSHOPS

One successful approach to the early phases of strategic management is to hold in-house strategy workshops. In such workshops, all members of the management team meet to exchange ideas and information; they design a strategy; they plan its implementation.

This approach has several important strengths:

- *It promotes the free flow of data* among contributors, thus bringing expertise from a variety of sources within the company.
- *It encourages "devil's advocate" roles* that can increase the chances of spotting potential problems before they occur.
- *It heightens team members' commitment* to the overall plan ultimately agreed upon.

The result of this workshop method is often a high level of participation during planning stages and a greater potential for success during implementation.

Here are three suggestions on how to organize a strategic management workshop:

- Before holding the workshop, *send each team member a questionnaire* eliciting opinions about the company's strengths and weaknesses, about the competitors' strengths and weaknesses, and about other significant issues to address in the course of strategic management.

- *Designate one member of the team to facilitate the process.* This should be someone who will encourage new concepts and effective group dynamics rather than foster orthodox company thinking.
- *Strive for eventual consensus on the strategic plan* rather than forcing an early decision that will alienate team players in the long run. Try to reach agreement on each level of strategy (mission, goals, objectives, and so on, as described in the next section).

The goal of these workshops—in fact, the goal of the planning process itself—is to do the company's strategic thinking as fully as possible in advance. Improvisation has its virtues, and your field staff may have to improvise at times; but the more completely your strategy takes contingencies into account, the more likely your company will be to succeed in its new venture.

A FRAMEWORK FOR STRATEGIC MANAGEMENT

A framework is an essential tool in organizing the tasks of strategic management. One such framework, which we call FOCUS*, has proven effective in a wide range of settings throughout the global marketplace. This framework provides a means for analyzing information, clarifying goals, and planning and implementing corporate strategies. Using this framework can help you create a brief, flexible, practical strategy rather than a long, rigid, overly theoretical strategy of the kind that has burdened many international ventures in the past.

What follows is an overview of this framework. You may prefer to use another method—perhaps your company's own in-house procedures—to map out a strategy. But one way or another, you should satisfactorily address the fundamental issues raised in the following discussion.

---

*FOCUS is a proprietary approach to strategic management developed by Arthur Young and its international affiliates.

The Three Phases of Developing a Strategy

The FOCUS framework organizes six tasks within three broad phases. These phases and their corresponding tasks are:

- the *foundation phase,* during which you (1) analyze the information compiled from testing the waters and learning the language, (2) define a mission, and (3) establish goals;
- the *strategic development phase,* during which you (4) develop objectives and (5) plan strategies; and
- the *pre-implementation phase,* during which you (6) create action plans.

Figure 3 shows this framework.

The Foundation Phase: Information Analysis, Mission, Goals

In the course of testing the waters and learning the language, you have amassed abundant information about target markets overseas; in addition, you have acquired new or more refined information about your company's operations. Now, during the foundation phase of mapping out a strategy, you analyze this information, with emphasis on the following three areas of concern:

- Environmental assessment
- Competitor assessment
- Corporate assessment

You then use the results of your analysis to define a mission and establish goals.

Information Analysis. The task of information analysis begins by assessing the environment in which your company will function overseas. This *environmental assessment* in turn focuses on three subareas: the general environment, the industry, and the market.

First, *the general environment.* What conditions in the host country will affect your venture? Will the climate require special storage facilities for the company's products? How good are the local

FIGURE 3. The FOCUS planning framework

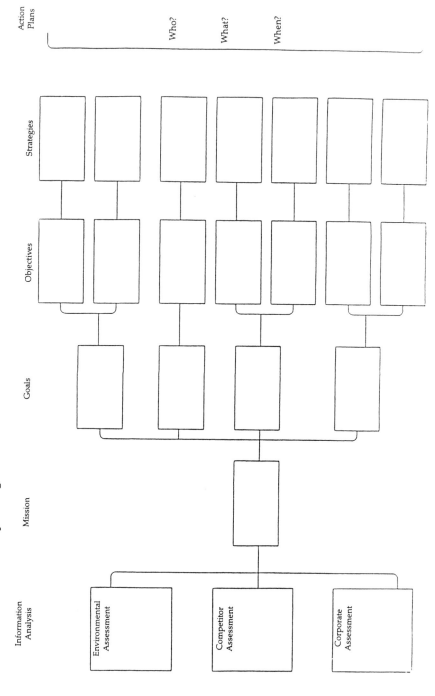

telecommunications resources? Will host-country financial or political conditions complicate the task of doing business overseas? During the course of testing the waters and learning the language, you have answered these and many similar questions; now you should examine the collected data in terms of how the general environment influences your strategy. Use the following checklist to summarize your data and assess whether each factor is an asset or a liability in relation to your company's plans.

Factor	Asset	Liability	N/A	Explanation
1. Ecological environment (describe):	( )	( )	( )	
2. Technological environment (describe):	( )	( )	( )	
3. Local economic environment (describe):	( )	( )	( )	
4. Demographic and sociopolitical environment (describe):	( )	( )	( )	
5. Legal environment (describe):	( )	( )	( )	

For each factor in the checklist, you should specify the most characteristic features of the target market. For example, a U.S. firm that specializes in alternative energy technology and that is exploring the possibilities of selling solar-powered water heaters in a large Southeast Asian country might specify these features:

1. *Ecological environment:* Tropical climate; two dominant seasons (wet/dry); varied topography (mostly hilly); good maritime access.

2. *Technological environment:* Developing technological base; good infrastructure in cities, uneven elsewhere; some high-tech industries.

3. *Local economic environment:* Current economic slump; potential improvement if tin and oil markets improve; governmental constraints.

4. *Demographic and sociopolitical environment:* Growing urban population; large rural population; good work force; ethnic tensions.

5. *Legal environment:* Strict governmental regulations on patent/trademark issues; strong trade barriers; risk of patent/trademark piracy.

The second stage of environmental assessment concentrates on *the industry.* How extensive is your industry worldwide? What corporate structures do other companies use (for example, joint ventures or subsidiaries) in the target market? How do other companies in the industry go about distributing their products? Analyzing these issues will help you identify the factors that influence your strategy for dealing with the industry overall. Use the following checklist in assessing the industry. (As before, you should tailor this checklist to fit the specialized circumstances your company faces overseas.)

Factor	Asset	Liability	N/A	Explanation
1. Industry structure (describe):	( )	( )	( )	
2. Customer base (describe):	( )	( )	( )	
3. Employment and competitive situation (describe):	( )	( )	( )	

(Continued)

Factor	Asset	Liability	N/A	Explanation
4. Business orientation (describe):	( )	( )	( )	
5. Distribution structure (describe):	( )	( )	( )	
6. Safety issues (describe):	( )	( )	( )	

The market is the third and final area to consider in an environmental assessment. If a cluster of two countries in a region has high market volume, and if another cluster of ten countries has a lower market volume, which cluster would make the better target market? The answer will vary, of course; but even a huge target market in terms of area may not be promising if the actual market volume is low. Similarly, the stability of demand influences the decision to enter a specific target market even if the level of demand is currently high. These and other considerations affect your assessment of the target market. Applying your data from testing the waters and learning the language, the following checklist—again, properly adjusted to reflect your specific circumstances—will help you assess the market and its effects on strategy.

Factor	Asset	Liability	N/A	Explanation
1. Market volume (describe):	( )	( )	( )	
2. Life cycle status of the market (describe):	( )	( )	( )	
3. Quantitative market growth (describe):	( )	( )	( )	

(Continued)

Factor	Asset	Liability	N/A	Explanation
4. Market share (describe):	( )	( )	( )	
5. Stability of demand (describe):	( )	( )	( )	
6. Market segmentation (describe):	( )	( )	( )	
7. Demand trends (describe):	( )	( )	( )	
8. Structure of customer requirements (describe):	( )	( )	( )	
9. Motivation for purchasing (describe):	( )	( )	( )	
10. Purchasing procedures (describe):	( )	( )	( )	

Having assessed the general environment, you should now focus on assessing your company's competition. Specific areas to analyze in this *competitor assessment* are each competitor's market share, market segments, recognizable strategies, financial strength, and so forth. Your goal in analyzing these factors is to answer the fundamental questions that will help you plot your strategy. What are your competitors doing? How strong are these companies? What sorts of distribution networks have they established? Why are they successful—or why aren't they? Can you outlast them? Sizing up these factors will clarify your strategy in terms of specific rivals. For each competitor, use a copy of the following checklist (modified in the ways already described) to assess its situation and how serious a threat it presents to your overseas venture.

Factor	Asset	Liability	N/A	Explanation
1. Market share (describe):	( )	( )	( )	
2. Market segments (describe):	( )	( )	( )	
3. Recognizable strategies (describe):	( )	( )	( )	
4. Present situation (describe):	( )	( )	( )	
5. Price range (describe):	( )	( )	( )	
6. Financial strength (describe):	( )	( )	( )	
7. Reasons for current success or failure (describe):	( )	( )	( )	

Finally, the third step in analyzing information is summarizing your own company's situation—the *corporate assessment*. While testing the waters and learning the language, you acquired data about the firm's plant capacity, product suitability, and other factors influencing performance overseas. You should now analyze these areas, with special emphasis on your company's financial resources, knowledge of marketing and distribution, and organizational structure, using the following checklist.

Factor	Asset	Liability	N/A	Explanation
1. Your company's capabilities (describe):	( )	( )	( )	
2. Current market situation (describe):	( )	( )	( )	
3. Research and development capacity (describe):	( )	( )	( )	
4. Production methods (describe):	( )	( )	( )	
5. Procurement methods (describe):	( )	( )	( )	
6. Management methods (describe):	( )	( )	( )	
7. Organization and personnel (describe):	( )	( )	( )	
8. Costs (describe):	( )	( )	( )	

(Continued)

Factor	Asset	Liability	N/A	Explanation
9. Earnings (describe):	( )	( )	( )	

One other crucial factor besides those in the preceding checklist deserves your special attention. This factor is your company's *strategic excellence positions.*

Your strategic excellence position (SEPs) are your company's or product's distinctive capabilities—whatever features make your company unique or remarkable. Properly recognized and cultivated, your SEPs *can give your company leverage to attain success in the marketplace.* For this reason, identifying SEPs lays the foundation for your strategy.

Strategic excellence positions are important because operational excellence alone is not sufficient to guarantee success. Your company's excellence must be in an area of strategic significance; that is, some feature or features of your product or service (or the way in which you deliver it) must be in a position to determine the outcome of competition in the marketplace. For this reason, you should take special care to identify the distinctive capabilities that you wish to emphasize as part of your strategy in going international. Remember in doing so that features that work well at home may not have the same value facing other competitors in other marketplaces.

How do you identify your company's strategic excellence positions? There are a variety of methods, but one of the most straightforward makes use of the checklists already provided in this chapter.

First, go back to the checklists you've used in this chapter. Note all the factors marked on the checklists as strengths. On a separate page, make a list of these strengths. This is your initial compilation of *potential* SEPs. Next, prioritize and clarify the individual strengths. Consider the following questions as you do so:

- Which features of the company are the strongest, the most remarkable, or the most unusual?
- Which features most fully support management's overall goals?
- Which features give the company the most leverage in its new overseas market?

Examples of Strategic Excellence Positions

We can look to a number of corporations for examples of strategic excellence positions. The following companies have achieved success by capitalizing on distinctive capabilities:

3M—product innovation

Chapparal Steel—production technology

Allersuisse—materials technology

Benetton—customer needs

IBM—customer service

Frito-Lay—distribution network

Rolls Royce—image

Disney—employee motivation

GE—strategic planning

As you proceed, you should discard factors that are less promising and retain those that are relatively more so. Narrow the list to three or four strengths. You may wish to regard several of these strengths as your company's SEPs; on the other hand, some firms (like those listed in the preceding boxed example) emphasize one predominant SEP. In any case, you *cannot* have a strategic excellence position that has not appeared initially as one of the strengths in the checklists you filled out.

This process determines your strategic excellence position or positions. In addition, by helping you clarify the issue of the company's strength, it also leads to the next task in the foundation phase.

Mission.   After having assessed the environment, the competition, and your own company, and after having identified your SEPs, your next task is to define the company's mission.

In broad conceptual terms, the mission statement defines your company's view of what drives its business activities. The statement may include references to product, target market, desired market position, financial goals, business methods, distribution channels, and geography. Unlike other components of your strategy, the mission statement is not quantifiable or measurable. It may consist of a statement about today's business, or about where the organization would like to be in the future. There are few rules for writing mission statements. A company's mission is, after all, an expression of corporate identity or philosophy, hence something that varies greatly from one organization to another.

Note that an effective mission statement is generally oriented primarily toward your company's customers rather than toward its owners; it does not apply equally well to your company's competitors; and it expresses a vision and purpose that employees are proud to work toward.

Sample Mission Statement

One company formulated the following mission statement: "To be the world leader in developing, manufacturing, and selling instruments for laser surgery." We'll call this company Las-Tech, Inc., and use it as a model to illustrate the remaining strategic management tasks.

Goals.   Goals elaborate and expand on key components of the mission statement. Although more specific than the mission statement, goals are nonetheless broad statements of the organization's aspirations for the future. They include the company's distinctive capabilities and, generally speaking, its enduring general features, often nonquantifiable. Most companies state their goals in terms of the external business environment, and often in relative terms—that is, "the leading," "the best," "the highest quality," and so forth.

There are several important aspects of goals:

- Goals can be product-, market-, or function-related.
- The number of goals that a company can achieve is limited, given finite resources. Ideally, a firm should attempt to set only four to six goals.
- Goals must harmonize with each other.

* If possible, goals should build on strengths already present within the organization.

Sample Goals Statement

Las-Tech formulated the following goals statement:

Product leadership: To be recognized as having the most innovative and highest-performance products.

Domestic growth: Expand the use of surgical laser technology until it becomes part of the American surgeon's standard equipment, while maintaining our market share.

International growth: Establish our firm as the premier supplier of laser surgery technology in the European market.

Profitability: Earn a return on investment sufficient to attract financial resources to fund our growth and product leadership.

**The Strategic Development Phase:
Objectives and Strategies**

Objectives and strategies provide the link between the general goals and the specific actions that you will take to accomplish those goals. During the strategic development phase, you create this link.

* *Objectives* quantify the goals.
* *Strategies* make it possible for you to attain these objectives.

Objectives.   Objectives are time-specific, measurable (or at least in some fashion quantifiable) achievements. Obtained from specific departments or people, they are internally focused, indicating desired results in financial or quantifiable terms. Performance against measurable objectives is the prime indicator of whether the company is attaining the related goals.

Sample Objectives Statement

Here is the objectives statement developed by Las-Tech:

New products: Introduce devices for use in at least three new major branches of surgery within three years.

Existing products: Reduce the user costs of existing devices by 20 percent per year over each of the next five years, while improving performance characteristics.

Domestic growth:

- Have one of our devices installed in 80 percent of U.S. teaching hospitals.
- Expand the use of the technology to at least five new major surgical applications within the next four years.

International market entry: Enter Europe by having one of our devices installed in at least 200 English, French, and German teaching hospitals by 1995.

Profitability: Maintain return on equity at above 20 percent.

Strategies. In contrast, strategies describe overall approaches to achieving goals and objectives. They identify the opportunities to be exploited and, in turn, the resources to be acquired and concentrated so that you can take advantage of the opportunities. Strategies are generally sustained over the long term, though they may require fine-tuning along the way. Strategies are not detailed action steps; instead, they define the framework for developing specific action plans and the responsibilities for getting things done.

Sample Strategies Statement

Las-Tech stated its strategies as follows:

New products:

- Double the funding level for our three existing product introduction teams
- Establish three new teams during the next twelve months

Existing products:

- Commit $250,000 to develop a long-term productivity improvement program
- Establish joint research projects with teaching hospitals and major university laser technology departments

Growth:

- Undertake demonstration educational programs covering target markets in the United States and abroad
- Develop innovative financing schemes for initial placements
- Complete substitution of own sales force for agencies by 1990
- Develop and implement a marketing program including advertising, speakers, and technical articles
- Selectively fund high-profile use of our devices

European market entry:

- Establish European hub office in London
- Establish branch offices in Frankfurt and Paris
- Hire and train sales force for all three offices
- Establish contacts in major English, French, and German hospitals

Sample Strategies Statement, continued

- Adapt sales materials to each language/culture, with individual marketing programs including advertising, speakers, and technical articles

Profitability:

- Actively seek external research financing and investigate R&D partnerships
- Raise debt/equity ratio limit to 3:1

The Pre-implementation Phase: Action Plans

We now arrive at the third phase of mapping out a strategy. Backing up each strategy is an action plan and, in turn, an appropriate allocation of resources.

Action plans are essentially the how-to of executing a strategy. They take the form of lists that specify who will do what and by what time. In the case of international ventures, action plans provide the means to track how personnel in the field are executing the instructions that will ultimately set up operations and keep them running.

Sample Action Plan

Here is the action plan Las-Tech formulated to implement one aspect of its goal of international growth.

Goal: Establish our firm as the premier supplier of laser surgery technology in the European market.

Objective: Enter Europe by having one of our devices installed in at least 200 English, French, and German teaching hospitals by 1995.

Strategy: Adapt sales materials to each language/culture, with individual marketing programs including advertising, speakers, and technical articles.

Action plan: Develop promotional materials

Action steps:	Person responsible:	Due date:
Retool promotional brochures to address specific cultural issues within target host countries.	C. Girard M. Flannery	May 1, 1990
Identify translation services and request bids for work; select best bidder.	R. Levine	May 1, 1990
Submit translated documents to objective third-party medical contact for quality control.	M. Flannery	June 8, 1990
Send appropriate materials to established contacts overseas.	C. Girard	September 1, 1990

Putting It All Together

The result of finishing the six tasks that comprise the FOCUS framework is typically a document that looks something like Figure 4.

This framework now provides a succinct, easily reviewed map for each officer in your company to follow according to his or her specific role. It also offers a reality check as you proceed to implement the strategy. The FOCUS framework allows easy reference to the chain of cause-and-effect relationships within a particular strategy; that is, the framework's structure facilitates the recurrent task of identifying problems during the course of implementation. A difficulty in executing a particular action plan, for instance, may jeopardize the company's ability to execute the relevant strategy. This in turn may delay or prevent meeting a particular objective, with implications for reaching a certain goal. The framework makes it easy for management to track events and to predict their likely consequences.

134

FIGURE 4. Typical FOCUS framework results

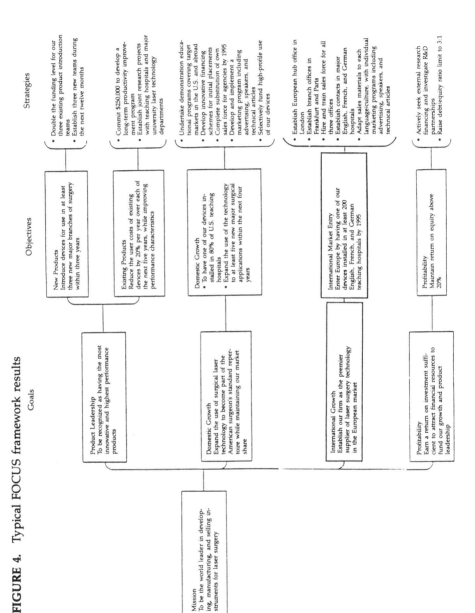

Goals

Objectives

Strategies

Mission
To be the world leader in developing, manufacturing, and selling instruments for laser surgery

Product Leadership
To be recognized as having the most innovative and highest performance products

New Products
Introduce devices for use in at least three new major branches of surgery within three years

- Double the funding level for our three existing product introduction teams
- Establish three new teams during the next twelve months

Existing Products
Reduce the user costs of existing devices by 20% per year over each of the next five years, while improving performance characteristics

- Commit $250,000 to develop a long-term productivity improvement program
- Establish joint research projects with teaching hospitals and major university laser technology departments

Domestic Growth
Expand the use of surgical laser technology to become part of the American surgeon's standard repertoire while maintaining our market share

Domestic Growth
- To have one of our devices installed in 80% of U.S. teaching hospitals
- Expand the use of the technology to at least five new major surgical applications within the next four years

- Undertake demonstration educational programs covering target markets in the U.S. and abroad
- Develop innovative financing schemes for initial placements
- Complete substitution of own sales force for agencies by 1995
- Develop and implement a marketing program including advertising, speakers, and technical articles
- Selectively fund high-profile use of our devices

International Growth
Establish our firm as the premier supplier of laser surgery technology in the European market

International Market Entry
Enter Europe by having one of our devices installed in at least 200 English, French, and German teaching hospitals by 1995

- Establish European hub office in London
- Establish branch offices in Frankfurt and Paris
- Hire and train sales force for all three offices
- Establish contacts in major English, French, and German hospitals
- Adapt sales materials to each language/culture, with individual marketing programs including advertising, speakers, and technical articles

Profitability
Earn a return on investment sufficient to attract financial resources to fund our growth and product leadership

Profitability
Maintain return on equity above 20%

- Actively seek external research financing and investigate R&D partnerships
- Raise debt/equity ratio limit to 3:1

IMPLEMENTATION

The final step of strategic management is implementation. More accurately stated, implementation is not a step so much as a process—the ongoing effort to put a company's agreed-upon strategy into action, to observe its results, to review the consequences of particular choices, and to modify the strategy along the way.

Implementation is ultimately the heart of the matter. Even the best strategy will come to grief if implemented in a halfhearted, indifferent manner. Likewise, even a flawed strategy has a chance of succeeding if its proponents execute it with great vigor, observe it carefully to identify its weaknesses, and correct the problems insightfully. The goal is not theoretical perfection. Rather, the goal is a dynamic strategy that proves itself responsive to the unpredictable nature of the global marketplace.

Before proceeding with actual implementation, however, you face what you have already confronted twice before: a go/no-go decision.

You should base this decision on your answers to the following questions:

- Have you mapped out a strategy that serves your purposes, makes good use of the best information available about your target market, builds on your company's strengths, minimizes its weaknesses, and allows room for change?
- Does this strategy seem in keeping with your company's financial, human, and logistical resources?
- Is top management unified in its acceptance of and enthusiasm for the strategy—and are all the principal players involved ready to commit themselves to the time and exertion necessary for success?
- Last, is the gut-level feeling that this strategy will "fly"?

If some or all the answers to these questions are negative, then you should at least regroup and analyze what may be lacking in the strategy itself. The "no" votes may also indicate a more fundamental hesitancy to proceed with the international venture. However painful and expensive a decision to scrap the venture may be at this point, it is almost certain to be cheaper and more pleasant than proceeding into a corporate fiasco.

On the other hand, if the answers to these questions are positive, then you should proceed to the fourth and final step of going international.

STEP 4 _____

BEATING THEM AT THEIR OWN GAME

Now comes the most difficult but at the same time the most potentially rewarding phase of going international.

You have tested the waters, learned the language, and mapped out a strategy. You have decided at each step that you have good reason to expand your operations into the global marketplace, and you have consequently made the necessary commitments of time, money, and personnel. You are ready to confront your competitors—and ready to beat them at their own game.

What are the final aspects of starting to do business abroad? What should you keep in mind as you proceed to establish your niche, make sales, reap profits, and attain whatever other goals you have set out to accomplish?

The sections that follow—unlike those preceding—are not a unified sequence of tasks. Rather, Step 4 is a survey of several important issues that U.S. companies too often ignore, neglect, or leave to last-minute improvisation. By considering these issues and determining how they may affect your international venture, you can avoid some potential problems and increase your chances for success overseas.

THE RULES OF THE GAME

On the most basic level, beating your competitors at their own game means implementing the strategy already mapped out during the third step of going international. Specifically, you must execute the action plans that constitute your strategy in its most detailed form; you must track the results of these action plans in both quantitative and qualitative terms; and you must take the results into consideration as part of the iterative process of strategic management. But you must, in addition, pay attention to the fundamental rules of doing business abroad.

These rules are as follows:

- *Commit the best available personnel to your international venture.* To beat the competition, you need people who are dedicated to the company and committed to understanding a new culture and a new market. The higher the quality of your officers (and the longer-term their commitment to the venture), the better the chances of their developing the contacts, personal relationships, and knowledge necessary for success.

- *Be flexible.* No matter how westernized the modern world may seem, cultural differences still run deep. Doing business in Beijing, Riyadh, Paris, or even London often bears little resemblance to doing business in Seattle, Dallas, Nashville, or Boston. Beating the competition means playing by local rules.

- *Above all, stay patient.* Your competitors will feel they have time on their side. In Asia, businesses routinely plan ten to twenty years in advance. In Europe, ten-year time horizons are common. Your commitment must be substantial, durable, and confident. Only those who play for the long haul will win.

Beating your competitors at their own game also means keeping a close watch on four issues that companies sidestep only at their own peril. Specifically, you should pay special attention to

- selecting and dealing with expatriates,
- training personnel in cross-cultural skills,
- considering special tips for success, and
- avoiding common pitfalls.

SELECTING AND DEALING WITH EXPATRIATES

Some companies set up successful overseas operations without employing an expatriate field staff. Frequent telecommunications with local representatives plus periodic trips abroad allow some corporate officers to manage their ventures essentially by remote control. In theory, there is nothing wrong with such arrangements; in practice, they often prove successful. Moreover, this method offers the advantage of being less expensive than methods involving an expatriate field staff.

However, three major benefits accrue from having expatriates in your overseas office, benefits so significant and substantial that they should not be overlooked.

- First, having an expatriate field officer allows you to monitor operations far better than you would be able to otherwise.
- Second, having an expatriate field officer simplifies the task of dealing with other American companies overseas, since the executives of these other firms may prefer to deal with fellow countrymen.
- Third, an expatriate field officer will presumably come from one of your existing domestic operations, and thus will know and understand your company culture, will already have established relationships with key executives in your home office, and will be experienced in your company's procedures.

The main goals of maintaining an expatriate presence in your overseas office are *monitoring* and *control* of the business environment. And the experience of many U.S. corporations suggests overwhelmingly that monitoring and control are more easily accomplished with an expatriate officer on site.

Sitting at a desk back home, you may find it difficult to interpret events in your overseas markets, no matter how closely you follow developments in foreign periodicals or company reports. Is your local rep energetically and accurately representing the firm to host-country clients? Or is he neglecting his commitment to you, perhaps making an effort only when you fly out for a visit? Your long-distance vantage point may leave you with an overly optimistic impression of how you're doing overseas.

Alternatively, the view from headquarters may distort your perceptions in the opposite direction. Is the rep actually working *harder* than sales figures would suggest? Is the task of getting yourself established in the target market more complicated than you first thought? If you feel frustrated by your sense of the rep's work so far, are you perhaps underestimating the difficulties he faces in doing business in the host country?

Whether the overall situation is going better or worse than you anticipated, you'll have a hard time knowing the reality of the matter without your own staffer in the field. By contrast, with a member of your home team overseas, you can learn more directly how your product sells, how your service team performs, how your clients react, and how other aspects of going international take shape. You can stay in tune with developments in market penetration, competitors' activities, political and economic risk, changes in the infrastructure, and so forth.

Expats—the Biggest Asset, the Biggest Problem

For these reasons, expats are your biggest asset in going international. You have your own person on the scene; you receive direct feedback. Your field officer speaks your corporate language, so you don't have to worry about the communication problems. He or she can provide you with the clearest insight into your foreign market short of spending your own time there at length. In short, expats are invaluable.

At the same time, expatriates are also the biggest problem. Expats can be demanding, unpredictable, or eccentric. Some grow more and more obsessive about their salaries or benefits. Some develop personal problems in the course of adjusting to another culture. Marital difficulties, depression, and alcoholism can develop among hastily selected, ill-prepared expats. A small minority of expats either can't adjust to life overseas at all or else adjust far too well and "go native."

(A brief aside about "going native." This term refers to the phenomenon in which someone stationed overseas takes on the customs, attitudes, and other attributes of the host-country populace. It isn't simply a question of cultural adaptation. Learning about and respecting the local customs is, of course, desirable and necessary. However, some expatriates make such complete adjustments that in some sense they cease to be expatriates at all. The problem here is not that your field officer now eats different food or wears different clothing. Rather, the problem is that if this person now chooses to do business in the host-country manner, or to follow the local time sense, or to hold the host-country values, your company ceases to have an "inside person" at all. You are now dealing with yet another outsider.)

Despite these risks, however, expatriates are worth the trouble to find, train, and place in overseas posts. Most carefully selected, well-prepared expats adjust to their foreign assignments and perform successfully. They learn the language, settle into their new roles, and thrive in unfamiliar environments. In short, expats are a tricky issue but often a major advantage in an international venture.

Financial Issues

Expatriates are expensive. You should be prepared to deal with a variety of costs from the outset:

- Salary
- Overseas premium
- Cost-of-living adjustments (from the city of origin to destination)
- Hardship or hazardous assignment pay (in a host country subject to political instability, military conflict, or other contingencies)

- Housing allowances
- Income tax adjustments
- Moving expenses and set-up costs
- Local transportation costs (company car, sometimes with driver included)
- Schooling for the employee's children
- Home leave for the family
- Emergency and compassionate leave (for a death or illness in the family)
- Medical leave

Estimating a specific dollar cost for these items requires a knowledge of each country. As a rough estimate, however, you can figure that an employee on assignment overseas will cost you between three and five times his or her U.S. salary plus benefits. The specifics of particular packages vary significantly. Banks and oil companies offer expatriates more generous packages than smaller private corporations. To attract and retain high caliber expatriates, you must offer terms that are at least competitive with typical middle-range packages; otherwise you may end up with an employee who spends most of his or her time unhappy with himself or herself, with the company, and with life in general. Ultimately, as the level of misery increases and productivity drops, the underpaid expat will cost you more than a well-chosen, properly paid employee would have in the first place.

Who Are You Looking For?

Identifying the ideal candidate for an overseas post is generally not a simple matter. Suppose you intend to open up an Indonesian distribution network. By luck, your vice president for marketing is a bright, energetic, flexible world traveler who revels in cultural diversity, learns easily, and just happens to speak fluent Javanese, Bahasa Indonesia, and Dutch. Without a doubt you've found your ideal employee. But this scenario is unlikely to the point of fantasy. More likely, you have a pool of candidates who are talented executives but who lack many of the skills that would ensure a perfect match. Who's the best bet? And what sorts of backgrounds should you look for as you pick and choose?

In addition to fundamental qualifications, these are the most important criteria for the potential expatriate officer:

- *Overall job performance.* High achievement in service to the company is, of course, the fundamental criterion for an expatriate field officer. Only first-rate employees will thrive in their new environment. The ideal candidate must fully understand the company's goals in going international, yet at the same time must be a highly motivated self-starter.

- *Past success overseas.* A candidate who has worked well overseas—even in a culture far different from your current target market—is a better bet than one who has never experienced the task of adjusting to another country.

- *Flexibility.* Since an overseas assignment will invariably present the expat with a new, different, and initially confusing cultural environment, a flexible attitude toward people and situations is a big plus.

- *Patience.* "Time-is-money" fanatics will have severe difficulties in most countries—and will frustrate host-country customers and business partners as well. Someone who is energetic but also aware of other people's time sense will get more done than a compulsive watch-tapper.

- *Sense of humor.* A candidate who seems unable or unwilling to laugh at the sometimes bumpy road to adjustment in another country is doomed to failure. Anyone who *can* laugh at cross-cultural adventures—or who *enjoys* laughing—will have a far easier time in the first place.

- *Marital and family stability.* Overseas assignments are often rough not just on the expat, but on the spouse and children as well. A rocky marriage will get rockier; unhappy children will end up still unhappier. The family's state of mind will heavily influence the expat's success or failure as much as his or her own abilities and attitudes as an employee.

- *An ability to handle stress.* Although many people find overseas work to be stimulating, even exhilarating, the initial adjustment is always emotionally stressful. Some posts will be physically stressful as well, depending on the climate, standard of living, and so forth. Finally, most people go through *culture shock,* the often confusing experience of adapting to another way of life.

What sorts of assessments can you make from these guidelines? That depends on the particular job, particular host country, and particular candidate. A promising candidate would be a flexible, open-minded person, ideally with some sort of previous experience in living overseas, whose spouse is supportive of the opportunity to live in another country. (From a cost standpoint, a candidate with few or no children is generally preferable to one with a larger family.) To some extent, single candidates may be more promising than married candidates.

People to avoid at all costs are the escapee, the total unknown, and the mercenary.

The Escapee. Watch out for candidates whose reason for going overseas is to escape something—a dead-end career, a sense of personal failure, or a bad marriage. Some people imagine that an overseas post will resemble a vacation in Tahiti. The shock of the actual situation has cost U.S. companies untold millions. Still more common are the people who expect a new setting to solve their marital problems, only to discover that even a satisfying post can further strain a shaky marriage.

The Total Unknown. Hiring someone from outside your company is also risky. You want someone who has worked in your organization for years—someone who knows the company culture, believes in the company values, and strives for the company well-being. If you feel tempted to hire an outsider, imagine the potential risks of having an unfamiliar officer reporting from unfamiliar territory, thus compounding all your uncertainties about what goes on in the field.

The Mercenary. Mercenaries don't want the job because the work challenges and interests them, or because the position contributes to their career path. They just want it for the money. If the expat's *sole* concern is money, then career advancement, pride in personal achievement, and the firm itself are ultimately of little consequence.

The mercenary is merely a corporate soldier of fortune exploiting the company.

The Spouse—the Most Frequently Overlooked Variable

In the past, many American companies focused only on the candidate for an overseas position and neglected a critical variable: the candidate's spouse. The spouse is as likely to determine the expat's success or failure as the expat himself or herself.

Consequently, U.S. firms are now tending to interview the candidate's spouse at the same time as the candidate. Moreover, in an increasing number of instances, companies arrange for a prospective expatriate officer *and* the spouse to visit the foreign post, spend a few weeks there, and get a feel for the host country firsthand. (Some companies limit these visits to a week; ideally, however, the visit should extend to at least two weeks. A shorter visit complicates the task of getting an accurate sense of the place and the local culture.) During these visits, the expat and the spouse spend time with other Americans, see the stores, visit the schools, and tour local residences. Although costly, these test visits generally prevent the far greater expense of hiring an expat whose spouse or family ends up unhappy, thus resulting in an abortive assignment.

The Expat Career Path

The final and critical consideration when dealing with expats is the career path. In the past, some American companies used foreign posts as places to send their misfits and has-beens. These companies tended to make their international divisions the corporate equivalent of Siberia. By no means all employees posted overseas were misfits and has-beens. Some were, however. As a result, receiving an overseas assignment subjected even first-rate, highly committed employees to questions like "They're sending you to the boonies?" and "What have you done wrong?"

Fortunately, the situation is now changing. Top management is understanding the importance of the international sector in its own right. But U.S. firms still have some distance to go in defining the expat career path as something that is not merely tolerable, but desirable as well.

To make overseas posts truly attractive to the company's most talented employees, you should build the importance of international ventures into the company culture itself. The message to employees should be the following:

- *To attain top management positions, middle managers* must *go overseas at some point in their careers.* A foreign assignment is crucial for them to understand and value the firm's international commitments and projects. International work is important and will become increasingly important in the future.

- *The officer who takes an overseas post is* not *being put out to pasture.* On the contrary, he or she is undertaking a critical aspect of the company's work.

- *All employees who go overseas are guaranteed a position with the firm afterward.* This doesn't mean that top management will write a contract guaranteeing the employee a particular job for a particular period upon his or her return from the foreign post; you do, however, want to build into the corporate culture a perception that going international is a desirable, creative path within the company.

To foster these perceptions, you should build a roster of people within the company who have served overseas, who have returned to the domestic office or offices, and who are now in leadership positions. Such changes in company culture are more a question of top management's attitudes than of specific provisions. The message to all talented managers should be: "Going overseas means that you are an important person within this company. We trust you. By letting you have the unprecedented amount of responsibility in the overseas office—responsibility that we wouldn't give to most people—we're preparing you for a greater leadership position when you return."

In the final analysis, you should pick your staff members for overseas asignments not just because you want *them* to believe this message, but because you believe it yourself. If you assign personnel to overseas posts just because you don't know what to do with them otherwise, or because they are problematic and you want them out of your sight, you're making a mistake. If your employee isn't succeeding in the United States, he or she certainly won't succeed overseas. Only the most dynamic, adaptable, and tenacious individuals succeed.

TRAINING PERSONNEL IN CROSS-CULTURAL SKILLS

Although the executives most likely to succeed overseas are those who are already successful at home, excellence here is *in itself* no guarantee of excellence there. Other factors contribute to the quality of performance in another culture: language skills, personal resilience, cultural sensitivity, and knowledge about the host country. Fortunately, qualified candidates for overseas posts can augment their qualifications through well-chosen cross-cultural training, which will in turn increase the chances for beating the competition at their own game.

Every business person going overseas should take a course in cross-cultural training specific to the host country or region. Experience in dealing with other nations is, of course, helpful. But countries differ from each other in such numerous and often dramatic ways that nothing can truly replace detailed information, advice, and coaching from knowledgeable sources. The cost of such training is often high; however, cross-cultural training almost always pays off in heightened confidence and new insights. Such confidence and insight will ultimately contribute to the bottom line.

Sources of Information and Assistance

You can obtain cross-cultural training from a variety of sources. The most common types of organizations that provide cross-cultural training are the following:

- Cross-cultural training specialists
- International management consultants
- Accounting firms
- Universities and business schools
- Some large language-instruction firms

tion, some banks and CPA firms in the host country may offer short courses about business customs in that setting.

Another source of information—useful both before and during an overseas assignment—is books about general or specific cultural issues. One of the best general guides is *Going International: How to Make Friends and Deal Effectively in the Global Marketplace* by Lennie Copeland and Lewis Griggs (Random House, 1985). (Copeland and Griggs have also produced a series of audio and video tapes by the same title.) More specific guides to individual cultures include various series with titles like *Doing Business in [Country]*, with separate volumes focusing on nations throughout Europe, Asia, and the Middle East. Note, however, that books are probably an insufficient means of orientation before an overseas assignment. More interactive, in-person coaching is a necessary complement to even the most thorough reading program.

What Helps—and How It Helps

The fact is, the better prepared your expatriate officer is upon arrival in the host country, the more quickly and easily that person will be able to adjust, to work efficiently, and to accomplish the company's goals. Certain specific components of cross-cultural training can make the whole process simpler and more successful for everyone concerned. The most critical of these components are the following:

- *Language training.* Learning the host country's native language is often the most crucial dimension of cross-cultural training, though of course the specific circumstances depend on the country in question. Generally speaking, the expat should start language lessons, even in relatively accessible languages (such as Spanish or French), at least several months before departure. Learning non-Western languages like Japanese, Thai, or Chinese requires far longer, more intensive effort.

- *Cultural orientation.* Expatriates who understand how people live in the host country will adjust far more easily than those who arrive unsure of what to expect. Personal etiquette, time sense, formalities, and other local customs are all far easier to grasp if they don't come as a complete surprise.

- *National or regional history.* Although relatively unimportant to many expats, local history is the focal point of so many misunder-standings that all Americans traveling overseas would benefit from a wider historical background. The resulting advantage isn't just more knowledge of why people do what they do and believe what they believe. In addition, host-country business partners and customers take the expat's knowledge of their history as a compliment, and often respond more openly as a result.

- *Religious issues.* The same holds true for knowledge of religious customs, including holidays, taboos, dietary issues, and any fac-tional, regional, or international disputes.

- *Lifestyle issues.* What sorts of houses do people live in? What kinds of food do they eat? How, when, and where do they shop? What side of the road do they drive on? These and other questions get at the lifestyle issues that make the details of daily living different from one culture to another.

In dealing with these various dimensions of another culture, the goal is *not* to identify every difference, to learn every custom, or to anticipate every difficulty. Such a goal would be unattainable, and perhaps undesirable as well. Rather, the goal is to gain an overall sense of the culture that the expat will encounter, and to some extent to identify easily avoided problem areas. Nothing totally prepares an expat for either the challenges or the delights of experiencing a new culture. Cross-cultural training can, how-ever, make the challenges less difficult and the delights more obvious.

SPECIAL TIPS FOR SUCCESS OVERSEAS

Beating competitors at their own game is most often the result of long-term, systematic planning of the sort sketched in this book. Heeding the variety of miscellaneous tips we are about to offer can give you an extra edge. These tips supplement the planning methods already described, and can help you identify potential problems before they arise.

Tip 1: Take sufficient time to select selling channels carefully.

One of the most bizarre and least explainable tendencies of American business people going international is the impulse to set up selling channels with little or no forethought. A high-level manager goes overseas for a week, talks with a few people, and quickly picks someone to represent the company. Later, this representative turns out to be disreputable or unreliable. The company is then stuck with a bad partner, bad operations, and a bad overall experience. All this can occur despite extensive experience in the domestic market.

Throughout the world it is possible to find first-rate business people who would make good partners. But finding these people takes a cautious search, because unfortunately, no country on earth suffers a shortage of incompetents, mediocrities, and scoundrels. Some potential representatives make false claims about their backgrounds or intentions. Others present you with falsified or unaudited financial statements. If you assume that such potential partners are honest and their companies are healthy, and if you commit yourself too fast, the facts will emerge eventually—and painfully.

To avoid problems of this sort, you should check every potential partner as thoroughly as (if not more so than) you would in the United States. At the very least, you should

- investigate the firm's board of directors,
- check all references,
- determine if the representative has the staff he claims to have, and
- verify that he has in fact acquired the contracts he claims to have.

Would you arrange a partnership in the United States without verifying your potential partner's background? Of course not. Yet many American firms close deals with overseas partners they scarcely know.

Ultimately, the question is the other person's integrity, qualifications, and reliability. You have to be hard-nosed. And to be effectively hard-nosed, you have to spend some time getting to know your potential partner.

Tip 2: When working with foreign representatives, grant them only as large a territory as they can cover effectively.

If your intention is to hire a representative to distribute your product overseas, you will probably find many people in any given country eager to work with you. However, some of these people may be unrealistic about how much territory they can cover effectively. They may even request the rights to represent you not just in one country, but in several, perhaps even throughout an entire region— throughout Europe, for example, or throughout Asia. Unfortunately, few companies have a staff sufficient for such wide-scale operations. (For instance, the rights for all of Asia would involve a market of two and a half *billion* people.)

The reasons for this lack of realism among potential representatives are varied. Some reps simply don't know their own limitations. They may purchase the rights for a large territory only to discover that they can't sell your product effectively. Others know their shortcomings yet bargain for extensive territory regardless, because they have additional, often problematic intentions. Either way, granting excessive rights can put you in a bind.

For example, suppose you have a franchise operation. You sell the rights for Asia for $500,000 to a company that ultimately proves incapable of handling the entire region. This company then sells the rights *for each individual country in Asia,* except for the rights for Hong Kong, and earns a total of $750,000. The company then turns around and pays you $500,000. Without having paid a dime for the franchise, the original representative has gained a profit of $250,000 and has retained a particularly promising Asian market. Meanwhile, you end up in a position of having no information about or control over the people representing your products elsewhere in Asia. Risky? Of course. Yet this sequence of events takes place time after time.

Given these risks, you should sell the rights to your product *only to someone capable of handling the designated terrain.* If necessary, you should limit the terrain outright. Alternatively, you might consider offering initial rights for a particular country, with rights for further countries or regions open for negotiation when the rep proves his ability to handle the first country to your satisfaction. One way of showing your good faith is to offer the rep rights of first refusal on other territories. But in any case the rep must prove himself.

The exception to this rule is, of course, an arrangement with a big, well-established trading organization. Under these circumstances, you may not be able to call the shots. You may, in fact, not need to: such trading companies may present fewer problems in the first place. But even under these conditions you should look at the size of the company in relation to the territory the rep wants to acquire.

Other considerations are

• the number of people on the representative's staff,
• the number of products represented,
• the overall track record, and
• the representative's corporate history.

Tip 3: Grant representation rights for the shortest time possible.

Even when you find a representative who seems capable and realistic about his plans for your product, make sure you grant the rights for the shortest possible time under the circumstances. Many reps would like to have a long-range contract, sometimes covering a term of twenty years or more. You should negotiate a more limited term instead. Suggest, for example, that you will initially grant the rep rights for a year. At the one-year point, you will review the situation and decide whether to continue or not. Such arrangements allow both you and the rep a chance to proceed or to withdraw, as necessary.

Understandably, many representatives will protest these terms. They are, after all, making an investment in representing you—both in terms of training and effort—and may therefore consider a brief term unfair. Such protests are not necessarily groundless. A year may in fact be too short a time, given the representative's own investment. If the rep does protest, you should attempt to negotiate an intermediate period—perhaps a three-to-five-year contract, with an opportunity to review progress at the end of that period. If you can arrange something shorter, so much the better. A two-year contract is fine. A three- to five-year contract is fair. Anything beyond that, however, is deep water.

Tip 4: Tie a continuing relationship to the representative's performance.

This tip provides a useful escape hatch for the situations discussed in tips 1 and 2. During negotiations, offer the potential representative a three- to five-year contract *provided he achieves a designated level of sales.* If his performance falls short of what you have agreed upon, then you have the right to terminate the contract with sixty days' notice. The agreement therefore includes concrete terms: the rep must meet certain sales goals. You set reasonable quotas; in turn the rep must meet them to continue the relationship.

Many smaller or medium-sized agents will agree to these terms. Larger firms will, of course, balk at them or refuse them entirely. If your product is particularly promising, however—such as some high-tech or otherwise innovative products—you may be able to set some of the terms even if your company is relatively small and unknown.

Tip 5: Review performance at least quarterly.

Ideally, you should have your own manager on the scene to review overseas performance. If an on-site manager is not feasible, then you should make sure that someone from headquarters visits the field at least once per quarter. Less frequent reviews will prevent you from realistically seeing, feeling, and understanding the foreign market.

Information for review should come from

- firsthand observation by an on-site expatriate manager or manager from headquarters visiting the field,
- monthly reports from your agents or distributors overseas, and
- direct feedback during visits with overseas customers.

Less direct and abundant information may prove insufficient or misleading. It may even prevent you from perceiving accurately whether customers are truly satisfied with your products, service, response to their requests for orders, and so forth.

Moreover, on-site observation will allow you to understand the situation in ways that would be impossible from a more remote vantage point. Have you turned your product over to someone who represents it inaccurately or insufficiently? Is the rep promising that the product can do things that it can't, or promising that the company will introduce a new version shortly (when in fact you aren't planning that at all)? Is sales support adequate? The only reliable way to answer these questions is to go out and talk with your customers. In addition, your on-site presence or quarterly visits keep your agents on their toes. They know that you will not be simply reading their reports, but will be on their own turf interviewing clients yourself.

Tip 6: Assume that communications will be different from—and perhaps more difficult than—in the United States.

In a world where all countries are increasingly interconnected by electronic communication systems, it's tempting to assume that exchanging data is as easy overseas as within the domestic arena. The truth is certainly more complex.

Communicating in the global marketplace continues to present a variety of difficulties. Some of the problems are technical. Other problems result from time differences. Some of the most significant problems are cultural. When these various difficulties compound each other, the likelihood of trouble increases exponentially.

However frustrating they may be, technical and time issues are often relatively simple to work around. Cultural issues, by contrast, can be difficult to work around but dangerously easy to ignore. The cultural aspects of communications cause some of the biggest and most frequent headaches in overseas ventures.

For example, when you give orders by phone to multilingual host-country employees and reps who speak English as a second or third language, there may be misunderstandings and ambiguities. Moreover, people in different cultures perceive telephone communication in varying ways. Not all business people use the phone in the same way (or for the same purposes) as Americans do. Generally speaking, phone exchanges aren't considered quite as definitive as in-person conversation. In some countries, the government taps telephones; people therefore communicate less openly by phone. And in many cultures, people simply don't feel as comfortable with the phone, but prefer to meet face-to-face instead.

For these reasons, you should be aware of how communications may differ between the United States and your overseas location, and you should respond accordingly. In general, you should

- stay alert to cultural differences in communication styles, even when the hardware in use makes interaction seem universal;
- back up conversations with a telex or FAX when it seems advisable; and
- above all, do not believe that a telephone conversation can substitute for an on-site presence or frequent visits.

Tip 7: Make as few changes as possible to your product.

Frequently, overseas representatives will ask you to modify your product to suit their real or imagined needs. These requests are often well-intentioned and helpful. However, you should make sure that all modifications are realistic, and that the market is large enough to justify the trouble and expense of making them.

The ideal way to change your product is to make it adaptable to a variety of different circumstances. Japanese electronics firms, for instance, provide switches on many electronic appliances to convert the appliance from 110 to 120, 220, or 240 volts, as needed. Many companies also provide purchasers with a box of adapters that enable the appliance to fit various kinds of outlets in different countries. Their instruction booklets come in multiple languages. As a result, these firms can ship their products to a wide range of countries without having to make modifications for each market.

The worst method, in contrast, is to modify the product repeatedly and unsystematically, ending up with a German version, a French version, a Japanese version, a Taiwanese version, and so forth.

To proceed in the most effective and least disruptive way, you should accumulate a list of the whole range of potential modifications, decide which are realistic and which are unrealistic, and then determine how to combine as many of them as possible. The ultimate goal should be to make the fewest and most minimal changes possible. Ideally, you will end up with one universal version of each of your products. The next-best case would be one version for Europe, one version for Asia, and so on. By all means stay sensitive to any special local requirements. But keep in mind that your product simply may not be suitable for every country because of unusual or expensive requirements. Otherwise you will end up with a different product, a different inventory, a different sales support service, and a different training program for each country you have targeted. Making profits under those circumstances will be difficult—if not virtually out of the question.

Tip 8: Avoid the temptation to take shortcuts.

Throughout this book, we have emphasized the need for staying patient while going international. At the risk of harping on the subject, we must stress this point once again. An appalling number of American business people spend vast amounts of money and time preparing for an international venture, then ruin their chances of success by making hasty moves.

You *must* invest in training. You *must* monitor the results. You *must* guide your representatives and on-site expatriate staff through the initial phases of operation. And you *must* make periodic visits to interview some of your customers in person. Taking the time to learn about the host-country culture, getting to know your representatives before you commit to them, checking their background, having your local personnel visit headquarters—all these efforts will pay off in the long run. Simply tossing your product out like a message in a bottle and hoping it ends up somewhere worthwhile is a guaranteed route to failure.

Export trading companies—discussed in Step 1—are admittedly an inexpensive way to get started. However, using them at length, or without restrictive terms, often means you forfeit your control over a given territory in exchange for avoiding the risks of setting up your own operations. Export trading companies are a valid way to proceed, but at a high price.

There are no cheap shortcuts when doing business abroad.

Tip 9: Expect the pace of business to be different overseas.

In a few countries—Hong Kong is a good example—the American pace of business is too slow. In most other places, however, it's far too fast. We Americans tend to arrive on foreign soil almost literally like invading commandos.

Time is different overseas. The American cliché that time is money strikes people in many cultures as offensive, even foolish. Time is time. Money is money. Time provides the opportunity to do many things, among them making money. But to equate time with money seems the height of arrogance and boorishness. Throughout most of the world, even the people most intent on making money see their business dealings in a wider, often complex context of relationships, social obligations, regional and local customs, even religious observances, many of which affect the sense of time. To succeed in doing business abroad, you should recognize these differences in time sense and honor them to the greatest degree possible.

Especially in Latin America and Asia, the pace and sequence of events differs dramatically from what seems familiar and sensible in the United States. Europe has its own variations: some countries—such as Germany and Switzerland—move a little faster, while others—such as France, Italy, and Spain—move at a more leisurely pace. Whatever else, business people overseas are more likely than Americans to want to get to know you before proceeding with major deals.

The crux of the matter is that *you can't do things overseas the way you do them at home.* Don't get frustrated by the speed at which things get done. The slower pace does *not* mean that your host-country partners and customers are uninterested in doing business with you. Rather, they just have different priorities and a different style.

AVOIDING COMMON PITFALLS

Finally, there are seven pitfalls that trap U.S. companies needlessly but often. You should keep these pitfalls in mind throughout the course of beating your competitors at their own game. The likelihood of encountering any particular threat is, of course, uncertain. The risks vary from industry to industry and from country to country.

Pitfall 1: Using Joint Venture Partners from the Start

Since many countries require local participation in foreign businesses, you may feel tempted to start off with a joint venture partner. After all, such a partner will already have built a business infrastructure within the host country. This approach involves two risks, however:

- Missing out on better terms for local participation
- Finding that an established company makes its own business its first priority

Countries requiring local participation may allow you to bargain for a phase-in of whatever arrangement you reach, often over an extended period of time. Moreover, some governments rescind local participation requirements when foreign investments start to dwindle. Accepting such requirements at face value is therefore unwise. You may reach better terms by holding off initially. Starting your operations unilaterally gives you time to make the best possible arrangements with the host-country government. If you ultimately decide to go ahead with a joint venture, the early delays—plus the firsthand experience you will have gained in the field—will work to your advantage when you actually choose a partner.

The other potential problem is that leaping headlong into a joint venture lands you with a company whose infrastructure puts your firm at an immediate disadvantage. Some companies may, in fact, want little more than to take your ideas, products, or technology for their own use, offering little or nothing to you in return.

As illustrated in the Case Study on page 159, you should arrange a joint venture as knowledgeably as possible. Allow yourself a long period of corporate courtship before agreeing to the terms; then factor in more time to reach the final commitment—if any. Ideally, you should go ahead with a joint venture only after several years of experience with local business practices and the consequent knowledge of who within the local business community can or cannot be trusted. Only then will you know enough about the host-country markets and methods of operation to identify the specific strategic advantages of linking up with a local firm.

Case Study

An electronics company set up a joint venture with a long-established firm in Malaysia. The Malaysian partner turned against the U.S. company, however, and eventually pulled enough strings within the local government to have the Americans expelled from the country. The upshot was that the U.S. firm relinquished control of its technology and product knowledge. The partner also used this arrangement to pick up other lines from competitors once they had learned the market through the advice and training that the Americans provided.

Case Study

Local representatives sponsor Lactoso Foods, Inc., in many parts of the world. Some of these reps talked the parent company into heavy investments for training the local staff and financing initial product inventories. The company has no U.S.-based managers on location with the representatives, however; as a result, the company's products tend to be either poorly displayed or not displayed at all. In many stores, the products seem all but swamped by the abundance of various competitors' goods.

Top management back in the U.S. cannot understand why sales are so poor. Every time they visit the region, their products are prominently displayed alongside rival brands. Little do they know that the local merchants dust off and display the firm's products only when the international vice president for marketing comes into town.

Pitfall 2: Using Representatives without Your Staffer on the Scene

For similar reasons, you should be wary of arrangements in which local business people represent your company without field supervision. Otherwise representatives may become more of a hindrance than a help, as shown in the Lactoso Foods Case Study.

As with joint ventures, you should consider using representatives only after an initial (and perhaps extended) period of learning the ins and outs of the local market, and after developing a firsthand knowledge of potential representatives' standing within the host-country business community.

Pitfall 3: Not Adequately Checking Out the Tax Situation—and Not Getting Guarantees on It

All too often, U.S. companies identify a target market and base their decision to enter it on current tax practices, since management feels safe for the period of tax holiday granted by the local government. However, many countries change their tax laws periodically—sometimes overnight. (Both Malaysia and the People's Republic of China, for example, recently passed laws that added a 20 percent withholding tax at source on remittances made overseas for consultancy services.) For this reason, you should take these precautions:

- Double-check the overall host-country tax situation as fully as possible.
- Include caveats as a part of any incentive program that you arrange with the local government.
- Make sure that caveats include statements that any subsequent changes made in tax laws will affect previous agreements, or, alternatively, that any changes will involve a penalty accruing to the government.

Remember at all times that your company is in its best bargaining position *before* you break ground in the host country or establish yourself in any formal way. During these initial phases, the government will be more receptive to you overall and will be more conciliatory in granting tax and other incentives. Once your company has started operations and has made some initial investment, you will generally find the local government less receptive to any pleas for changes or improvements to the original agreement. Such inflexibility once the investment has begun is often called the "international *gotcha*."

Pitfall 4: Glibly Accepting the Comment "It Isn't Done That Way Here"

Although many American business people have, in fact, tended to be insensitive to foreign business practices, some host-country business people may use the issue of cultural differences as a device for manipulating you. By all means keep your radar finely tuned to local customs and protocol. But don't take every assertion at face value. If someone tells you that a certain business practice simply isn't acceptable locally, double-check the facts as carefully as possible.

Case Study

An American consultant reviewed cash management procedures for a large company in Europe. He wondered whether the company should ask for bids on banking services. In the course of interviewing twenty-five of the largest banks in the country, he heard from each contact that their organization would never entertain the notion of such an unprofessional way of developing banking relationships.

Nevertheless, the consultant recommended to his client that the company prepare a request for banking services and submit it to the banks for a response. Each of the banks responded with offers of banking services at more competitive rates than the client had received in the past. The winning bank even offered to open a branch in the client's own building, thus giving the company quicker recognition of foreign and local checks, plus a reduced rate on the long-term and working capital debt. The company ultimately saved more than $2 million a year on its cash management.

Many times the claim doesn't hold up under scrutiny. Ask other reliable sources their opinions. Also, ask every source for *specific examples* of where other companies have attempted to do what is supposedly unacceptable and have failed in their efforts.

In short, accepting at face value all comments on how to do business in a particular setting *may* be a mistake. Consider the possibilities. Ask around. Check with your local contacts. And under some conditions, go ahead and try out your alternative.

Pitfall 5: Not Developing a Fallback Position

As part of your overall strategy, you should identify a second target market as a fallback position just in case something goes wrong with your first choice. Many companies doing business in the Middle East, for example, use Athens, Greece, as a fallback. A variety of firms retreated to Greece from Iran and Libya as political problems developed in those countries; the result was that their regional operations could continue with relatively minor disruption.

Similarly, countries doing business in either Hong Kong or Singapore—or, for that matter, companies doing business in Southeast Asia but headquartered in Hong Kong or Singapore—sometimes use the other nation as a fallback. This is especially true for companies in Hong Kong. With the People's Republic of China scheduled to take over governance of Hong Kong in 1997, Hong Kong is both a high-risk and high-opportunity location. Many companies are establishing headquarters there, poising themselves for intensive work with China. Under the circumstances, these firms would be wise to consider Singapore as an alternative headquarters, since tax or financial conditions may change unpredictably when the PRC takes over.

Pitfall 6: Starting Too Big

Many American companies succumb to a classic misconception: to succeed overseas, you must open a big plant with a cast of thousands. Here as in other aspects, impatience and grandiosity often lead to disaster. Slow initial sales disappoint the company's top executives, who, resenting low returns on high investment, close down the operation and permanently drop the idea of ever going international.

By contrast, more successful firms generally start off on a smaller scale. They build only as the market expands, with on-site staff gaining knowledge of the local culture and markets that makes growth steady and more reliable than the flash-in-the-pan approach.

One of the best ways to start up reliable, productive operations is the "one-plus-one" approach. In this approach, you station one of your best people in your target market. This person's first responsibility is to find one good local counterpart. That local counterpart then helps the American to understand the local environment, business practices, legal issues, and so forth. In short, one expatriate plus one local business person form a team to get business operations started. Only then—and only little by little—does your company build its presence overseas. This approach provides flexibility and reliability at a relatively low cost. It also allows the company to build for the future by training the local counterpart to take a leadership role in the long run.

An added advantage of this approach is that if the government requires local participation at a later date, the local counterpart will be the ideal candidate. Through stock options, training, a long-term personal relationship, and other incentives, you will have established many inducements for the local counterpart to feel primary allegiance to your company.

Pitfall 7: Losing Control

Many American companies lose control of their overseas operations through lack of prudence—specifically, through failure to imagine all the ways in which their competitors may act or react.

Some nations' lax laws concerning copyrights and trademarks also allow foreign manufacturers to copy products and to sell them at a fraction of the original's cost. American companies whose products have been pirated in this manner receive no compensation. For this reason, you should give special consideration to safeguarding your products in these countries. Even with weak copyright and trademark laws, you can find ways to protect your products. One software company, for example, asks every buyer to sign a non-copying agreement, enforceable in both the United States and the country of origin of the buyer.

Case Study

TNT Tobacco Corporation decided to enter several Latin American markets. Upon doing so, however, management discovered that a major competitor had recently entered Latin America as well, and had *registered all the brand names for all major American tobacco companies,* including those for TNT. This preemptive move may have been unethical, but it turned out to be legal. TNT Tobacco could not use its own brand names in Latin America. Prudent strategizing would have saved TNT from severe legal and marketing headaches.

THE COMMITMENT TO WINNING

Step 4 has addressed a wide range of issues—wider, perhaps, than the range of those addressed in the previous three steps. But if any single statement encapsulates the variety of issues in question, it is this: *If you really want to beat your competitors at their own game, then you must select your personnel with utmost care, take them seriously, and give them the resources to do the job right.*

Does this all go without saying? Perhaps. But perhaps not. Otherwise why would so many American companies select their expatriate staffers without much forethought? Why would too many firms treat their overseas personnel with a mixture of disdain and envy, as if they were tourists on a junket? Why would a regrettable number of corporations set up international ventures, only to expect their executives and agents to work with limited funds and unreasonably tight time frames? The sad fact is that U.S. businesses want to beat the competition without committing themselves to a degree that makes success possible.

But you can go about things differently. You can approach your competition as if in a game of chess. You can move carefully and wisely. You can wait patiently.

And you can win the complex, challenging, often profitable game of going international.

PART 3

CONCLUSION—AH, SUCCESS!

Going international is rarely easy; on the contrary, it requires clear thinking, careful planning, strenuous effort, and durable patience. Going international is not risk-free; it is usually expensive, complex, and unpredictable. Yet going international is often eminently worthwhile. In an age of economic interdependence, global communication, and heightened cultural interaction, many U.S. companies already feel a growing need to see not just the United States, but the entire world, as their marketplace.

The Arthur Young International Business Guide has attempted to provide an overview of the process of going international. No single book can address all the issues relevant to such an intricate subject; however, our hope is that this book has provided an outline and sourcebook to help your company master the necessary tasks as you take your products or services to customers in other countries. As mentioned throughout the text, the Appendixes offer additional leads to information, guidance, and funding.

Is going international worth the time, money, and effort required? There is, of course, no single answer to that question. Your company's goals, products, and financial circumstances are the biggest variables affecting the outcome. But the current trend is unquestionably for U.S. companies to consider the option of international ventures, and the trend is there for good reasons.

Perhaps the most convincing evidence that going international can be worthwhile is the experience of companies that have done so successfully. We therefore conclude by hearing what imaginative corporate officers in three small or medium-sized companies have done to expand their operations into overseas markets. Their experiences are good examples of how going international can be manageable, profitable, and even enjoyable.

PATTON ELECTRIC COMPANY, INC.

At a recent National Hardware Show in Chicago, a Taiwanese distributor approached the Patton Electric Company's booth and expressed interest in representing the firm's products in his country. Patton Electric, a manufacturer of small appliances, had previously sold its products almost entirely within the United States. But gradually an international contract took shape.

"This gentleman represented a group of Taiwanese retail department stores," according to William Hunt III, Patton's vice president for sales and marketing. "He inquired about our heaters and became quite intrigued with the quality, design, and features of our products. After our initial discussion, we had further conversations, and as a result of our negotiations we received letters of credit for two large forty-foot shipping containers to be filled with seven thousand portable electric heaters bound for Taiwan."

This sale was a coup in more ways than one. Selling seven thousand units was, of course, a worthwhile sale for the company in its own right. But selling these appliances to the Taiwanese seemed surprising, since most portable electric heater fans available in the United States are in fact *made* in Taiwan. William Hunt says, "This is unusual. We haven't found any manufacturer of portable electric appliances who's shipping *any* electric appliances to Taiwan. Our sale is a first, as far as we've been able to determine."

Moreover, the sale has marked a change of direction for Patton Electric. Hunt notes that until recently, the company has focused almost entirely on the U.S. domestic market. However, recent changes in currency exchange rates have prompted executives at Patton to reconsider their marketing strategies. "Opportunities are just now beginning to open up," he explains, "due to the devaluation of the dollar. This makes our products more attractive. For many years, there was a demand for American-made products because of the worldwide perception that they are more modern, up-to-date, and of a little higher quality. They've been a kind of status symbol. But the problem has been that American products have always been too expensive. Now we are starting to see the trade situation change a little. We're getting new opportunities for export."

In addition, Patton has had to deal with a variety of engineering issues, issues that now seem worth addressing. "The biggest problem for Patton is not so much the problem of the dollar, it's the problem of electrical systems," according to William Hunt. "Different countries have different kinds of electrical systems, and they require different voltages and use different types and speeds of motors. These countries also have different types of electrical commissions and governmental authorities. So there's quite an array of constraints to selling electrical appliances. The technical types of problems that we are working to overcome can't be solved overnight just because the dollar drops."

The result is therefore not so much that Patton Electric anticipates a quick fix to these technical issues, but rather that the company now finds an incentive to deal with them over the long haul. "We are actually allocating resources to engineering projects designed to configure our products to work in 220-volt markets. The 220-volt market is, after all, the largest market in terms of the world's population. And the motors, of course, have to be 50 cycles instead of the 60-cycle motors we have in the U.S."

Modifying its products in these ways, Patton Electric intends to move carefully into overseas markets. "Since the time of our business expansion into Taiwan," Hunt explains, "we have been shipping merchandise into Mexico. Mexico has a similar current to ours. At the same time, we're having a representative attend the Domotechnica Trade Show in Cologne, West Germany, where we hope to attract new interest in our 220-volt configurations. We are also working on a joint venture for producing components in China, and we're working with the Chinese government to produce products for consumption inside of China."

Hunt summarizes how Patton has experienced going international. "Quite frankly, in this business you pretty much respond to a window of opportunity, but you respond in a way that's greater than just to that one window. When you have responded to that window, you say, 'Okay, let's see if we can enter other windows along the same line.' But there are a lot of unknowns. No one just instantly knows about all the barriers and restraints to trade in every country in the world. You have to investigate the most promising areas of opportunity, then develop the product, the design, and the means for moving the product into that country, and for selling it through."

What advice would William Hunt offer to other companies taking their products overseas for the first time?

"First of all, answer all requests. So many foreigners request information and send inquiries to U.S. manufacturers, but hardly any of them are ever answered. Even if your answer is, 'We can't do it,' or 'We can't do it right now, but maybe later'—always answer the request.

"Second, when someone shows an interest in your product or company, follow up. Even if they don't speak English, or if their ways are different, take the time to follow up. Because you have everything to gain and nothing to lose.

"Third, learn a little about your customers' country and their customs. So many times, we accidentally insult people because we don't take time to learn the simplest things about their culture. Our Taiwanese customers were fluent in English. Their trading representative had a U.S. office, so he spoke good English. But you're dealing with issues of politeness, respect, and care and understanding. This is how international trade is done. It's not the same as how many people do business in the United States with U.S. companies. You shouldn't come on too strong."

Patton Electric has found its international ventures challenging, requiring new plans, new ideas, and new ways of doing business; but the experience has also been a source of tremendous satisfaction throughout the whole company.

"In manufacturing those heater fans for Taiwan, I sensed a great sense of pleasure in the general work force of our company. There was a sense of pride for our workers in our plants. In fact, when they filled the last container with Patton heater fans, they actually went out and made a big sign that said, 'Proudly Made in the U.S.A. for the People of Taiwan.' And they put that sign in the container with the heater fans."

KATHY MULLER TALENT AND MODELING AGENCY

While in high school and college, Kathy Muller worked as a model and actress in Hawaii and California. Later, following a stint with an advertising firm in San Francisco, she founded the Kathy Muller Talent and Modeling Agency in her native Honolulu. Her company is now the largest theatrical, commercial, and modeling agency in Hawaii.

"After I'd been in business about a year," Muller explains, "I took a trip to Tokyo for P.R. purposes. From that point on, clients heard that we had quality models with the right look for Japan—and business just started exploding. The basis of my business became the Japanese market. Perhaps 65 percent of our revenue still comes from Japanese clients."

What sorts of arrangements has she made with these clients?

"We work with agencies that are already established in Tokyo and have a good track record. On my trips to Tokyo, I meet with the staff, take a look at their financial backing, make sure that their apartments are in safe areas, and see that everything is set up properly for our models. Then we rotate our models into the individual agency. They pay us a mother-agency commission—in other words, they pull a 20 percent commission, and they send either 5 percent or 10 percent back to us, depending on the model."

Muller goes on to explain that "the *hapa-haole* models—half-Caucasian, half-Japanese—are our management stars in the Japanese market. They are the girls who will get a one-year exclusive contract for $10,000 to $20,000, plus the shoot rate. That special half-half look is what the Japanese like. That is a major part of the Japanese market for us. We also book many Caucasian fashion models into Japan to make the whole package profitable for us."

More recently, Muller has expanded operations to send models to countries other than Japan. "We realized that in order to grow—to take the next step—we had to work with other markets in other parts of the world. About five years ago, we set up our international division and started sending models to Australia, Hong Kong, and most major agencies in Europe. So we now have Japanese clients who come to work with our models here in Hawaii; we have our models who go to Japan and rotate in for a two-month modeling stint with the agencies in Tokyo; and we have Caucasian-European models who head off to Australia, Paris, London, Milan, Munich, Hamburg, and Switzerland. A few years ago, we also added Spain to our circuit."

Muller plans other expansions of overseas work. "We're just starting to get our models into Hong Kong. The Hong Kong economy is very strong, and European-Caucasian models are very popular there. We're opening that area up this year. We have not tapped the Scandinavian countries yet, but that will be our next step, along with Taiwan and Korea."

Kathy Muller has obviously done well overseas. In just nine years, she has not only succeeded beyond her own expectations; she has also helped to make Hawaii one of the major centers for modeling in the world. How does she explain her success in the global marketplace?

"Each country has its own personality that you have to adjust to," Muller says. "Going into Tokyo, I took a while to understand what they were looking for. I had to research the 'look' they were interested in. I developed an eye for the type of face they wanted—small and delicate, with some of the Japanese characteristics, yet with some Caucasian characteristics, too. Basically, you need to go into each area and find out what the need is, and then try to find that in your own community and supply it."

Cultural issues are also paramount. "With the Japanese, you have to learn to be patient. The way they do business takes more time than doing business in the U.S. You often sit down and enjoy the tea ceremony before discussing business. Americans are so used to rushing in, putting the papers on the table, completing the deal, and moving on to the next project. I've learned so much from the Japanese. Loyalty is important, and once they trust you, they trust you forever. They will never go around you once you set up that relationship. Business is done on a much more personal and structured basis."

She goes on to say, "We have a lot of companies in this country that fizzled because they didn't take the time to visit their international market; they didn't go and meet people face to face. It's imperative that you do that. You can't carry on a business relationship just by mail. Your clients need to know the person they're working with. Internationally, that's a very important point—*the personal connection.*"

The Kathy Muller Talent and Modeling Agency now brings in about $1 million annually in revenues. Muller has expanded the business from an out-of-the-home operation to a multifaceted company representing approximately one thousand models and actors. She sees no immediate limits to her endeavors. "To run this sort of business," she concludes, "you should look around and see what the needs are. If people ask, 'Can you get me this or that?' then you say, 'Yes,' hang up the phone, and go get it. Every time a door has opened, we've just walked through it."

MRS. FIELDS COOKIES

Founded in 1977, Mrs. Fields Cookies is a food specialty company whose stores are a common sight on city streets and in shopping malls throughout the United States. The firm currently maintains 650 domestic outlets, with annual revenues reaching $115 million in 1987.

"We opened our first foreign store in 1984, in Australia," explains Randy Fields, chairman of the board. "About a year later, we opened in Japan, Hong Kong, and Canada. Last year we opened in the United Kingdom. We now have about forty outlets in these countries." Mrs. Fields Cookies did not initially plan these international operations. "We just perceived it as an opportunity. There was an individual in the company who felt these foreign outlets would be something he could do well, so we just turned him loose to do it."

What has been the response to the firm's products overseas? Fields says that "in each country we've opened, sales have been relatively slow initially, compared to the U.S. Not only is Mrs. Fields an unknown brand name—*cookies* are an unknown concept. It normally takes about a year to get rolling. Beyond the first year, we've done just terrific everywhere."

Mrs. Fields Cookies' success has involved a somewhat unusual marketing decision, given the issues of selling unfamiliar food items in different cultures. "We generally source our materials in each of the countries. But if we can't get materials to our specifications, then we export them from the U.S.," according to Fields. "It would not be possible to distinguish between our products made anywhere in the world. This is not necessarily true of other companies' products." On the other hand, the company may consider slight alterations in the future. "Our muffins in Australia, for example, may contain fruits indigenous to that country, such as sour cherries."

Mrs. Fields Cookies has followed a clear pattern in introducing products in each new market. As Randy Fields states, "For the first several years in each market, we've sold only cookies, though here in the U.S. we sell brownies and now muffins. In Australia, we now sell the full product line, but it's taken us three-plus years to do that. In Canada we sell our brownies. Within the next twelve months, each of the countries will be fully integrated with the U.S. product line."

What delights and frustrations has the company found in going international?

"The biggest delight was the ability to open Japan without a partner," Fields says. "We're the only wholly-owned American company with an outlet on the Ginza. The frustrations are just the usual frustrations you'd expect. In each case, they are the frustrations of the start-up versus what you have with a domestic addition. Here in the U.S., we just add units. When we go into a new country, there's a tremendous front-end effort to start up. It's not a question of finances—it's the logistical effort. But everything else is very much like doing business here, except that the distances are greater."

Mrs. Fields Cookies intends to remain and, in fact, to expand in the global marketplace. "We would anticipate that over the course of the next ten years, the international part of our business ought to be a very significant portion overall."

Mrs. Fields Cookies has tempted the world with its goodies and found a big appetite waiting everywhere the company has gone. According to Randy Fields, "You shouldn't underestimate the complexity of going international. On the other hand, there's a market out there as big as the U.S. for many if not most products. If you're opportunistic and want to take advantage of that, I don't think there's really an option, is there?"

WANTED: THE ORIGINAL AMERICAN CAN-DO ATTITUDE

In closing, it seems important to reflect on these companies' success stories and on their implications for the general task of doing business abroad.

When I left the United States almost fourteen years ago to take my first overseas assignment, Americans routinely expressed pride in their country's products, services, and overall business practices. This pride was often entirely appropriate. U.S. businesses did, in fact, manufacture excellent products and provide first-rate services; and in response to such excellence, consumers throughout the world coveted and admired American goods and skills. Working among other expatriate Americans, I sensed confidence in our nation, our technology, and our future. Many expats would compliment a high-quality item or service in the host country by calling it "positively Stateside."

Upon returning home, however, I learned quickly that times had changed. Many Americans now criticize our own products, services, and business practices. It's common wisdom that U.S. goods are shoddy, our services are indifferent, and both our goods and our services cost far too much.

It goes without saying that American business people have learned a lot from our competitors in other countries. We aren't perfect, and we know it. Foreign competitors have created admirable innovations in technology, management, marketing, and other aspects of business. There's nothing wrong with learning from others' experience. However, the often blindly accepted clichés about American mediocrity are disturbing and, worse yet, counterproductive. The litany of complaints tends to become a self-fulfilling prophecy.

Since my recent return to the United States, I've made a point of buying U.S.-made products. I find little justification for the widespread complaints about their quality. Neither do I find that they are generally or disproportionately more expensive than their foreign-made equivalents. American service firms, meanwhile, offer a wide range of services that equal or exceed (and often far exceed) what I encountered overseas. So much for the decline of American craftsmanship.

What strikes me as truly unfortunate about this situation is that it need not have developed in the first place. To the extent that American products and services can be made better or sold cheaper than they are at present, we should pursue—both as individual executives and as a nation—the necessary means to increase U.S. excellence and competitiveness abroad. To the extent that our products and services are already good, we should grasp the reality of the situation, call a spade a spade, and stop running ourselves into the ground. The alternative to common sense in this regard is commercial decline. If we don't stop distorting the present, we stand no chance of facing the future with any chance of success.

Patton Electric Company, Inc., Kathy Muller Talent and Modeling Agency, and Mrs. Fields Cookies are three examples of American companies that have accepted the challenge of doing business abroad. As success stories, these firms deserve admiration and emulation. Yet these three are only a few of the U.S. companies that produce excellent goods or services. Countless others have achieved their own levels of excellence. Still, as noted at the beginning of this book, only a small minority of American firms take their products and services overseas.

The fact remains: American companies can succeed in the global marketplace. They can earn profits, attain greater name recognition, and increase competitiveness at home as well as abroad. But success requires not only completing the tasks outlined in this book; success also depends on the original American can-do attitude.

Randy Fields of Mrs. Fields Cookies noted that *there's a market out there as big as the United States*. In fact, the global marketplace is even bigger than the huge market we have at home.

Are you willing to take advantage of that global marketplace? Are you willing to take the risks and do the work? Are you willing to seek and find the opportunities awaiting you overseas?

Is there really an option?

PART 4

APPENDIXES

APPENDIX A: GLOSSARY OF COMMON INTERNATIONAL BUSINESS TERMS*

The following glossary defines terms that are common in international business ventures. Some of these terms have appeared in the preceding text; others have not.

Acceptance—This term has several related meanings:

1. A time draft (or bill of exchange) which the drawee has accepted and is unconditionally obligated to pay at maturity. The draft must be presented first for acceptance—the drawee becomes the "acceptor"—then for payment. The word "accepted" and the date and place of payment must be written on the face of the draft.

2. The drawee's act in receiving a draft and thus entering into the obligation to pay its value at maturity.

3. (Broadly speaking) Any agreement to purchase goods under specified terms. An agreement to purchase goods at a stated price and under stated terms.

Ad valorem—According to value. See **Duty.**

Advance against documents—A loan made on the security of the documents covering the shipment.

Advising bank—A bank, operating in the exporter's country, that handles letters of credit for a foreign bank by notifying the exporter that the credit has been opened in his or her favor. The advising bank fully informs the exporter of the conditions of the letter of credit without necessarily bearing responsibility for payment.

Advisory capacity—A term indicating that a shipper's agent or representative is not empowered to make definitive decisions or adjustments without approval of the group or individual represented. Compare **Without reserve.**

Agent—See **Foreign sales agent.**

Air waybill—A bill of lading that covers both domestic and international flights trans-

* Source: U.S. Department of Commerce

177

porting goods to a specified destination. This is a non-negotiable instrument of air transport that serves as a receipt for the shipper, indicating that the carrier has accepted the goods listed and obligates itself to carry the consignment to the airport of destination according to specified conditions. Compare **Inland bill of lading, Ocean bill of lading,** and **Through bill of lading.**

Alongside—A phrase referring to the side of a ship. Goods to be delivered "alongside" are to be placed on the dock or barge within reach of the transport ship's tackle so that they can be loaded aboard the ship.

Antidiversion clause—See **Destination control statement.**

Arbitrage—The process of buying **Foreign exchange,** stocks, bonds, and other commodities in one market and immediately selling them in another market at higher prices.

Asian dollars—U.S. dollars deposited in Asia and the Pacific Basin. Compare **Eurodollars.**

ATA Carnet—See **Carnet.**

Balance of trade—The difference between a country's total imports and exports; if exports exceed imports, a favorable balance of trade exists; if not, a trade deficit is said to exist.

Barter—Trade in which merchandise is exchanged directly for other merchandise without use of money. Barter is an important means of trade with countries using currency that is not readily convertible.

Beneficiary—The person in whose favor a **Letter of credit** is issued or a **Draft** is drawn.

Bill of exchange—See **Draft.**

Bill of lading—A document that establishes the terms of a contract between a shipper and a transportation company under which freight is to be moved between specified points for a specified charge. Usually prepared by the shipper on forms issued by the carrier, it serves as a document of title, a contract of carriage, and a receipt for goods. Also see **Air waybill, Inland bill of lading, Ocean bill of lading,** and **Through bill of lading.**

Bonded warehouse—A warehouse authorized by **Customs** authorities for storage of goods on which payment of **Duties** is deferred until the goods are removed.

Booking—An arrangement with a steamship company for the acceptance and carriage of freight.

Buying agent—See **Purchasing agent.**

Carnet—A customs document permitting the holder to carry or send merchandise temporarily into certain foreign countries (for display, demonstration, or similar purposes) without paying duties or posting bonds.

Cash against documents (C.A.D.)—Payment for goods in which a commission house or other intermediary transfers title documents to the buyer upon payment in cash.

Cash in advance (C.I.A.)—Payment for goods in which the price is paid in full before shipment is made. This method is usually used only for small purchases or when the goods are built to order.

Cash with order (C.W.O.)—Payment for goods in which the buyer pays when ordering and in which the transaction is binding on both parties.

Certificate of inspection—A document certifying that merchandise (such as perishable goods) was in good condition immediately prior to its shipment.

Certificate of manufacture—A statement (often notarized) in which a producer of goods certifies that manufacture has been completed and that the goods are now at the disposal of the buyer.

Certificate of origin—A document, required by certain foreign countries for tariff purposes, certifying the country of origin of specified goods.

C & F—"Cost and freight." A pricing term indicating that the cost of the goods and freight charges are included in the quoted price; the buyer arranges for and pays insurance.

Charter party—A written contract, usually on a special form, between the owner of a vessel and a "charterer" who rents use of the vessel or a part of its freight space. The contract generally includes the freight rates and the ports involved in the transportation.

C & I—"Cost and insurance." A pricing term indicating that the cost of the product and insurance are included in the quoted price. The buyer is responsible for freight to the named port of destination.

C.I.F.—"Cost, insurance, freight." A pricing term indicating that the cost of the goods, insurance, and freight are included in the quoted price.

Clean bill of lading—A receipt for goods issued by a carrier that indicates that the goods were received in "apparent good order and condition," without damages or other irregularities. Compare **Foul bill of lading.**

Clean draft—A **Draft** to which no documents have been attached.

Collection papers—All documents (**Commercial invoices, Bills of lading,** etc.) submitted to a buyer for the purpose of receiving payment for a shipment.

Commercial attache—The commerce expert on the diplomatic staff of his or her country's embassy or large consulate.

Commercial invoice—An itemized list of goods shipped, usually included among an exporter's **Collection papers.**

Commission agent—See **Purchasing agent.**

Common carrier—An individual, partnership, or corporation that transports persons or goods for compensation.

Confirmed letter of credit—A letter of credit, issued by a foreign bank, with validity confirmed by a U.S. bank. An exporter who requires a confirmed letter of credit from the buyer is assured of payment by the U.S. bank even if the foreign buyer or the foreign bank defaults. See **Letter of credit.**

Consignment—Delivery of merchandise from an exporter (the consignor) to an agent (the consignee) under agreement that the agent sell the merchandise for the account of the exporter. The consignor retains title to the goods until the consignee has sold them. The consignee sells the goods for commission and remits the net proceeds to the consignor.

Consular declaration—A formal statement, made to the consul of a foreign country, describing goods to be shipped.

Consular invoice—A document, required by some foreign countries, describing a shipment of goods and showing information such as the consignor, consignee, and value of the shipment. Certified by a consular official of the foreign country, it is used by the country's customs officials to verify the value, quantity, and nature of the shipment.

Convertible currency—A currency that can be bought and sold for other currencies at will.

Correspondent bank—A bank that, in its own country, handles the business of a foreign bank.

Countertrade—The sale of goods or services that are paid for in whole or in part by the transfer of goods or services from a foreign country. (See **Barter.**)

Credit risk insurance—Insurance designed to cover risks of nonpayment for delivered goods. Compare **Marine insurance.**

Customs—The authorities designated to collect duties levied by a country on imports and exports. The term also applies to the procedures involved in such collection.

Customhouse broker—An individual or firm licensed to enter and clear goods through Customs.

Date draft—A draft that matures in a specified number of days after the date it is issued, without regard to the date of **Acceptance** (Definition 2). See **Draft, Sight draft** and **Time draft.**

Deferred payment credit—Type of **Letter of credit** providing for payment some time after presentation of shipping documents by exporter.

Demand draft—See **Sight draft.**

Destination control statement—Any of various statements that the U.S. Government requires to be displayed on export shipments and that specify the destinations for which export of the shipment has been authorized.

Devaluation—The official lowering of the value of one country's currency in terms of one or more foreign currencies. (E.g., if the U.S. dollar is devalued in relation to the French franc, one dollar will "buy" fewer francs than before.)

Discrepancy—Letter of credit—When documents presented do not conform to the letter of credit, it is referred to as a "discrepancy."

Dispatch—An amount paid by a vessel's operator to a charterer if loading or unloading is completed in less time than stipulated in the charter party.

Distributor—A foreign agent who sells for a supplier directly and maintains an inventory of the supplier's products.

Dock receipt—A receipt issued by an ocean carrier to acknowledge receipt of a shipment at the carrier's dock or warehouse facilities. Also see **Warehouse receipt.**

Documentary draft—A **Draft** to which documents are attached.

Documents against acceptance (D/A)—Instructions given by a shipper to a bank indicating that documents transferring title to good should be delivered to the buyer (or drawee) only upon the buyer's acceptance of the attached draft.

Draft (or Bill of exchange)—An unconditional order in writing from one person (the drawer) to another (the drawee), directing the **Drawee** to pay a specified amount to a named **Drawer** at a fixed or determinable future date. See **Date draft, Sight draft, Time draft.**

Drawback—Articles manufactured or produced in the United States with the use of imported components or raw materials and later exported are entitled to a refund of up to ninety-nine percent of the duty charged on the imported components. The refund of duty is known as a "drawback."

Drawee—The individual or firm on whom a draft is drawn and who owes the stated amount. Compare **Drawer.** Also see **Draft.**

Drawer—The individual or firm that issues or signs a draft and thus stands to receive payment of the stated amount from the drawee. Compare **Drawee.** Also see **Draft.**

Dumping—Exporting/importing merchandise into a country below the costs incurred in production and shipment.

Duty—A tax imposed on imports by the customs authority of a country. Duties are generally based on the value of the goods (ad valorem duties), some other factor such as weight or quantity (specific duties), or a combination of value and other factors (compound duties).

EMC—See **Export management company.**

ETC—See **Export trading company.**

Eurodollars—U.S. dollars placed on deposit in banks outside the United States; usually refers to deposits in Europe.

EX—**"From."** When used in pricing terms such as "Ex Factory" or "Ex Dock," it signifies that the price quoted applies only at the point of origin (in the two examples, at the seller's factory or a dock at the import point). In practice, this kind of quotation indicates that the seller agrees to place the goods at the disposal of the buyer at the specified place within a fixed period of time.

Exchange permit—A government permit sometimes required by the importer's government to enable the importer to convert his or her own country's currency into foreign currency with which to pay a seller in another country.

Exchange rate—The price of one currency in terms of another, i.e., the number of units of one currency that may be exchanged for one unit of another currency.

Eximbank—The Export-Import Bank of the United States.

Export broker—An individual or firm that brings together buyers and sellers for a fee but does not take part in actual sales transactions.

Export commission house—An organization which, for a commission, acts as a purchasing agent for a foreign buyer.

Export declaration—See **Shipper's export declaration.**

Export license—A government document that permits the "Licensee" to engage in the export of designated goods to certain destinations. (See **General and Validated licenses.**)

Export management company—A private firm that serves as the export department for several manufacturers, soliciting and transacting export business on behalf of its clients in return for a commission, salary, or retainer plus commission.

Export trading company—A firm similar or identical to an export management company.

F.A.S.—**"Free alongside."** A pricing term indicating that the quoted price includes the cost of delivering the goods alongside a designated vessel.

F.I.—**"Free in."** A pricing term indicating that the charterer of a vessel is responsible for the cost of loading and unloading goods from the vessel.

Floating policy—See **Open policy.**

F.O.—**"Free out."** A pricing term indicating that the charterer of a vessel is responsible for the cost of loading goods from the vessel.

F.O.B.—**"Free on board."** A pricing term indicating that the quoted price includes the cost of loading the goods into transport vessels at the specified place.

Force majeure—The title of a standard clause in marine contracts exempting the parties for nonfulfillment of their obligations as a result of conditions beyond their control, such as earthquakes, floods, or war.

Foreign exchange—The currency or credit instruments of a foreign country. Also, transactions involving purchase and/or sale of currencies.

Foreign freight forwarder—See **Freight forwarder.**

Foreign sales agent—An individual or firm that serves as the foreign representative of a domestic supplier and seeks sales abroad for the supplier.

Foreign sales corporation (FSC)—An organization formed by American manufacturers or export groups to obtain U.S. tax incentives for export sales. FSCs are a valuable tool for increasing export profits.

Foreign trade zone—See **Free trade zone.**

Foul bill of lading—A receipt for goods issued by a carrier with an indication that the goods were damaged when received. Compare **Clean bill of lading.**

Free port—An area such as a port city into which merchandise may legally be moved without payment of duties.

Free trade zone—A port designated by the government of a country for duty-free entry of any non-prohibited goods. Merchandise may be stored, displayed, used for manufacturing, etc., within the zone and reexported without duties being paid. Duties are imposed on the merchandise (or items manufactured from the merchandise) only when the goods pass from the zone into an area of the country subject to the Customs Authority.

Freight forwarder—An independent business which handles export shipments for compensation. (A freight forwarder is among the best sources of information and assistance on U.S. export regulations and documentation, shipping methods, and foreign import regulations.)

GATT—**"General Agreement on Tariffs and Trade."** A multilateral treaty intended to help reduce trade barriers between the signatory countries and to promote trade through tariff concessions.

General export license—Any of various export licenses covering export commodities for which **Validated export licenses** are not required. No formal application or written authorization is needed to ship exports under a General export license.

Gross weight—The full weight of a shipment, including goods and packaging. Compare **Tare weight.**

Import license—A document required and issued by some national governments authorizing the importation of goods into their individual countries.

Inland bill of lading—A bill of lading used in transporting goods overland to the exporter's international carrier. Although a **Through bill of lading** can sometimes be used, it is usually necessary to prepare both an inland bill of lading and an **Ocean bill of lading** for export shipments. Compare **Air waybill, Ocean bill of lading,** and **Through bill of lading.**

International freight forwarder—See **Freight forwarder.**

Irrevocable letter of credit—A letter of credit in which the specified payment is guaranteed by the bank if all terms and conditions are met by the drawee. Compare **Revocable letter of credit.**

Letter of credit (L/C)—A document, issued by a bank per instructions by a buyer of goods, authorizing the seller to draw a specified sum of money under specified terms, usually the receipt by the bank of certain documents within a given time.

Licensing—A business arrangement in which the manufacturer of a product (or a firm with proprietary rights over certain technology, trademarks, etc.) grants permission to some other group or individual to manufacture that product (or make use of that proprietary material) in return for specified royalties or other payment.

Manifest—See **Ship's manifest.**

Marine insurance—Insurance that compensates the owners of goods transported overseas in the event of loss that cannot be legally recovered from the carrier. Also covers air shipments. Compare **Credit risk insurance.**

Marking (or marks)—Letters, numbers, and other symbols placed on cargo packages to facilitate identification.

Ocean bill of lading—A **Bill of lading (B/L)** indicating that the exporter consigns a shipment to an international carrier for transportation to a specified foreign market. Unlike an **Inland B/L**, the **Ocean B/L** also serves as a collection document. If it is a "straight" **B/L**, the foreign buyer can obtain the shipment from the carrier by simply showing proof of identity. If a "negotiable" **B/L** is used, the buyer must first pay for the goods, post a bond, or meet other conditions agreeable to the seller. Compare **Air waybill, Inland bill of lading,** and **Through bill of lading.**

On board bill of lading (B/L)— A **Bill of lading** in which a carrier certifies that goods have been placed on board a certain vessel.

Open account—A trade arrangement in which goods are shipped to a foreign buyer without guarantee of payment. The obvious risk this method poses to the supplier makes it essential that the buyer's integrity be unquestionable.

Open insurance policy—A marine insurance policy that applies to all shipments made by an exporter over a period of time rather than to one shipment only.

"Order" bill of lading (B/L)—A negotiable **Bill of lading** made out to the order of the shipper.

Packing list—A list showing the number and kinds of items being shipped, as well as other information needed for transportation purposes.

Parcel post receipt—The postal authorities' signed acknowledgment of delivery to receiver of a shipment made by parcel post.

PEFCO (Private Export Funding Corporation)—lends to foreign buyers to finance exports from U.S.

Perils of the sea—A marine insurance term used to designate heavy weather, stranding, lightning, collision, and sea water damage.

Phytosanitary Inspection Certificate—A certificate, issued by the U.S. Department of Agriculture to satisfy import regulations for foreign countries, indicating that a U.S. shipment has been inspected and is free from harmful pests and plant diseases.

Political risk—In export financing the risk of loss due to such causes as currency inconvertibility, government action preventing entry of goods, expropriation or confiscation, war, etc.

Pro forma invoice—An invoice provided by a supplier prior to the shipment of merchandise, informing the buyer of the kinds and quantities of goods to be sent, their value, and important specifications (weight, size, etc.).

Purchasing agent—An agent who purchases goods in his or her own country on behalf of foreign importers such as government agencies and large private concerns.

Quota—The quantity of goods of a specific kind that a country permits to be imported without restriction or imposition of additional **Duties.**

Quotation—An offer to sell goods at a stated price and under specified conditions.

Remitting bank—Bank that sends the **Draft** to overseas bank for collection.

Representative—See **Foreign sales agent.**

Revocable letter of credit—A **Letter of credit** that can be cancelled or altered by the **Drawee** (buyer) after it has been issued by the drawee's bank. Compare **Irrevocable letter of credit.**

Schedule B—Refers to "Schedule B, Statistical Classification of Domestic and Foreign Commodities Exported from the United States." All commodities exported from the United States must be assigned a seven-digit Schedule B number.

Shipper's export declaration—A form required by the U.S. Treasury Department for all shipments and prepared by a shipper, indicating the value, weight, destination, and other basic information about an export shipment.

Ship's manifest—An instrument in writing, signed by the captain of a ship, that lists the individual shipments constituting the ship's cargo.

Sight draft (S/D)—A draft that is payable upon presentation to the drawee. Compare **Date draft, Time draft.**

Spot exchange—The purchase or sale of foreign exchange for immediate delivery.

Standard Industrial Classification (SIC)—A standard numerical code system used by the U.S. Government to classify products and services.

Standard International Trade Classification (SITC)—A standard numerical code system developed by the United Nations to classify commodities used in international trade.

Steamship conference—A group of steamship operators that operate under mutually agreed upon freight rates.

Straight bill of lading—A non-negotiable **Bill of lading** in which the goods are consigned directly to a named consignee.

Tare weight—The weight of a container and packing materials without the weight of the goods it contains. Compare **Gross weight.**

Tenor (or a Draft)—Designation of a payment as being due at sight, a given number of days after sight, or a given number of days after date.

Through bill of lading—A single **Bill of lading** converting both the domestic and international carriage of an export shipment. An **Air waybill,** for instance, is essentially a through bill of lading used for air shipments. Ocean shipments, on the other hand, usually require two separate documents—an **Inland bill of lading** for domestic carriage and an **Ocean bill of lading** for international carriage. **Through bills of lading** are insufficient for ocean shipments. Compare **Air waybill, Inland bill of lading, Ocean bill of lading.**

Time draft—A draft that matures either a certain number of days after acceptance or a certain number of days after the date of the draft. Compare **Date draft, Sight draft.**

Tramp steamer—A ship not operating on regular routes or schedules.

Transaction statement—A document that delineates the terms and conditions agreed upon between the importer and exporter.

Trust receipt—Release of merchandise by a bank to a buyer in which the bank retains title to the merchandise. The buyer, who obtains the goods for manufacturing or sales purposes, is obligated to maintain the goods (or the proceeds from their sale) distinct from the remainder of his or her assets and to hold them ready for repossession by the bank.

Validated export license—A required document issued by the U.S. Government authorizing the export of specific commodities. This license is for a specific transaction or time period in which the exporting is to take place. Compare **General export license.**

Warehouse receipt—A receipt issued by a warehouse listing goods received for storage.

Wharfage—A charge assessed by a pier or dock owner for handling incoming or outgoing cargo.

Without reserve—A term indicating that a shipper's agent or representative is empowered to make definitive decisions and adjustments abroad without approval of the group or individual represented. Compare **Advisory capacity.**

APPENDIX B: DIRECTORY OF FEDERAL ASSISTANCE*

1. U.S. Department of Commerce
2. Small Business Administration
3. Export-Import Bank
4. U.S. Department of Agriculture
5. Overseas Private Investment Corporation (OPIC)
6. Department of the Treasury/U.S. Customs Service
7. Agency for International Development
8. U.S. Trade Representative

1. U.S. Department of Commerce

The U.S. Department of Commerce can provide a wealth of information to exporters. The first step an exporter should take is to contact the nearest US&FCS District Office. For more specific information on who to contact in Washington, DC, the Export Counseling Center (below) can help guide the exporter to the right person or office.

* Source: U.S. Department of Commerce

To send inquiries to or to communicate with the following offices, the address should include the office name, the office room number, followed by: U.S. Department of Commerce, Washington, DC 20230 (exceptions noted).

Area Code: 202

U.S. and Foreign Commercial Service

Office of Domestic Operations
- Export Counseling Center: Room 1066 (Export counseling and marketing assistance) 377-3181

Export Promotion Services
- Office of Information Product Development and Distribution: P.O. Box 14207, Washington, DC 20044 (Information on foreign markets, customers, and trade leads) . . . 377-2432
- Office of Marketing Programs: (Trade show and trade mission information) Room 2116 377-4231
- Information on *Commercial News USA* and other Commerce export-related publications) 377-5367

Office of Foreign Operations

Regional Coordinators for:

- Africa, Near East and South Asia: Room 3104 377-2736
- East Asia and Pacific: Room 3104 377-2736
- Europe: Room 3122 377-1599
- Western Hemisphere: Room 3122 377-1599

Trade Development

Product/Service Specialists:
- Aerospace: Room 6877 377-8228

- Automotive Affairs and Consumer
  Goods: Room 4324 377-0823
- Basic Industries:
  Room 4045 377-0614
- Capital Goods & International
  Construction: Rm 2001B . . . 377-5023
- Export Trading Company Affairs:
  Room 5618 377-5131
- International Major Projects:
  Room 2007 377-5225
- Science and Electronics:
  Room 1001A 377-4466
- Services:
  Room 1128 377-5261
- Textiles and Apparel:
  Room 3100 377-3737
- Trade Information and Analysis:
  Room 3814B 377-1316

Trade Administration

Office of Export Administration

- Exporter's Service Staff: (Export licensing, controls, etc.)
  Room 1099 377-4811

Office of Antiboycott Compliance:
Room 3886 377-2381

Minority Business Development Agency

Minority Export Development Consulting
Program Office:
Room 5093 377-2881

International Economic Policy

Country Desk Officers can provide specific
country information relating to international
trade. The following is a list of country desk
officers.

Listing of ITA desk officers

Country	Phone	Room
Afghanistan	377-2954	2029-B
Albania	377-2645	3419
Algeria	377-4652	2033

Country	Phone	Room
Angola	377-0357	3317
Argentina	377-5427	3021
ASEAN	377-3875	2032
Australia	377-3646	2310
Austria	377-2434	3411
Bahamas	377-2527	3029-A
Bahrain	377-5545	2039
Bangladesh	377-2954	2029-B
Barbados	377-2527	3029-A
Belgium	377-2920	3415
Belize	377-3527	3029-A
Benin	377-4564	3317
Bermuda	377-2527	3029-A
Bhutan	377-2954	2029-B
Bolivia	377-4302	3314
Botswana	377-5148	3317
Brazil	377-3871	3017
Brunei	377-3875	2310
Bulgaria	377-2645	3419
Burkina Faso	377-4564	3317
Burma	377-5334	3820
Burundi	377-0357	3318
Cambodia	377-4681	2323
Cameroon	377-0357	3317
Canada	377-3101	3314
Cape Verde	377-4564	3317
Caymans	377-2527	3029-A
Central African Rep.	377-0357	3317
Chad	377-4564	3317
Chile	377-4302	3027
Columbia	377-4302	3027
Comoros	377-4564	3317
Congo	377-0357	3317
Costa Rica	377-2527	3029-A
Cuba	377-2527	3029-A
Cyprus	377-3945	3044
Czechoslovakia	377-2645	3419
Denmark	377-3254	3413
D'Jibouti	377-4564	3320
Dominican Rep.	377-2527	3016
East Caribbean	377-2527	3022
Ecuador	377-4302	3027
Egypt	377-4652	2033
El Salvador	377-5563	3029-A
Equatorial Guinea	377-0357	3318
Ethiopia	377-4564	3320
European Community	377-5276	3034

Listing of ITA desk officers

Country	Phone	Room
Finland	377-3254	3413
France	377-8008	3042
French Guyana	377-2523	3029-A
Gabon	377-0357	3317
Gambia	377-4564	3317
German Democratic Rep.	377-2645	3419
Germany (West)	377-2434	3411
Ghana	377-4564	3317
Greece	377-3945	3044
Grenada	377-2527	3029-A
Guatemala	377-5563	3022
Guadeloupe	377-2527	3029-A
Guinea	377-4564	3317
Guinea-Bissau	377-4564	3317
Guyana	377-2527	3029-A
Haiti	377-2521	3029-A
Honduras	377-2527	3029-A
Hong Kong	377-2462	2323
Hungary	377-2645	3421
Iceland	377-3254	3413
India	377-2954	2029-B
Indonesia	377-3875	2032
Iran	377-5767	2039
Iraq	377-5767	2039
Ireland	377-2920	3415
Israel	377-4652	2039
Italy	377-2177	3045
Ivory Coast	377-4388	3317
Jamaica	377-2527	3029-A
Japan	377-4527	2318
Jordan	377-5767	2038
Kampuchea	377-4681	2323
Kenya	377-4564	3317
Korea	377-4399	2034
Kuwait	377-5767	2039
Laos	377-3583	2325
Lebanon	377-5767	2039
Lesotho	377-5148	3317
Liberia	377-4564	3317
Libya	377-5737	2039
Luxembourg	377-2920	3415
Macao	377-3853	2325
Madagascar	377-0357	3317
Malaysia	377-3875	2310
Malawi	377-3875	2310
Maldives	377-2954	2029-B

Country	Phone	Room
Mali	377-4564	3320
Malta	377-5401	3415
Martinique	377-2527	3029-A
Mauritania	377-4564	3317
Mauritius	377-0357	3317
Mexico	377-2332	3028
Mongolia	377-3932	3217
Morocco	377-5737	2039
Mozambique	377-5148	3317
Namibia	377-5148	3319
Nepal	377-2954	2029-B
Netherlands	377-5401	3415
Netherlands Antilles	377-2527	3029-A
New Zealand	377-3647	2310
Nicaragua	377-2527	3029-A
Niger	377-4564	3317
Nigeria	377-4388	3321
Norway	377-4414	3413
Oman	377-5545	2039
Pacific Islands	377-3647	2310
Pakistan	377-2954	1029-B
Panama	377-2527	3029-A
Paraguay	377-5427	3021
People's Republic of China	377-3583	2317
Peru	377-4302	3027
Philippines	377-3875	2310
Poland	377-2645	3419
Portugal	377-8010	3042
Puerto Rico	377-2527	3029-A
Qatar	377-5545	2039
Romania	377-2645	3419
Rwanda	377-0357	3317
Sao Tome & Principe	377-0357	3317
Saudi Arabia	377-5767	2039
Senegal	377-4564	3317
Seychelles	377-4564	3320
Sierra Leone	377-4564	3317
Singapore	377-3875	2310
Somalia	377-4564	3317
South Africa	377-5148	3317
Spain	377-4509	3042
Sri Lanka	377-2954	2029-B
St. Barthelemy	377-2527	3029-A
St. Martin	377-2527	3029-A
Sudan	377-4564	3317
Suriname	377-2527	3029-A

Listing of ITA desk officers

Country	Phone	Room
Swaziland	377-5148	3317
Sweden	377-4414	3413
Switzerland	377-2897	3044
Syria	377-5767	2039
Taiwan	377-4957	2034
Tanzania	377-4564	3317
Thailand	377-3875	2032
Togo	377-4564	3317
Trinidad & Tobago	377-2527	3029-A
Tunisia	377-5737	2039
Turks & Caicos Islands	377-2527	3029-A
Turkey	377-2434	3042
Uganda	377-4564	3317
U.S.S.R.	377-4655	3414
United Arab Emirates	377-5545	2039
United Kingdom	377-4104	4212
Uruguay	377-5427	3021
Venezuela	377-4302	3027
Vietnam	377-4681	2323
Virgin Islands (U.K.)	377-2527	3029-A
Virgin Islands (U.S.)	377-2912	3016
Yemen	377-5767	2039
Yugoslavia	377-5373	3046
Zaire	377-0357	3317
Zambia	377-5148	3317
Zimbabwe	377-5148	3317

2. Small Business Administration (SBA)

All export programs administered through SBA are available through SBA Field Offices. More information about the programs can be obtained through:

Small Business Administration
(SBA) . . . . (202) 653-7794
Office of International Trade
1441 L Street, NW.
Washington, DC 20416

3. Export Import Bank

Export Import Bank
811 Vermont Ave., NW.
Washington, DC 20571   Area Code: 202

Export Trading Company
Assistance 566-8944

Engineering Division 566-8802

Small Business Assistance
Hotline 800-424-5201

4. U.S. Department of Agriculture

U.S. Department of Agriculture
14th Street and Independence Avenue, SW.
Washington, DC 20250   Area Code: 202

Foreign Agricultural Service

Commodity and Marketing Programs:

Dairy, Livestock
and   Poultry 447-8031
Grain and Feed
Division 447-6219
Horticulture and
Tropical Plants 447-6590
Oilseed and Oilseed
Products 447-7037
Tobacco, Cotton and Seed 382-9516
Forest Products 382-8138

Export Programs
Division 447-3031

Minority and Small Business
Coordinator 447-3833

Agricultural Information &
Marketing Service (AIMS) 447-7103

5. Overseas Private Investment Corporation (OPIC)

Overseas Private Investment Corporation
(OPIC) . . . . (202) 457-7200
1615 M St., NW., Suite 400
Washington, DC 20527

6. U.S. Department of Treasury

U.S. Department of Treasury
15th Street and Pennsylvania Ave., NW.
Washington, DC 20220

U.S. Customs Strategic
Investigation Division (Exodus
Command Center) . . . . . (202) 566-9464

7. Agency for International Development (AID)

Agency for International
Development (AID)
Department of State Building
320 21st Street, NW.
Washington, DC 20523

Office of Business
Relations . . . . (202) 235-1840

8. Office of the United States Trade Representative

Winder Building
600 17th Street, NW.
Washington, DC 20506   Area Code: 202

General Counsel 395-3150
Private Sector Liaison 395-6120
Agricultural Affairs & Commodity
Policy 395-6127
The Americas Trade
Policy 395-6135
East-West & Non-Market
Economies 395-4543
Europe & Japan 395-4620
General Agreement on Tariff &
Trade (GATT) 395-6843
Industrial & Energy
Trade Policy 395-7320
Investment Policy 395-3510
Pacific, Asia, Africa & North-South
Trade Policy 395-3430

APPENDIX C: COMMERCE DEPARTMENT DISTRICT OFFICES*

ALABAMA, Birmingham - 2015 2nd Ave.
N., 3rd Flr., Berry Bldg., 35203. Tel:
(205) 264-1331.

ALASKA, Anchorage - 701 C Street, P.O.
Box 32, 99513. Tel: (907) 271-5041.

ARIZONA, Phoenix - Fed. Bldg. & U.S. Courthouse, 230 N. 1st Ave., Rm. 3412, 85025.
Tel: (602) 254-3285.

ARKANSAS, Little Rock - Savers Fed. Bldg.,
Ste. 635, 320 W. Capitol Ave., 72201. Tel:
(501) 378-5794.

CALIFORNIA, Los Angeles - Rm. 800, 11777
San Vicente Blvd., 90049. Tel: (213) 209-
6707.

Santa Ana - 116-A, W. 4th St., Ste. 1, 92701.
Tel: (714) 836-2461.

San Diego - P.O. Box 81404, 92138, Tel:
(619) 293-5395.

San Francisco - Fed. Bldg. Box 36013, 450
Golden Gate Ave., 94102. Tel: (415) 556-
5860.

COLORADO, Denver - Room 119, U.S.
Customhouse, 721 19th St., 80202, Tel:
(303) 844-3246.

CONNECTICUT, Hartford - Rm. 610-B, Fed.
Bldg., 450 Main St., 06103. Tel: (203) 722-
3530.

DELAWARE, Serviced by Philadelphia D.O.

DISTRICT OF COLUMBIA, Serviced by Baltimore D.O.

FLORIDA, Miami - 224 Fed. Bldg., 51 SW. 1st
Ave., 33130. Tel: (305) 536-5267.

Clearwater - 128 N. Osceola Ave., 33515.
Tel: (813) 461-0011.

Jacksonville - 3 Independent Dr., 32202. Tel:
(904) 791-2796.

Orlando - 75 E. Ivanhoe Blvd., 32802. Tel:
(305) 425-1247.

Tallahassee - 107 W. Gaines St., Rm. G-20,
32304. Tel: (904) 488-6469.

*Source: National Association of State Development Agencies, State Export Program Database, January 1985.

GEORGIA, Atlanta - Suite 504, 1365 Peachtree St., NE., 30309. Tel: (404) 881-7000.

Savannah - Fed. Bldg., Rm. A-107, 120 Bernard St., 31401. Tel: (912) 944-4204.

HAWAII, Honolulu - 4106 Fed. Bldg., P.O. Box 50026, 300 Ala Moana Blvd., 96850. Tel: (808) 546-8694.

IDAHO, Boise - Statehouse, Rm 113, 83720. Tel: (208) 334-2470.

ILLINOIS, Chicago - 1406 Mid Continental Plaza Bldg., 55 East Monroe St., 60603. Tel: (312) 353-4450.

Palatine - Harper College, Algonquin & Roselle Rd., 60067. Tel: (312) 397-3000.

Rockford - 515 N. Court St., P.O. Box 1747, 61110-0247. Tel: (815) 987-8100.

INDIANA, Indianapolis - 357 U.S. Courthouse & Fed. Bldg., 46 E. Ohio St., 46204. Tel: (317) 269-6214.

IOWA, Des Moines - 817 Fed. Bldg., 210 Walnut St., 50309. Tel: (515) 284-4222.

KANSAS, Wichita (Kansas City, MO, District) - River Park Pl., Ste. 565, 727 N. Waco, 67203. Tel: (316) 269-6160.

KENTUCKY, Louisville - Rm 636B, U.S. Post Office and Courthouse Bldg., 40202. Tel: (502) 582-5066.

LOUISIANA, New Orleans - 432 Intl. Trade Mart, No. 2 Canal St. 70130. Tel: (504) 589-6546.

MAINE, Augusta (Boston, MA, Districts) - 1 Memorial Circle, Casco Bank Bldg., 04330. Tel: (207) 622-8249.

MARYLAND, Baltimore - 415 U.S. Customhouse, Gay & Lombard Sts., 21202. Tel: (301) 962-3560.

Rockville - 101 Monroe St., 15th Flr., 20850. Tel: (301) 251-2345.

MASSACHUSETTS, Boston - 10th Flr., 441 Stuart St., 02116. Tel: (617) 223-2312.

MICHIGAN, Detroit - 445 Fed. Bldg., 231 W. Lafayette, 48226. Tel: (313) 226-3650.

Grand Rapids - 300 Monroe N.W., Rm. 409, 49503. Tel: (616) 456-2411.

MINNESOTA, Minneapolis - 108 Fed. Bldg., 110 S. 4th St., 55401. Tel: (612) 349-3338.

MISSISSIPPI, Jackson - 300 Woodrow Wilson Blvd., Ste. 328, 39213. Tel: (601) 965-4388.

MISSOURI, St. Louis - 120 S. Central Ave. 63105. Tel: (314) 425-3302.

Kansas City - Rm. 635, 601 E. 12th St., 64106. Tel: (816) 374-3142.

MONTANA, Serviced by Denver D.O.

NEBRASKA, Omaha - 1st Flr., 300 S. 19th St., 68102. Tel: (402) 221-3664.

NEVADA, Reno - 1755 E. Plumb Ln., #152, 89502. Tel: (702) 784-5203.

NEW HAMPSHIRE, Serviced by Boston D.O.

NEW JERSEY, Trenton - 3131 Princeton Pike, 4-D, Ste. 211, 08648. Tel: (609) 989-2100.

NEW MEXICO, Albuquerque - 517 Gold, SW., Ste. 4303, 87102. Tel: (505) 766-2386.

NEW YORK, Buffalo - 1312 Fed. Bldg., 111 W. Huron St., 14202. Tel: (716) 846-4191.

Rochester - 121 E. Ave., 14604. Tel: (716) 263-6480.

New York - Fed. Bldg., 26 Fed. Plaza, Foley Sq., 10278. Tel: (212) 264-0634.

NORTH CAROLINA, Greensboro - 203 Fed. Bldg., 324 W. Market St., P.O. Box 1950, 27402. Tel: (919) 378-5345.

NORTH DAKOTA, Serviced by Omaha D.O.

OHIO, Cincinnati - 9504 Fed. Bldg., 550 Main St., 45202. Tel: (513) 684-2944.

Cleveland - Rm. 600, 666 Euclid Ave., 44114. Tel: (216) 522-4750.

OKLAHOMA, Oklahoma City - 6601 Broadway Ext., Ste. 200, 73116. Tel: (405) 231-5302.

Tulsa - 440 S. Houston St., 74127. Tel: (918) 581-7650.

OREGON, Portland - Rm. 618, 1220 SW. 3rd Ave., 97204. Tel: (503) 221-3001.

PENNSYLVANIA, Philadelphia - 9448 Fed. Bldg., 600 Arch St., 19106. Tel: (215) 597-2866.

Pittsburgh - 2002 Fed. Bldg., 1000 Liberty Ave., 15222. Tel: (412) 644-2850.

PUERTO RICO, San Juan (Hato Rey) - Rm. 659-Fed. Bldg., 00918. Tel: (809) 753-4555.

RHODE ISLAND, Providence (Boston, MA, District) - 7 Jackson Walkway, 02903. Tel: (401) 528-5104.

SOUTH CAROLINA, Columbia - Fed. Bldg., Suite 172, 1835 Assembly St. 29201. Tel: (803) 765-5345.

Charleston - 17 Lockwood Dr., 29401. Tel: (803) 724-4361.

SOUTH DAKOTA, Serviced by Omaha D.O.

TENNESSEE, Nashville - Ste. 1114 Parkway Towers, 404 Jas. Robertson Pkwy., 37219-1505. Tel: (615) 736-5161.

Memphis - 3876 Central Ave., 38111. Tel: (901) 521-4826.

TEXAS, Dallas - Rm. 7A5, 1100 Commerce St., 75242. Tel: (214) 767-0542.

Austin - P.O. Box 12728, Capitol Station, 78711. Tel: (512) 472-5059.

Houston - 2625 Fed. Courthouse, 515 Rusk St., 77002. Tel: (713) 229-2578.

UTAH, Salt Lake City - Rm. 340 U.S. Courthouse, 350 S. Main St., 84101. Tel: (801) 524-5116.

VERMONT, Serviced by Boston D.O.

VIRGINIA, Richmond - 8010 Fed. Bldg., 400 N. 8th St., 23240. Tel: (804) 771-2246.

WASHINGTON, Seattle - Rm. 706, Lake Union Bldg., 1700 Westlake Ave. N., 98109. Tel: (206) 442-5616.

Spokane - P.O. Box 2170, 99210, Tel: (509) 838-8202.

WEST VIRGINIA, Charleston - 3000 New Fed. Bldg., 500 Quarrier St., 25301. Tel: (304) 347-5123.

WISCONSIN, Milwaukee - Fed. Bldg., U.S. Courthouse, 517 E. Wisc. Ave., 53202. Tel: (414) 291-3473.

WYOMING, Serviced by Denver D.O.

	ALABAMA	ALASKA	ARIZONA	ARKANSAS	CALIFORNIA	COLORADO	CONNECTICUT	DELAWARE	FLORIDA	GEORGIA	HAWAII	IDAHO	ILLINOIS	INDIANA	IOWA	KANSAS	KENTUCKY	LOUISIANA (d)	MAINE	MARYLAND	MASSACHUSETTS	MICHIGAN	MINNESOTA
Seminars/ conferences	●		●	●	●	●	●	●	●	●	●	●	●	●	●	●	●	●		●	●	●	●
One-on-one counseling	●		●	●	●	●	●		●	●	●		●	●		●	●			●	●	●	●
Market studies prepared			●	●		●	●		●	●			●		●						●	●	
Language bank				●	●										●	●							
Referrals to local export services	●			●		●	●	●		●	●		●			●	●			●		●	●
Newsletter			●	●	● (a)		●										●			●		●	●
How-to handbook	●				● (b)										●	●	●					●	
Sales leads disseminated	●		●	●	●	●	●	●	●	●	●	●	●	●	●	●	●	●	●	●		●	●
Trade shows	●	●	●	●	●	●	●		●	●	●	●	●	●	●	●	●	●			●	●	●
Trade missions	●	●	●	●		●	●		●	●	●	●	●	●	●	●	●		●	●		●	●
Foreign offices reps.	●	●		●			●		●	● (c)			●	●	●		●			●		●	●
Operational financing program					●							●	●										●

*Source: National Association of State Development Agencies, State Export Program Database, January 1985.

MISSISSIPPI	MISSOURI	MONTANA	NEBRASKA	NEVADA	NEW HAMPSHIRE	NEW JERSEY	NEW MEXICO	NEW YORK	NORTH CAROLINA	NORTH DAKOTA	OHIO	OKLAHOMA	OREGON	PENNSYLVANIA	RHODE ISLAND	SOUTH CAROLINA	SOUTH DAKOTA	TENNESSEE	TEXAS	UTAH	VERMONT	VIRGINIA	WASHINGTON	WEST VIRGINIA	WISCONSIN	WYOMING
•	•	•	•	•	•	•	•	•	•	•	•	•	•	•	•	•	•	•	•	•	•	•	•	•	•	
•	•	•	•		•	•	•	•	•	•	•	•	•	•	•	•	•	•	•	•		•	•		•	
•	•	•						•		•	•	•	•	•	•	•	•					•	•			
			•	•				•		•	•	•					•					•				
	•	•	•		•	•	•	•	•		•	•		•	•	•			•			•		•		
•	•			•		•		•	•		•	•	•	•	•							•		•		
•	•	•	•		•		•	•		•								•	•	•		•	•		•	
•	•	•	•		•	•	•	•	•	•	•	•	•	•	•	•	•	•	•	•		•		•		
•	•	•	•			•		•	•	•	•	•	•	•	•		•	•	•	•		•	•		•	
•	•	•		•		•		•	•	•		•	•		•	•		•		•		•		•	•	•
	•						•	•	•		•			•	•	•		•	•	•	•	•		•		
•											•															

Notes: See next page for notes and explanation of programs.

State trade development services explanation and footnotes

• **Seminars/conferences**—State sponsors seminars for exporters, either basic, specific function, or specific market.

• **One-on-one counseling**—State staff provides actual export counseling to individual businesses in addition to making appropriate referrals.

• **Market studies prepared**—State staff prepares specific market studies for individual companies.

• **Language bank**—State program to match foreign-speaking visitors with bilingual local residents who provide volunteer translation services.

• **Referrals to local export services**—Matching exporters with exporter services, e.g. matchmaker fair, export service directory, individual referrals, etc.

• **Newsletter**—State publishes an international trade newsletter.

• **How-to handbook**—State publishes a basic how-to-export handbook.

• **Sales leads disseminated**—State collects and distributes sales leads to in-state businesses.

• **Trade shows**—State assists with and accompanies or represents businesses on trade shows.

• **Trade missions**—State assists with and accompanies businesses on trade missions.

• **Foreign offices/reps**—State office or contractual representative located abroad.

• **Operational financing program**—State export financing assistance program that is currently operational.

Footnotes:

(a) California issues a bimonthly column to local chambers and trade groups for publication in their newsletters.

(b) California produces a "road map" to low cost and free trade services.

(c) Georgia's foreign offices are only active in attracting reverse investment.

(d) Louisiana has recently established a new Office of International Trade, Finance and Development within the Department of Commerce and Industry. The office is expected to offer a full range of trade promotion services.

State & local sources of assistance

Alabama

U.S. Department of Commerce
US&FCS District Office
3rd Floor, Berry Building
2015 2nd Avenue North
Birmingham, Alabama 35203
(205) 254-1331

U.S. Small Business Administration
908 South 20th Street, Suite 202
Birmingham, Alabama 35205
(205) 254-1344

Alabama World Trade Association
777 Central Bank Building
Huntsville, Alabama 35801
(205) 539-8121

Office of International Trade
Department of Economic and
  Community Affairs
P.O. Box 2939
Montgomery, Alabama 36105-0939
(205) 284-8721

Alaska

U.S. Department of Commerce
US&FCS District Office
701 C Street
P.O. Box 32
Anchorage, Alaska 99513
(907) 271-5041

U.S. Small Business Administration
701 C Street, Room 1068
Anchorage, Alaska 99501
(907) 271-4022

U.S. Small Business Administration
101 12th Avenue, Box 14
Fairbanks, Alaska 99701
(907) 452-0211

Alaska State Chamber of Commerce
310 Second Street
Juneau, Alaska 99801
(907) 586-2323

Anchorage Chamber of Commerce
415 F Street
Anchorage, Alaska 99501
(907) 272-2401

Department of Commerce
and Economic Development
Pouch D
Juneau, Alaska 99811
(907) 465-3580

Fairbanks Chamber of Commerce
First National Center
100 Cushman Street
Fairbanks, Alaska 99707
(907) 452-1105

Arizona

U.S. Department of Commerce
US&FCS District Office
Fed. Bldg. & U.S. Courthouse
230 N. 1st Ave., Rm. 3412
Phoenix, Arizona 85025
(602) 254-3285

U.S. Small Business Administration
3030 N. Central Avenue, Suite 1201

Phoenix, Arizona 85012
(602) 241-2200

U.S. Small Business Administration
301 W. Congress Street, Room 3V
Tucson, Arizona 85701
(602) 762-6715

Arizona World Trade Association
34 West Monroe, Suite 900
Phoenix, Arizona 85003
(602) 254-5521

Director of International Trade
Office of Economic Planning
and Development
1700 W. Washington Street,
Room 505
Phoenix, Arizona 85007
(602) 255-3737

Foreign Trade Zone No. 48
Papago Agency
P.O. Box 578
Sells, Arizona 85634
(602) 383-2611

Foreign Trade Zone No. 60
Border Industrial Development, Inc.
P.O. Box 578
Nogales, Arizona 85621
(602) 281-0600

Arkansas

U.S. Department of Commerce
US&FCS District Office
320 West Capitol Avenue,
Room 635
LIttle Rock, Arkansas 72201
(501) 378-5794

U.S. Small Business Administration
320 W. Capitol Avenue, Room 601
Little Rock, Arkansas 72201
(501) 378-5871

Arkansas Exporters Round Trade
1660 Union National Plaza
Little Rock, Arkansas 72201
(501) 375-5377

International Marketing
Department of Economic Development
1 Capitol Mall
Little Rock, Arkansas 72201
(501) 371-7678

World Trade Club of Northeast Arkansas
P. O. Box 2566
Jonesboro, Arkansas 72401
(501) 932-7550

California

U.S. Department of Commerce
US&FCS District Office
11777 San Vicente Boulevard
Room 800
Los Angeles, California 90049
(213) 209-6707

U.S. Department of Commerce
US&FCS District Office
Federal Building, Room 15205
450 Golden Gate Avenue
Box 36013
San Francisco, California 94102
(415) 556-5860

U.S. Small Business Administration
2202 Monterey Street, Room 108
Fresno, California 93721
(209) 487-5189

U.S. Small Business Administration
350 South Figueroa Street, 6th Floor
Los Angeles, California 90071
(213) 688-2956

U.S. Small Business Administration
660 J Street, Room 215
Sacramento, California 95814
(916) 440-4461

U.S. Small Business Administration
880 Front Street, Room 4-S-29
San Diego, California 85701
(619) 293-5540

U.S. Small Business Administration
450 Golden Gate Avenue, Room 15307
San Francisco, California 94102

U.S. Small Business Administration
211 Main Street, 4th Floor
San Francisco, California 94105
(415) 556-0642

U.S. Small Business Administration
111 W. St. John Street, Room 424
San Jose, California 95113
(408) 275-7584

U.S. Small Business Administration
2700 N. Main Street, Room 400
Santa Ana, California 92701
(714) 836-2494

California State World Trade
Commission
1121 L Street, Suite 310
Sacramento, California 95814
(916) 324-5511

Department of Economic and Business
Development
1030 13th Street, Room 200
Sacramento, California 95814
(916) 322-1394

California Chamber of Commerce
International Trade Department
1027 10th Street
P.O. Box 1736
Sacramento, California 95808
(916) 444-6670

Century City Chamber of Commerce
International Business Council
2020 Avenue of the Stars, Plaza Level
Century City, California 90067
(213) 553-4062

Custom Brokers & Freight Forwarders
Association
303 World Trade Center
San Francisco, California 94111
(415) 982-7788

Economic Development Corporation
of Los Angeles County
1052 W. 6th Street, Suite 510
Los Angeles, California 90017
(213) 482-5222

Export Managers Association of California
10919 Vanowen Street
North Hollywood, California 91605
(213) 985-1158

Foreign Trade Association of Southern
 California
350 S. Figueroa Street, #226
Los Angeles, California 90071
(213) 627-0634

Inland International Trade Association, Inc.
Bob Watson
World Trade Center
W. Sacramento, California 95691
(916) 371-8000

International Marketing Association
 of Orange County
Cal State Fullerton
Marketing Department
Fullerton, California 92634
(714) 773-2223

Long Beach Area Chamber of Commerce
International Business Association
50 Oceangate Plaza
Long Beach, California 90802
(213) 436-1251

Los Angeles Area Chamber of Commerce
International Commerce Division
404 S. Bixel Street
Los Angeles, California 90017
(213) 629-0722

Los Angeles International Trade
 Development Corporation
555 S. Flower Street, #2014
Los Angeles, California 90071
(213) 622-4832

Oakland World Trade Association
1939 Harrison Street
Oakland, California 94612
(415) 388-8829

San Diego Chamber of Commerce
101 West "C" Street
San Diego, California 92101
(619) 232-0124

San Francisco Chamber of Commerce
San Francisco World Trade Association
465 California Street, 9th Floor
San Francisco, California 94104
(415) 392-4511

Santa Clara Valley World Trade
 Association
P. O. Box 6178
San Jose, California 95150
(408) 998-7000

Valley International Trade Association
 (San Fernando Valley)
1323 Carmelina Avenue,
Suite 214
Los Angeles, California 90025
(213) 207-1802

World Trade Association
 of Orange County
Hutton, 200 E. Sandpointe #480
Santa Ana, California 92707
(714) 549-8151

World Trade Association of
 San Diego
P. O. Box 81404
San Diego, California 92138
(619) 298-6581

World Trade Council of
 San Mateo Co.
4 West Fourth Avenue, Suite 501
San Mateo, California 94402
(415) 342-7278

Colorado

U.S. Department of Commerce
US&FCS District Office
U.S. Customhouse, Room 119
721 19th Street
Denver, Colorado 80202
(303) 837-3246

U.S. Small Business Administration
U.S. Customhouse, Room 407
721 19th Streeet
Denver, Colorado 80202
(303) 844-2607

Colorado Association of Commerce
and Industry
1390 Logan Street
Denver, Colorado 80202
(303) 831-7411

Denver Chamber of Commerce
1301 Welton Street
Denver, Colorado 80204
(303) 534-3211

Foreign Trade Office
Department of Commerce &
Development
1313 Sherman Street, Room 523
Denver, Colorado 80203
(303) 866-2205

Connecticut

U.S. Department of Commerce
US&FCS District Office
Federal Building, Room 610-B
450 Main Street
Hartford, Connecticut 06103
(203) 722-3530

U.S. Small Business Administration
One Hartford Square West
Hartford, Connecticut 06106
(203) 722-3600

International Division
Department of Economic
Development
210 Washington Street
Hartford, Connecticut 06106
(203) 566-3842

Delaware

U.S. Department of Commerce
US&FCS District Office
—See listing for Philadelphia,
Pennsylvania

U.S. Small Business Administration
844 King Street, Room 5207
Wilmington, Delaware 19801
(302) 573-6294

Delaware State Chamber of Commerce
One Commerce Center, Suite 200
Wilmington, Delaware 19801
(302) 655-7221

Delaware-Eastern Pennsylvania
Export Council
9448 Federal Building
600 Arch Street
Philadelphia, Pennslyvania 19106
(215) 597-2850

Division of Economic Development
Box 1401
630 State College Road
Dover, Delaware 19901
(302) 736-4271

Florida

U.S. Department of Commerce
US&FCS District Office
Federal Building, Suite 224
51 SW. First Avenue
Miami, Florida 33130
(305) 350-5267

U.S. Small Business Administration
400 W. Bay Street, Room 261
Jacksonville, Florida 32202
(904) 791-3782

U.S. Small Business Administration
2222 Ponce de Leon Boulevard, 5th Floor
Miami, Florida 33134
(305) 350-5521

U.S. Small Business Administration
700 Twigs Street, Room 607
Tampa, Florida 33602
(813) 228-2594

U.S. Small Business Administration
3550 45th Street, Suite 6
West Palm Beach, Florida 33407
(305) 689-2223

Bureau of International Trade and
Development
Department of Commerce
Collins Building

Tallahassee, Florida 32301
(904) 488-6124

Georgia

U.S. Department of Commerce
US&FCS District Office
1365 Peachtree Street, NE, Suite 504
Atlanta, Georgia 30309
(404) 881-7000

U.S. Department of Commerce
US&FCS District Office
Federal Building, Room A-107
120 Barnard Street
Savannah, Georgia 31401
(912) 944-4204

U.S. Small Business Administration
1720 Peachtree Road, NW.,
6th Floor
Atlanta, Georgia 30309
(404) 881-4749

U.S. Small Business Administration
52 North Main Street, Room 225
Statesboro, Georgia 30458
(912) 489-8719

Department of Industry and Trade
1400 N. OMNI International
Atlanta, Georgia 30303
(404) 656-3746

International Trade Division
Division of Marketing
Department of Agriculture
19 Martin Luther King, Jr., Drive
Atlanta, Georgia 30334
(404) 656-3600

Hawaii

U.S. Department of Commerce
US&FCS District Office
4106 Federal Building

300 Ala Moana Boulevard
P.O. Box 50026
Honolulu, Hawaii 96850
(808) 546-8694

U.S. Small Business Administration
2213 Federal Building
300 Ala Moana Boulevard
Honolulu, Hawaii 96850
(808) 546-8950

Chamber of Commerce of
 Hawaii
World Trade Association
735 Bishop Street
Honolulu, Hawaii 96813
(808) 531-4111

Economic Development Corporation
 of Honolulu
1001 Bishop Street
Suite 855, Pacific Tower
Honolulu, Hawaii 96813
(808) 545-4533

International Services Agency
Department of Planning &
 Economic Development
P. O. Box 2359
Honolulu, Hawaii 96804
(808) 548-3048

Idaho

U.S. Department of Commerce
US&FCS District Office
—See listing for Salt Lake City,
 Utah

U.S. Small Business Administration
1005 Main Street, 2nd Floor
Boise, Idaho 83701
(208) 334-1696

Division of Economic & Community
 Affairs
Office of the Governor
State Capitol, Room 108
Boise, Idaho 83720
(208) 334-2470

Department of Agriculture
International Trade Division
120 Klotz Lane
P.O. Box 790
Boise, Idaho 83701

District Export Council
Statehouse, Room 225
Boise, Idaho 83720
(208) 334-2200

Idaho International Institute
1112 South Owyhee
Boise, Idaho 83705
(208) 342-4723

Idaho World Trade Association
Box 660
Twin Falls, Idaho 83301
(208) 326-5116

World Trade Committee
Greater Boise Chamber of Commerce
P.O. Box 2368
Boise, Idaho 83701
(208) 344-5515

Illinois

U.S. Department of Commerce
US&FCS District Office
Mid-Continental Plaza Building
Room 1406
55 East Monroe Street
Chicago, Illinois 60603
(312) 353-4450

U.S. Small Business Administration
219 South Dearborn Street
Room 838
Chicago, Illinois 60604
(312) 886-0848

U.S. Small Business Administration
Four North, Old State Capitol Plaza
Springfield, Illinois 62701
(217) 492-4416

American Association of Exporters
and Importers
7763 S. Kedzie Avenue
Chicago, Illinois 60652
(312) 471-1958

Chamber of Commerce of
Upper Rock Island County
622 19th Street

Moline, Illinois 61265
(309) 762-3661

Chicago Association of Commerce
and Industry
World Trade Division
130 S. Michigan Avenue
Chicago, Illinois 60603
(312) 786-0111

Chicago Economic Development
Commission
International Business Division
20 N. Clark Street, 28th Floor
Chicago, Illinois 60602
(312) 744-8666

Customs Brokers and Foreign Freight
Forwarders Association of Chicago, Inc.
P.O. Box 66365
Chicago, Illinois 60666
(312) 992-4100

Department of Commerce &
Community Affairs
International Business Division
310 South Michigan Avenue
Suite 1000
Chicago, Illinois 60604
(312) 793-7164

Foreign Credit Insurance Association
20 North Clark Street, Suite 910
Chicago, Illinois 60602
(312) 641-1915

Illinois Department of Agriculture
1010 Jorie Boulevard
Oak Brook, Illinois 60521
(312) 920-9256

Illinois Manufacturers' Association
175 West Jackson Boulevard
Suite 1321
Chicago, Illinois 60604
(312) 922-6575

Illinois State Chamber of Commerce
International Trade Division
20 N. Wacker Drive, Suite 1960
Chicago, Illinois 60606
(312) 372-7373

International Business Council
 MidAmerica (IBCM)
401 North Wabash Avenue
Suite 538
Chicago, Illinois 60611
(312) 222-1424

Mid-America International Agri-Trade
 Council (MIATCO)
300 West Washington Boulevard
Suite 1001
Chicago, Illinois 60606
(312) 368-4448

Northwest International Trade Club
P.O. Box 454
Elk Grove Village, Illinois 60007
(312) 793-2086

Overseas Sales & Marketing Association
 of America, Inc.
3500 Devon Avenue
Lake Bluff, Illinois 60044
(312) 679-6070

Peoria Area Chamber of Commerce
230 SW. Adams Street
Peoria, Illinois 61602
(309) 676-0755

World Trade Club of
 Northern Illinois
515 N. Court
Rockford, Illinois 61101
(815) 987-8100

Indiana

U.S. Department of Commerce
US&FCS District Office
One North Capitol
Indianapolis, Indiana 46204-2248
(317) 232-8846

U.S. Department of Commerce
US&FCS District Office
357 U.S. Courthouse & Federal
 Office Building
46 East Ohio Street
Indianapolis, Indiana 46204
(317) 269-6214

U.S. Small Business Administration
575 N. Pennsylvania Street
Room 578
Indianapolis, Indiana 46204
(317) 269-7272

U.S. Small Business Administration
501 East Monroe Street, Room 160
South Bend, Indiana 46601
(219) 232-8361

Fort Wayne Chamber of Commerce
International Development Group
826 Ewing Street
Fort Wayne, Indiana 46802
(219) 434-1435

Greater Lafayette
Tippecanoe World Trade Council
Chamber of Commerce
P.O. Box 348
Lafayette, Indiana 47902
(317) 742-4041

Indiana Manufacturers Association
115 N. Pennsylvania Street, No. 950
Indianapolis, Indiana 46204
(317) 632-2474

Indiana State Chamber of Commerce
1 North Capitol, No. 200
Indianapolis, Indiana 46204
(317) 634-6407

Indianapolis Chamber of Commerce
Development and World Trade
320 N. Meridan
Indianapolis, Indiana 46204
(317) 267-2900

Indianapolis Economic Development
 Corporation
48 Monument Circle
Indianapolis, Indiana 46204
(317) 236-6363

Michiana World Trade Club
230 W. Jefferson Boulevard
P.O. Box 1677
South Bend, Indiana 46634
(219) 234-0051

TransNational Business Club
College of Business
Ball State University
Muncie, Indiana 47306
(317) 285-5207

Tri State World Trade Council
329 Main Street
Evansville, Indiana 47708
(812) 425-8147

World Trade Club of Indiana, Inc.
P.O. Box 986
Indianapolis, Indiana 46206
(317) 261-1169

Iowa

U.S. Department of Commerce
US&FCS District Office
817 Federal Building
210 Walnut Street
Des Moines, Iowa 50309
(515) 284-4222

U.S. Small Business Administration
373 Collins Road, N.E.
Cedar Rapids, Iowa 52402
(319) 399-2571

U.S. Small Business Administration
749 Federal Building
210 Walnut Street
Des Moines, Iowa 50309
(515) 284-4222

International Trade
Iowa Development Commission
600 East Court Avenue, Suite A
Des Moines, Iowa 50309
(515) 281-3581

Iowa Association of Business
 & Industry
706 Employers Mutual Building
Des Moines, Iowa 50309
(515) 281-3138

Iowa-Illinois International Trade
 Association
112 East Third Street

Davenport, Iowa 52801
(319) 322-1706

Siouxland Int. Trade Association
Legislative & Agriculture Affairs
101 Pierce Street
Sioux City, Iowa 51101
(712) 255-7903

Kansas

U.S. Department of Commerce
US&FCS District Office
—See listing for Kansas City, Missouri

U.S. Small Business Administration
110 East Waterman Street
Wichita, Kansas 67202
(316) 269-6571

Department of Economic Development
International Trade Development
 Division
503 Kansas Avenue, 6th Floor
Topeka, Kansas 66603
(913) 296-3483

International Trade Institute
1627 Anderson
Manhattan, Kansas 66502
(913) 532-6799

Kansas District Export Council
c/o Sunflower Manufacturing Company
Box 628
Beloit, Kansas 67420
(913) 738-2261

Kentucky

U.S. Department of Commerce
US&FCS District Office
U.S. Post Office & Courthouse
 Building, Room 636-B
Louisville, Kentucky 40202
(502) 582-5066

U.S. Small Business Administration
600 Federal Place, Room 188
Louisville, Kentucky 40201
(502) 582-5971

Kentuckiana World Commerce Council
P.O. Box 58456
Louisville, Kentucky 40258
(502) 583-5551

Kentucky District Export Council
601 West Broadway, Room 636-B
Louisville, Kentucky 40202
(502) 582-5066

Louisville Economic Development
  Cabinet
609 West Jefferson Street
Louisville, Kentucky 40201
(502) 586-3051

Office of International Marketing
Kentucky Commerce Cabinet
Capitol Plaza Tower, 24th Floor
Frankfort, Kentucky 40601
(502) 564-2170

TASKIT (Technical Assistance to Stimulat-
  ing Kentucky International Trade)
College of Business and Economics
University of Kentucky
Lexington, Kentucky 40506-0205
(606) 257-7663

Louisiana

U.S. Department of Commerce
US&FCS District Office
432 International Trade Mart
2 Canal Street
New Orleans, Louisiana 70130
(504) 589-6546

U.S. Small Business Administration
1661 Canal Street, Suite 2000
New Orleans, Louisiana 70112
(504) 589-6685

U.S. Small Business Administration
500 Fannin Street
Room 6B14
Shreveport, Louisiana 71101
(318) 226-5196

Chamber of Commerce/New
  Orleans and the River Region

301 Camp Street
New Orleans, Louisiana 70130
(504) 527-6900

Office of International Trade
  Finance and Development
Louisiana Department of Commerce
P.O. Box 44185
Baton Rouge, Louisiana 70804
(504) 342-5361

World Trade Club of
  Greater New Orleans
1132 International Trade Mart
2 Canal Street
New Orleans, Louisiana 70130
(504) 525-7201

Maine

U.S. Department of Commerce
US&FCS District Office
—See listing for Boston,
  Massachusetts

U.S. Small Business Administration
40 Western Avenue, Room 512
Augusta, Maine 04333
(207) 622-8378

State Development Office
State House, Station 59
Augusta, Maine 04333
(207) 289-2656

Maryland

U.S. Department of Commerce
US&FCS District Office
415 U.S. Customhouse
Gay and Lombard Streets
Baltimore, Maryland 21202
(301) 962-3560

U.S. Small Business Administration
8600 La Salle Road, Room 630
Towson, Maryland 21204
(301) 962-4392

Baltimore Economic Development Corp.
36 S. Charles Street, Suite 2400

Baltimore, Maryland 21201
(301) 837-9305

Division of Economic Development
45 Calvert Street
Annapolis, Maryland 21401
(301) 269-3944

The Export Club
326 N. Charles Street
Baltimore, Maryland 21201
(301) 727-8831

Massachusetts

U.S. Department of Commerce
US&FCS District Office
441 Stuart Street, 10th Floor
Boston, Massachusetts 02116
(617) 223-2312

U.S. Small Business Administration
150 Causeway Street, 10th Floor
Boston, Massachusetts 02114
(617) 223-3224

U.S. Small Business Administration
1550 Main Street
Springfield, Massachusetts 01103
(413) 785-0268

Associated Industries of Massachusetts
462 Boylston Street
Boston, Massachusetts 02116
(617) 262-1180

Brockton Regional Chamber of Commerce
One Centre Street
Brockton, Massachusetts 02401
(617) 586-0500

Central Berkshire Chamber of Commerce
Berkshire Common
Pittsfield, Massachusetts 01201
(413) 499-4000

Chamber of Commerce of the
 Attleboro Area
42 Union Street
Attleboro, Massachusetts 02703
(617) 222-0801

Fall River Area Chamber of Commerce
P.O. Box 1871
200 Pocasset Street
Fall River, Massachusetts 02722
(617) 676-8226

Greater Boston Chamber of Commerce
125 High Street
Boston, Massachusetts 02110
(617) 426-1250

Greater Fitchburg Chamber of Commerce
344 Main Street
Fitchburg, Massachusetts 01420
(617) 343-6487

Greater Gardner Chamber of Commerce
301 Central Street
Gardner, Massachusetts 01440

Greater Lawrence Chamber of Commerce
300 Essex Street
Lawrence, Massachusetts 01840
(617) 687-9404

Greater Springfield Chamber of Commerce
600 Bay State West Plaza, Suite 600
1500 Main Street
Springfield, Massachusetts 01115
(413) 734-5671

Massachusetts Department of Commerce
 & Development
100 Cambridge Street
Boston, Massachusetts 02202
(617) 727-3218

Massachusetts Department of Food
 & Agriculture
100 Cambridge Street
Boston, Massachusetts 02202
(617) 727-3108

New Bedford Area Chamber of Commerce
Room 407, First National Bank Building
New Bedford, Massachusetts 02742
(617) 999-5231

North Suburban Chamber of Commerce
25-B Montvale Avenue
Woburn, Massachusetts 01801
(617) 933-3499

Office of Economic Affairs
One Ashburton Place
Boston, Massachusetts 02108
(617) 367-1830

South Middlesex Area
  Chamber of Commerce
615 Concord Street
Framingham, Massachusetts 01701
(617) 879-5600

South Shore Chamber of Commerce
36 Miller Stile Road
Quincy, Massachusetts 02169
(617) 479-1111

Waltham/West Suburban
  Chamber of Commerce
663 Main Street
Waltham, Massachusetts 02154
(617) 894-4700

Watertown Chamber of Commerce
75 Main Street
Watertown, Massachusetts 02172
(617) 926-1017

Worcester Chamber of Commerce
Suite 350—Mechanics Tower
100 Front Street
Worcester, Massachusetts 01608
(617) 753-2924

Michigan

U.S. Department of Commerce
US&FCS District Office
445 Federal Building
231 West Lafayette
Detroit, Michigan 48226
(313) 226-3650

U.S. Small Business Administration
515 Patrick V. McNamara Building
477 MIchigan Avenue, Room 515
Detroit, Michigan 48226
(313) 226-6075

U.S. Small Business Administration
220 W. Washington Street, Room 310
Marquette, Michigan 49885
(906) 225-1108

Ann Arbor Chamber of Commerce
207 East Washington
Ann Arbor, Michigan 48104
(313) 665-4433

City of Detroit
Community & Economic
  Development Department
150 Michigan Avenue, 7th Floor
Detroit, Michigan 48226
(313) 224-6533

Detroit Customhouse Brokers & Foreign
  Freight Forwarders Association
1237-45 First National Building
Detroit, Michigan 48226
(313) 961-4130

Downriver Community Conference
15100 Northline
Southgate, Michigan 48195
(313) 283-8933

Flint Area Chamber of Commerce
708 Root
Flint, Michigan 49503
(313) 232-7101

(Greater) Detroit
  Chamber of Commerce
150 Michigan Avenue
Detroit, Michigan 48226
(313) 964-4000

(Greater) Grand Rapids
  Chamber of Commerce
17 Fountain Street, NW.
Grand Rapids, Michigan 49502
(616) 459-7221

(Greater) Port Huron-Marysville
  Chamber of Commerce
920 Pine Grove Avenue
Port Huron, Michigan 48060
(313) 985-7101

(Greater) Saginaw
  Chamber of Commerce
901 S. Washington
Saginaw, Michigan 48606
(517) 752-7161

Kalamazoo Chamber of Commerce
500 W. Crosstown Parkway
Kalamazoo, Michigan 49008
(616) 381-4000

Macomb County Chamber of Commerce
10 North Avenue
P.O. Box 855
Mt. Clemens, Michigan 48043
(313) 463-1528

Michigan Department of Agriculture
Office of International Trade
P.O. Box 30017
Lansing, Michigan 48909
(517) 373-1054

Michigan Manufacturers Association
124 East Kalamazoo
Lansing, Michigan 48933
(517) 372-5900

Michigan State Chamber of Commerce
Small Business Programs
200 N. Washington Square, Suite 400
Lansing, Michigan 48933
(517) 371-2100

Muskegon Area Chamber of Commerce
1065 Fourth Street
Muskegon, Michigan 49441
(616) 722-3751

Office of International Development
Michigan Department of Commerce
Law Building, 5th Floor
Lansing, Michigan 48909
(517) 373-6390

Twin Cities Area Chamber of Commerce
777 Riverview Drive, Building V
Benton Harbor, Michigan 49022
(616) 925-0044

West Michigan World Trade Club
445 Sixth Street, NW.
Grand Rapids, Michigan 49504
(616) 451-7651

World Trade Club of Detroit
150 Michigan Avenue

Detroit, Michigan 48226
(313) 964-4000

Minnesota

U.S. Department of Commerce
US&FCS District Office
108 Federal Building
110 S. 4th Street
Minneapolis, Minnesota 55401
(612) 349-3338

U.S. Small Business Administration
100 North 6th Street, Suite 610
Minneapolis, Minnesota 55403
(612) 349-3550

Minnesota Export Finance Authority
90 W. Plato Boulevard
St. Paul, Minnesota 55107
(612) 297-4659

Minnesota World Trade Association
33 E. Wentworth Avenue, 101
West St. Paul, Minnesota 55118
(612) 457-1038

Minnesota Trade Office
90 W. Plato Boulevard
St. Paul, Minnesota 55107
(612) 297-4222

Mississippi

U.S. Department of Commerce
US&FCS District Office
300 Woodrow Wilson Boulevard
Suite 328
Jackson, Mississippi 39213
(601) 960-4388

U.S. Small Business Administration
100 West Capitol Street, Suite 322
Jackson, Mississippi 39269
(601) 960-4378

U.S. Small Business Administration
111 Fred Haise Boulevard, 2nd Floor
Biloxi, Mississippi 39530
(601) 435-3676

International Trade Club of
Mississippi, Inc.
P.O. Box 16673
Jackson, Mississippi 39236
(601) 981-7906

Marketing Division
Mississippi Department of
Economic Development
P.O. Box 849
Jackson, Mississippi 39205
(601) 359-3444

Missouri

U.S. Department of Commerce
US&FCS District Office
120 South Central, Suite 400
St. Louis, Missouri 53105
(314) 425-3301

U.S. Department of Commerce
US&FCS District Office
601 E. 12th Street, Room 635
Kansas City, Missouri 64106
(816) 374-3142

U.S. Small Business Administration
818 Grande Avenue
Kansas City, Missouri 64106
(816) 374-3419

U.S. Small Business Administration
309 North Jefferson, Room 150
Springfield, Missouri 65803
(417) 864-7670

International Business Development
Department of Commerce &
Economic Development
P.O. Box 118
Jefferson City, Missouri 65102
(314) 751-4855

International Trade Club
of Greater Kansas City
920 Main Street, Suite 600
Kansas City, Missouri 64105
(816) 221-1460

Missouri Department of Agriculture
International Marketing Division

P.O. Box 630
Jefferson City, Missouri 65102
(314) 751-5611

Missouri District Export Council
120 S. Central, Suite 400
St. Louis, Missouri 63105
(314) 425-3302

World Trade Club of St. Louis, Inc.
111 North Taylor Avenue
Kirkwood, Missouri 63122
(314) 965-9940

Montana

U.S. Department of Commerce
US&FCS District Office
—See listing for Denver, Colorado

U.S. Small Business Administration
301 South Park, Room 528
Helena, Montana 59626
(406) 449-5381

U.S. Small Business Administration
Post-of-Duty
2601 First Avenue North, Room 216
Billings, Montana 59101
(406) 657-6047

Governor's Office of Commerce &
Small Business Development
State Capitol
Helena, Montana 59620
(406) 444-3923

Nebraska

U.S. Department of Commerce
US&FCS District Office
Empire State Building, 1st Floor
300 South 19th Street
Omaha, Nebraska 68102
(402) 221-3664

U.S. Small Business Administration
Empire State Building
300 South 19th Street
Omaha, Nebraska 68102
(402) 221-4691

International Division
Nebraska Department of
Economic Development
P.O. Box 94666
301 Centennial Mall South
Lincoln, Nebraska 68509
(402) 471-3111

Midwest International Trade Association
c/o NBC, 13th & 0 Streets
Lincoln, Nebraska 68108
(402) 472-4321

Omaha Chamber of Commerce
International Affairs
1301 Harney Street
Omaha, Nebraska 68102
(402) 346-5000

Nevada

U.S. Department of Commerce
US&FCS District Office
1755 East Plumb Lane, Room 152
Reno, Nevada 89502
(702) 784-5203

U.S. Small Business Administration
301 East Steward Street
Las Vegas, Nevada 89125
(702) 385-6611

U.S. Small Business Administration
50 South Virginia Street, Room 238
Reno, Nevada 89505
(702) 784-5268

Commission on Economic Development
600 East Williams, Suite 203
Carson City, Nevada 89710
(702) 885-4325

Department of Economic Development
Capitol Complex
Carson City, Nevada 89701
(701) 885-4325

Economic Development Authority of
Western Nevada
P.O. Box 11710
Reno, Nevada 89510
(702) 322-4004

Latin Chamber of Commerce
P.O. Box 7534
Las Vegas, Nevada 89125-2534
(702) 835-7367

Nevada Development Authority
P.O. Box 11128
Las Vegas, Nevada 89111

Nevada District Export Council
P.O. Box 11007
Reno, Nevada 89520
(702) 784-3401

New Hampshire

U.S. Department of Commerce
US&FCS District Office
—See listing for
Boston, Massachusetts

U.S. Small Business Administration
55 Pleasant Street, Room 211
Concord, New Hampshire 03301
(603) 244-4041

Foreign Trade &
Commercial Development
Department of Resources &
Economic Development
105 Loudon Road, Building 2
Concord, New Hampshire 03301
(603) 271-2591

New Jersey

U.S. Department of Commerce
US&FCS District Office
3131 Princeton Pike, 4-D, Ste. 211
Trenton, New Jersey 08648
(609) 989-2100

U.S. Small Business Administration
60 Park Place, 4th Floor
Newark, New Jersey 07102
(201) 645-2434

U.S. Small Business Administration
1800 East Davis Street, Room 110
Camden, New Jersey 08104
(609) 757-5183

Department of Commerce &
Economic Development
Division of International Trade
744 Broad Street, Room 1709
Newark, New Jersey 07102
(201) 648-3518

World Trade Association of New Jersey
5 Commerce Street
Newark, New Jersey 07102
(201) 623-7070

New Mexico

U.S. Department of Commerce
US&FCS District Office
517 Gold, SW., Ste 4303
Albuquerque, New Mexico 87102
(505) 766-2386

Department of Development
International Trade Division
Bataan Memorial Building
Santa Fe, New Mexico 87503
(505) 827-6208

New Mexico Department of Agriculture
P.O. Box 5600
Las Cruces, New Mexico 88003
(505) 646-4929

New Mexico Foreign Trade and
Investment Council
Mail Stop 150, Alvarado Square
Albuquerque, New Mexico 87158
(505) 848-4632

New Mexico Industry
Development Corporation
5301 Central Avenue, NE., Suite 705
Albuquerque, New Mexico 87110
(505) 262-2247

New York

U.S. Department of Commerce
US&FCS District Office
1312 Federal Building
111 West Huron Street
Buffalo, New York 14202
(716) 846-4191

U.S. Department of Commerce
US&FCS District Office
Federal Office Building, Room 3718
26 Federal Plaza, Foley Square
New York, New York 10278
(212) 264-0634

U.S. Small Business Administration
26 Federal Plaza, Room 3100
New York, New York 10278
(212) 264-4355

U.S. Small Business Administration
35 Pinelawn Road, Room 102E
Melville, New York 11747
(516) 454-0750

U.S. Small Business Administration
100 S. Clinton Street, Room 1071
Syracuse, New York 13260
(315) 423-5383

U.S. Small Business Administration
111 West Huron Street, Room 1311
Buffalo, New York 14202
(716) 846-4301

U.S. Small Business Administration
333 East Water Street
Elmira, New York 14901
(607) 733-4686

U.S. Small Business Administration
445 Broadway, Room 2368
Albany, New York 12207
(518) 472-6300

U.S. Small Business Administration
100 State Street, Room 601
Rochester, New York 14614
(716) 263-6700

Albany-Colonie Regional
Chamber of Commerce
14 Corporate Woods Boulevard
Albany, New York 12211
(518) 434-1214

American Association of
Exporters and Importers
11 West 42nd Street
New York, New York 10036
(212) 944-2230

Buffalo Area Chamber of Commerce
Economic Development
107 Delaware Avenue
Buffalo, New York 14202
(716) 849-6677

Buffalo World Trade Association
146 Canterbury Square
Williamsville, New York 14221
(716) 634-8439

Foreign Credit Insurance Association
One World Trade Center, 9th Floor
New York, New York 10048
(212) 432-6300

International Business Council of the
  Rochester Area Chamber of Commerce
International Trade & Transportation
55 St. Paul Street
Rochester, New York 14604
(716) 451-2220

Long Island Association, Inc.
80 Hauppage Road
Commack, New York 11725
(516) 499-4400

Long Island Association, Inc.
World Trade Club
Legislative & Economic Affairs
80 Hauppage Road
Commack, New York 11725
(516) 499-4400

Mohawk Valley World Trade Council
P.O. Box 4126
Utica, New York 13540
(315) 797-9530 ext. 319

National Association of
  Export Companies
200 Madison Avenue
New York, New York 10016
(212) 561-2025

New York Chamber of Commerce
  & Industry
200 Madison Avenue
New York, New York 10016
(212) 561-2028

New York State Department
  of Commerce
International Division
230 Park Avenue
New York, New York 10169
(212) 309-0502

Rochester Area
  Chamber of Commerce
World Trade Department
International Trade
  & Transportation
55 St. Paul Street
Rochester, New York 14604
(716) 454-2220

Tappan Zee International
  Trade Association
1 Blue Hill Plaza
Pearl River, New York 10965
(914) 735-7040

U.S. Council of the International
  Chamber of Commerce
1212 Avenue of the Americas
New York, New York 10036
(212) 354-4480

Westchester County Association, Inc.
World Trade Club of Westchester
235 Mamaroneck Avenue
White Plains, New York 10605
(914) 948-6444

World Commerce Association of
  Central New York
1 MONY Plaza
Syracuse, New York 13202
(315) 470-1343

World Trade Club of
  New York, Inc.
200 Madison Avenue
New York, New York 10016
(212) 561-2028

World Trade Institute
1 World Trade Center
New York, New York 10048
(212) 466-4044

North Carolina

U.S. Department of Commerce
US&FCS District Office
203 Federal Building
324 West Market Street
P.O. Box 1950
Greensboro, North Carolina 27402
(919) 378-5345

U.S. Small Business Administration
230 South Tryon Street, Room 700
Charlotte, North Carolina 28202
(704) 371-6563

U.S. Small Business Administration
215 South Evans Street, Room 102E
Greenville, North Carolina 27834
(919) 752-3798

Department of Commerce
International Division
430 North Salisburg Street
Raleigh, North Carolina 27611
(919) 733-7193

North Carolina Department of Agriculture
P.O. Box 27647
Raleigh, North Carolina 27611
(919) 733-7912

North Carolina World Trade Association
AMF Marine International
P.O. Box 2690
High Point, North Carolina 27261
(919) 899-6621

North Dakota

U.S. Department of Commerce
US&FCS District Office
—See listing for Omaha, Nebraska

U.S. Small Business Administration
657 2nd Avenue, North, Room 218
Fargo, North Dakota 58108
(701) 237-5771

North Dakota Economic
  Development Commission

International Trade Division
1050 E. Interstate Avenue
Bismarck, North Dakota 58505
(701) 224-2810

Fargo Chamber of Commerce
321 N. 4th Street
Fargo, North Dakota 58108
(701) 237-5678

Ohio

U.S. Department of Commerce
US&FCS District Office
9504 Federal Building
550 Main Street
Cincinnati, Ohio 45202
(513) 684-2944

U.S. Department of Commerce
US&FCS District Office
666 Euclid Avenue, Room 600
Cleveland, Ohio 44114
(216) 522-4750

U.S. Small Business Administration
1240 East 9th Street, Room 317
Cleveland, Ohio 44199
(216) 552-4180

U.S. Small Business Administration
85 Marconi Boulevard
Columbus, Ohio 43215
(614) 469-6860

U.S. Small Business Administration
550 Main Street, Room 5028
Cincinnati, Ohio 45202
(513) 684-2814

Cleveland World Trade Association
690 Huntington Building
Cleveland, Ohio 44115
(216) 621-3300

Columbus Area Chamber of Commerce
Economic Development
37 N. High Street
Columbus, Ohio 43216
(614) 221-1321

Columbus Council on World Affairs
57 Jefferson Street
Columbus, Ohio 43215
(614) 461-0632

Commerce & Industry Association
 of Greater Elyria
Elyria, Ohio 44036
(216) 322-5438

Dayton Council on World Affairs
300 College Park
Dayton, Ohio 45469
(513) 229-2319

Dayton Development Council
1880 Kettering Tower
Dayton, Ohio 45423
(513) 226-8222

Department of Development
International Trade Division
30 East Broad Street
P.O. Box 1001
Columbus, Ohio 43216
(614) 466-5017

(Greater) Cincinnati
 Chamber of Commerce
Export Development
120 West 5th Street
Cincinnati, Ohio 45202
(513) 579-3122

(Greater) Cincinnati World Trade Club
120 W. 5th Street
Cincinnati, Ohio 45202
(513) 579-3122

International Business & Trade
 Association of Akron
 Regional Development Board
Akron, Ohio 44308
(216) 376-5550

North Central Ohio Trade Club
Chamber of Commerce
Mansfield, Ohio 44902
(419) 522-3211

Ohio Department of Agriculture
Ohio Department Building, Room 607

65 South Front Street
Columbus, Ohio 43215
(614) 466-8789

Ohio Foreign Commerce Association,
 Inc.
26250 Euclid Avenue, Suite 333
Cleveland, Ohio 44132
(216) 696-7000

Toledo Area International Trade
 Association
Toledo, Ohio 43604
(419) 243-8191

Oklahoma

U.S. Department of Commerce
US&FCS District Office
4024 Lincoln Boulevard
Oklahoma City, Oklahoma 73105
(405) 231-5302

U.S. Small Business Administration
200 NW. 5th Street, Suite 670
Oklahoma City, Oklahoma 73102
(405) 231-4301

Department of Economic Development
International Trade Division
4024 N. Lincoln Boulevard
P.O. Box 53424
Oklahoma City, Oklahoma 73152
(405) 521-3501

(Metropolitan) Tulsa
 Chamber of Commerce
Economic Development Division
616 South Boston Avenue
Tulsa, Oklahoma 74119
(918) 585-1201

Oklahoma City Chamber of Commerce
Economic and Community Development
One Santa Fe Plaza
Oklahoma City, Oklahoma 73102
(405) 278-8900

Oklahoma City International Trade
 Association
c/o Ditch Witch International
P.O. Box 66

Perry, Oklahoma 73077
(405) 336-4402

Oklahoma District Export Council
4024 Lincoln Boulevard
Oklahoma City, Oklahoma 73105
(405) 231-5302

Oklahoma State Chamber of Commerce
4020 Lincoln Boulevard
Oklahoma City, Oklahoma 73105
(405) 424-4003

Tulsa World Trade Association
1821 N. 106th East Avenue
Tulsa, Oklahoma 74116
(918) 836-0338

Oregon

U.S. Department of Commerce
US&FCS District Office
1220 SW. 3rd Avenue, Room 618
Portland, Oregon 97204
(503) 221-3001

U.S. Small Business Administration
1220 SW. 3rd Avenue, Room 676
Portland, Oregon 97204
(503) 221-5221

Department of Economic Development
International Trade Division
921 SW. Washington, Suite 425
Portland, Oregon 97205
(503) 229-5625 or (800) 452-7813

Eugene Area Chamber of Commerce
1401 Willamette
P.O. Box 1107
Eugene, Oregon 97440
(503) 484-1314

Institute for International Trade
 and Commerce
Portland State University
1912 SW. 6th Avenue, Room 260
Portland, Oregon 97207
(503) 229-3246

Oregon District Export Council
1220 SW. 3rd Avenue, Room 618

Portland, Oregon 97209
(503) 292-9219

Western Wood Products Association
Yem Building
Portland, Oregon 97204
(503) 224-3930

Pennsylvania

U.S. Department of Commerce
US&FCS District Office
9448 Federal Building
600 Arch Street
Philadelphia, Pennsylvania 19106
(215) 597-2866

U.S. Department of Commerce
US&FCS District Office
2002 Federal Building
1000 Liberty Avenue
Pittsburgh, Pennsylvania 15222
(412) 644-2850

U.S. Small Business Administration
231 St. Asaphs Road, Suite 400
Philadelphia, Pennsylvania 19004
(215) 596-5889

U.S. Small Business Administration
 Branch Office
100 Chestnut Street, Suite 309
Harrisburg, Pennsylvania 17101
(717) 782-3840

U.S. Small Business Administration
 Branch Office
20 North Pennsylvania Avenue
Wilkes-Barre, Pennsylvania 18701
(717) 826-6497

U.S. Small Business Administration
 District Office
960 Pennsylvania Avenue, 5th Floor
Pittsburgh, Pennsylvania 15222
(412) 644-2780

American Society of International
 Executives, Inc.
Dublin Hall, Suite 419
Blue Bell, Pennsylvania 19422
(215) 643-3040

(City of) Philadelphia
Municipal Services Bldg.
Room 1660
Philadelphia, Pennsylvania 19102
(215) 686-3647

Economic Development Council of
  Northwestern Pennsylvania
1151 Oak Street
Pittston, Pennsylvania 18640
(717) 655-5581

Erie Manufacturers Association
P.O. Box 1779
Erie, Pennsylvania 16507
(814) 453-4454

(Greater) Pittsburgh Chamber of
  Commerce
411 Seventh Avenue
Pittsburgh, Pennsylvania 15219
(412) 392-4500

International Trade Development
  Association
Box 113
Furlong, Pennsylvania 18925
(215) 822-6993

Pennsylvania Department of Agriculture
Bureau of Agricultural Development
2301 North Cameron Street
Harrisburg, Pennsylvania 17110
(717) 783-8460

Pennsylvania Department of Commerce
Bureau of Domestic & International
  Commerce
408 South Office Building
Harrisburg, Pennsylvania 17120
(717) 787-6500

Philadelphia Export Network
3508 Market Street, Suite 100
Philadelphia, Pennsylvania 19104
(215) 898-4189

Reading Foreign Trade Association
35 N. 6th Street
Reading, Pennsylvania 19603
(215) 320-2976

Smaller Manufacturers Council
339 Boulevard of the Allies
Pittsburgh, Pennsylvania 15222
(412) 391-1622

Southwestern Pennsylvania Economic
  Development District
355 Fifth Avenue, Room 1411
Pittsburgh, Pennsylvania 15222
(412) 391-1240

Western Pennsylvania District Export
  Council
1000 Liberty Avenue, Room 2002
Pittsburgh, Pennsylvania 15222
(412) 644-2850

Women's International Trade Association
P.O. Box 40004
Continental Station
Philadelphia, Pennsylvania 19106
(215) 923-6900

World Trade Association of
  Philadelphia, Inc.
820 Land Title Building
Philadelphia, Pennsylvania 19110
(215) 563-8887

World Trade Club of Northwest
  Pennsylvania
P.O. Box 1232
Kingston, Pennsylvania 18704
(717) 287-9624

Rhode Island

U.S. Department of Commerce
US&FCS District Office
—See listing for Boston, Massachusetts

U.S. Small Business Administration
380 Westminster Mall
Providence, Rhode Island 02903
(401) 351-7500

Department of Economic
  Development
7 Jackson Walkway
Providence, Rhode Island 02903
(401) 277-2601

South Carolina

U.S. Department of Commerce
US&FCS District Office
Strom Thurmond Federal Building
Suite 172
1835 Assembly Street
Columbia, South Carolina 29201
(803) 765-5345

U.S. Small Business Administration
Strom Thurmond Federal Building
Suite 172
1825 Assembly, 3rd Floor
Columbia, South Carolina 29202
(803) 765-5376

South Carolina District Export Council
Strom Thurmond Federal Building
Suite 172
1835 Assembly Street
Columbia, South Carolina 29201
(803) 765-5345

South Carolina International
 Trade Club
Strom Thurmond Federal Building
Suite 172
1835 Assembly Street
Columbia, South Carolina 29201
(803) 765-5345

South Carolina State Development Board
International Division
P.O. Box 927
Columbia, South Carolina 29202
(803) 758-2235

South Dakota

U.S. Department of Commerce
US&FCS District Office
—See listing for Omaha, Nebraska

U.S. Small Business Administration
101 South Main Avenue, Suite 101
Sioux Falls, South Dakota 57102
(605) 336-2980

Rapid City Area Chamber of Commerce
P.O. Box 747

Rapid City, South Dakota 57709
(605) 343-1774

Sioux Falls Chamber of Commerce
127 E. 10th Street
Sioux Falls, South Dakota 57101
(605) 336-1620

South Dakota Bureau of Industrial
 and Agricultural Development
221 S. Central
Pierre, South Dakota 57501
(605) 773-5032

Tennessee

U.S. Department of Commerce
US&FCS District Office
Suite 1114, Parkway Towers
404 James Robertson Parkway
Nashville, Tennessee 37219-1505
(615) 736-5161

U.S. Small Business Administration
404 James Robertson Parkway
Suite 1012
Nashville, Tennessee 37219
(615) 251-5881

Chattanooga World Trade Council
1001 Market Street
Chattanooga, Tennessee 37402
(615) 765-2121

Department of Economic & Community
 Development
Export Promotion Office
Andrew Jackson State Building, Room 10
Nashville, Tennessee 37219
(615) 741-5870

East Tennessee International Trade Club
c/o United American Bank
P.O. Box 280
Knoxville, Tennessee 37901
(615) 971-2027

Memphis World Trade Club
P.O. Box 3577
Memphis, Tennessee 38103
(901) 346-1001

Mid-South Exporters' Roundtable
P.O. Box 3521
Memphis, Tennessee 38103
(901) 761-3490

Middle Tennessee World Trade Council
P.O. Box 17367
Nashville, Tennessee 37202
(615) 329-4931

Tennessee Department of Agriculture
Ellington Agricultural Center
P.O. Box 40627, Melrose Station
Nashville, Tennessee 37204
(615) 360-0103

Tennessee District Export Council
c/o Aladdin Industries
P.O. Box 100255
Nashville, Tennessee 37210
(615) 748-3575

Texas

U.S. Department of Commerce
US&FCS District Office
1100 Commerce Street, Room 7A5
Dallas, Texas 75242
(214) 767-0542

U.S. Department of Commerce
US&FCS District Office
2625 Federal Building
515 Rusk Street
Houston, Texas 77002
(713) 229-2578

U.S. Small Business Administration
300 East 8th Street, Room 780
Austin, Texas 78701
(512) 482-5288

U.S. Small Business Administration
400 Mann Street, Suite 403
Corpus Christi, Texas 78408
(512) 888-3331

U.S. Small Business Administration
1100 Commerce Street, Room 3C36
Dallas, Texas 75242
(214) 767-0605

U.S. Small Business Administration
4100 Rio Bravo, Suite 300
El Paso, Texas 79902
(915) 543-7586

U.S. Small Business Administration
221 West Lancaster Avenue, Room 1007
Ft. Worth, Texas 76102
(817) 334-5463

U.S. Small Business Administration
222 East Van Buren Street, Room 500
Harlingen, Texas 78550
(512) 423-8934

U.S. Small Business Administration
2525 Murworth, Room 112
Houston, Texas 77054
(713) 660-4401

U.S. Small Business Administration
1611 Tenth Street, Suite 200
Lubbock, Texas 79401
(806) 762-7466

U.S. Small Business Administration
100 South Washington Street
Room 3C36
Marshall, Texas 75670
(214) 935-5257

U.S. Small Business Administration
727 East Duranyo Street, Room A-513
San Antonio, Texas 78206
(512) 229-6250

Amarillo Chamber of Commerce
Amarillo Building
1301 S. Polk
Amarillo, Texas 79101
(806) 374-5238

Dallas Chamber of Commerce
1507 Pacific
Dallas, Texas 75201
(214) 954-1111

Dallas Council on World Affairs
The Fred Lange Center
1310 Annex, Suite 101
Dallas, Texas 75204
(214) 827-7960

El Paso Chamber of Commerce
10 Civic Center Plaza
El Paso, Texas 79944
(915) 544-7880

Foreign Credit Insurance Association
600 Travis
Suite 2860
Houston, Texas 77002
(713) 227-0987

Fort Worth Chamber of Commerce
700 Throckmorton
Fort Worth, Texas 76102
(817) 336-2491

Greater San Antonio Chamber of
  Commerce
P.O. Box 1628
San Antonio, Texas 78296
(512) 227-8181

Houston Chamber of Commerce
1100 Milam Building, 25th Floor
Houston, Texas 77002
(713) 651-1313

Houston World Trade Association
1520 Texas Avenue, Suite 239
Houston, Texas 77002
(713) 225-0967

Lubbock Chamber of Commerce
14th Street & Avenue K
P.O. Box 561
Lubbock, Texas 79408
(806) 763-4666

North Texas Customs Brokers &
  Foreign Freight Forwarders Association
P.O. Box 225464
DFW Airport, Texas 75261
(214) 456-0730

Odessa Chamber of Commerce
P.O. Box 3626
Odessa, Texas 79760
(915) 322-9111

Texas Department of Agriculture
Export Services Division
P.O. Box 12847, Capitol Station

Austin, Texas 78711
(512) 475-2760

Texas Economic Development Commission
International Trade Department
P.O. Box 13561
Austin, Texas 78711
(512) 475-6156

Texas Industrial Development Council, Inc.
P.O. Box 1002
College Station, Texas 77841
(409) 845-2911

U.S. Chamber of Commerce
4835 LBJ Freeway, Suite 750
Dallas, Texas 75324
(214) 387-0404

World Trade Association of
  Dallas/Fort Worth
P.O. Box 29334
Dallas, Texas 75229
(214) 760-9105

Utah

U.S. Department of Commerce
US&FCS District Office
U.S. Post Office Building
Room 340
350 South Main Street
Salt Lake City, Utah 84101
(801) 524-5116

U.S. Small Business Administration
125 South State Street
Room 2237
Salt Lake City, Utah 84138
(314) 524-5800

Salt Lake Area Chamber of Commerce
Export Development Committee
19 E. 2nd Street
Salt Lake City, Utah 84111

Utah Economic & Industrial Development
  Division
6150 State Office Building
Salt Lake City, Utah 84114
(801) 533-5325

World Trade Association of Utah
10 Exchange Place
Suite 301–302
Salt Lake City, Utah 84111
(801) 531-1515

Vermont

U.S. Department of Commerce
US&FCS District Office
—See listing for Boston, Massachusetts

U.S. Small Business Administration
87 State Street, Room 204
Montpelier, Vermont 05602
(802) 229-0538

Department of Economic Development
Pavilion Office Building
Montpelier, Vermont 05602
(802) 828-3221

Virginia

U.S. Department of Commerce
US&FCS District Office
8010 Federal Building
400 North 8th Street
Richmond, Virginia 23240
(804) 771-2246

U.S. Small Business Administration
3015 Federal Building
400 North 8th Street
Richmond, Virginia 23240
(804) 771-2617

International Trade Association of
  Northern Virginia
P.O. Box 2982
Reston, Virginia 22090

International Trade Development
Division of Industrial Development
1010 Washington Building
Richmond, Virginia 23219
(804) 786-3791

Newport News Export Trading System
Department of Development
Peninsula Export Program

2400 Washington Avenue
Newport News, Virginia 32607
(804) 247-8751

Piedmont Foreign Trade Council
P.O. Box 1374
Lynchburg, Virginia 24505
(804) 782-4231

Vextrac/Export Trading Company of
  the Virginia Port Authority
600 World Trade Center
Norfolk, Virginia 23510
(804) 623-8000

(Virginia) Chamber of Commerce
611 E. Franklin Street
Richmond, Virginia 23219
(804) 644-1607

Virginia Department of Agriculture &
  Consumer Services
1100 Bank Street
Room 710
Richmond, Virginia 23219
(804) 786-3501

Virginia District Export Council
P.O. Box 10190
Richmond, Virginia 23240
(804) 771-2246

Washington

U.S. Department of Commerce
706 Lake Union Building
1700 Westlake Avenue North
Seattle, Washington 98109
(206) 442-5616

U.S. Small Business Administration
915 Second Avenue
Room 1792
Seattle, Washington 98174
(206) 442-5534

U.S. Small Business Administration
W920 Riverside Avenue
Room 651
Spokane, Washington 99210
(509) 456-5310

Department of Commerce & Economic
Development
International Trade & Investment Division
312 1st Avenue North
Seattle, Washington 89109
(206) 348-7149

Economic Development Council of
Puget Sound
1218 Third Avenue, Suite 1900
Seattle, Washington 98101
(206) 622-2868

Inland Empire World Trade Club
P.O. Box 3727
Spokane, Washington 99220
(509) 489-0500

Seattle Chamber of Commerce
Trade & Transportation Division
One Union Square, 12th Floor
Seattle, Washington 98101
(206) 447-7263

Washington Council on International
Trade
Suite 420
Fourth and Vine Building
Seattle, Washington 98121
(206) 621-8485

Washington State Department of
Agriculture
406 General Administration Building
Olympia, Washington 98504
(206) 753-5046

Washington State International Trade Fair
312 First Avenue North
Seattle, Washington 98109
(206) 682-6911

World Affairs Council
Mayflower Park Hotel
405 Olive Way
Seattle, Washington 98101
(206) 682-6986

World Trade Club of Bellevue
100 116th Avenue S.E.
Bellevue, Washington 98005
(206) 454-2464

World Trade Club of Seattle
1402 Third Avenue, Suite 414
Seattle, Washington 98101
(206) 621-0344

West Virginia

U.S. Department of Commerce
US&FCS District Office
3000 New Federal Office Building
500 Quarrier Street
Charleston, West Virginia 25301
(304) 347-5123

U.S. Small Business Administration
168 West Main Street
Clarksburg, West Virginia 26301
(304) 923-3706

U.S. Small Business Administration
628 Charleston National Plaza
Charleston, West Virginia 25301
(304) 347-5220

Governor's Office of Economic
& Community Development
State Capitol, Room B-517
Charleston, West Virginia 25305
(304) 348-2234

West Virginia Chamber of Commerce
P.O. Box 2789
Charleston, West Virginia 25330
(304) 342-1115

West Virginia District Export Council
P.O. Box 26
Charleston, West Virginia 25321
(304) 343-8874

West Virginia Manufacturers Association
1313 Charleston National Plaza
Charleston, West Virginia 25301
(304) 342-2123

Wisconsin

U.S. Department of Commerce
US&FCS District Office
605 Federal Building
517 East Wisconsin Avenue

Milwaukee, Wisconsin 53202
(414) 291-3473

U.S. Small Business Administration
212 East Washington Avenue
Room 213
Madison, Wisconsin 53703
(608) 264-5261

U.S. Small Business Administration
500 South Barstow Street
Room 17
Eau Claire, Wisconsin 54701
(715) 834-9012

U.S. Small Business Administration
310 West Wisconsin Avenue, Room 400
Milwaukee, Wisconsin 53203
(414) 291-3941

Milwaukee Association of Commerce
756 N. Milwaukee Street
Milwaukee, Wisconsin 53202
(414) 273-3000

Small Business Development Center
602 State Street
Madison, Wisconsin 53703
(608) 263-7766

Wisconsin Department of Development
123 West Washington Avenue
Madison, Wisconsin 53702
(608) 266-1767

Wyoming

U.S. Department of Commerce
US&FCS District Office
—See listing for Denver, Colorado

U.S. Small Business Administration
100 East "B" Street, Room 4001
Casper, Wyoming 82602
(307) 261-5761

Department of Economic Planning
Industrial Development Division
Barrett Building, 3rd Floor

Cheyenne, Wyoming 82002
(307) 777-7285

APPENDIX E: CONTACTS FOR TOP OVERSEAS MARKETS*

Argentina

American Embassy Commercial Section
4300 Columbia, 1425
Buenos Aires, Argentina
APO Miami 34034
Tel: 744-7611/8811/9911
Telex: 18156 USICA AR

American Chamber of Commerce
  in Argentina
Virrey Loreto 2477/81
1426 Buenos Aires, Argentina
Tel: 782-6016
Telex: 21517 CIARG AR

Embassy of Argentina Commercial
  Section
1667 K ST., NW., Suite 610
Washington, DC 20006
Tel: (202) 939-6400
Telex: 89-2537 EMBARG WSH

Australia

American Embassy Commercial Section
Moonah Pl.
Canberra, A.C.T. 2600, Australia
APO San Francisco 96404
Tel: (062) 705000
Telex: 62104 USAEMB

American Consulate General—
  Melbourne Commercial Section
24 Albert Rd.
South Melbourne, Victoria 3205
Australia
APO San Francisco 96405
Tel: (03) 699-2244
Telex: 30982 AMERCON

* Source: U.S. Department of Commerce

American Consulate General—Sydney
Commercial Section
36th Fl., T&G Tower, Hyde Park Square
Park and Elizabeth Sts.
Sydney 2000, N.S.W., Australia
APO San Francisco 96209
Tel: 264-7044
Telex: 74223 FCSSYD

American Consulate General—Perth
Commercial Section
246 St. George's Ter.
Perth, WA 6000, Australia

American Chamber of Commerce in
Australia
60 Margaret Street
Sydney, N.S.W., 2000 Australia
Tel: 221-3055
Telex: 72729

Embassy of Australia Commercial Section
1601 Massachusetts Ave., NW.
Washington, DC 20036
Tel: (202) 797-3201

Bahamas

American Embassy Commercial Section
Mosmar Building
Queen Street
P.O. Box N-8197
Nassau, Bahamas
Tel: (809) 322-1181/1700
Telex: 20-138 AMEMB NS 138

Embassy of the Bahamas Commercial
Section
600 New Hampshire Avenue, NW.
Suite 865
Washington, DC 20037
Tel: (202) 338-3940
Telex: 440 244 BHMS

Belgium

American Embassy Commercial Section
27 Boulevard du Regent
B-1000 Brussels, Belgium
APO New York 09667-1000
Tel: (02) 513-3830
Telex: 846-21336

American Chamber of Commerce
in Belgium
c/o Essochem, Europe, Inc.
B-1040 Brussels, Belgium
Tel: (02) 720-9130
Telex: 62788

Embassy of Belgium Commercial Section
3330 Garfield Street, NW.
Washington, DC 20008
Tel: (202) 333-6900
Telex: 89 566 AMBEL WSH

Brazil

American Embassy Commercial Section
Avenida das Nocoes, Lote 3
Brasilia, Brazil
APO Miami 34030
Tel: (061) 223-0120
Telex: 061-1091

American Consulate General—
Rio de Janeiro Commercial Section
Avenida Presidente Wilson, 147
Rio de Janeiro, Brazil
APO Miami 34030
Tel: (021) 292-7117
Telex: AMCONSUL 021-21466

American Consulate General—Sao Paulo
Commercial Section
Rua Padre Joao Manoel, 933
Caixa Postal 8063
Sao Paulo, Brazil
APO Miami 34030
Tel: (011) 881-6511
Telex: 011-22183

American Chamber of Commerce in
Brazil—Sao Paulo
Caixa Postal 1980
01051, Sao Paulo, SP—Brazil
Tel: (011) 212-3132
Telex: 1132311 CASE BR

American Chamber of Commerce in
Brazil—Rio de Janeiro
20.040 Rio de Janiero, RJ—Brazil
Tel: 203-2477
Telex: 2123539 RJRT BR
Cable: REYNOTABA

American Chamber of Commerce in
Brazil—Salvador
c/o TABARAMA—Tabacos do Brazil Ltda.
Caixa Postal 508
40.000 Salvador, Bahia—Brazil
Tel: 241-1844

Embassy of Brazil Commercial Section
3006 Massachusetts Avenue, NW.
Washington, DC 20008
Tel: (202) 745-2700
Telex: 440371 BRASMB 89430 BRASMB

Canada

American Embassy Commercial Section
100 Wellington Street
Ottawa, Canada, K1P5T1
Tel: (613) 238-5335
Telex: 0533582

American Consulate General—Calgary
Commercial Section
615 Macleod Trail S.E., Rm. 1050
Calgary, Alberta, Canada T2G 4T8
Tel: (403) 266-8962
Telex: 038-21332

American Consulate General—Montreal
Commercial Section
Suite 1122
South Tower
Place Desjardins
Montreal, Quebec
Canada, H5B1G1
Tel: (514) 281-1886
Telex: 05-268751

American Consulate General—Toronto
Commercial Section
360 University Avenue
Toronto, Ontario
Canada, M5G1S4
Tel: (416) 595-1700
Telex: 065-24132

American Consulate General—
Vancouver Commercial Section
1075 West Georgia Street, 21st Floor
Vancouver, British Columbia
Canada, V6E4E9

Tel: (604) 685-4311
Telex: 04-55673

Embassy of Canada Commercial Section
1746 Massachusetts Avenue, NW.
Washington, DC 20036
Tel: 785-1400
Telex: 8 9664 DOMCAN A WSH

Chile

American Embassy Commercial Section
Edificio Codina
Agustinas 1343
Santiago, Chile
APO Miami 34033
Tel: 710133/90 or 710326/75
Telex: 240062-ICA-CL

American Chamber of Commerce in Chile
Pedro de Valdivia 291
Santiago, Chile
Tel: 223-3037
Telex: 645129 CMDLC CZ

Embassy of Chile Commercial Section
1732 Massachusetts Avenue, NW.
Washington, DC 20036
Tel: (202) 785-1746
Telex: 89-2663 EMBACHILE WSH

China, People's Republic of

American Embassy Commercial Section
Guang Hua Lu 17
Beijing, China
FPO San Francisco 96655
Tel: 52-2033
Telex: AMEMB CN 22701

American Consulate General—
Guangzou Commercial Section
Dong Fang Hotel
Box 100
FPO San Francisco 96659
Tel: 69900 x 1000

American Consulate General—
Shanghai Commercial Section
1469 Huai Hai Middle Rd.
Box 200

FPO San Francisco 96659
Tel: 379-880

American Consulate General—Shenyang
  Commercial Section
40 Lane 4, Section 5
Sanjing St., Heping District
Box 45
FPO San Francisco 96659-0002
Tel: 2 90038/34/54/68
Telex: 80011 AMCS CN

American Chamber of Commerce
  in China
Jian Guo Hotel
Jian Guo Men Wai
Beijing, People's Republic of China
Tel: 59-5261
Telex: 210179 GJPEK CN

Embassy of the People's Republic of China
  Commercial Section
2300 Connecticut Avenue, NW.
Washington, DC 20008
Tel: (202) 328-2520

Colombia

American Embassy Commercial
  Section
Calla 38, No. 8-61
Bogota, Colombia
APO Miami 34038
Tel: 285-1300/1688
Telex: 44843

American Chamber of Commerce in
  Colombia—Bogota
Trv. 18, No. 78-80
Apartado Aereo 75240
Bogota, Colombia
Tel: 256-8800
Telex: 44635

American Chamber of Commerce
  in Colombia—Cali
Apartado Aereo 101
Cali, Valle, Colombia
Tel: 689-506, 689-409
Telex: 55442

Embassy of Colombia Commercial Section
2118 Leroy Place, NW.
Washington, DC 20008
Tel: (202) 387-8338
Telex: 197 624 COLE UT

Denmark

American Embassy Commercial Section
Dag Hammarskjolds Alie 24
2100 Copenhagen, Denmark
APO New York 09170
Tel: (01) 423144
Telex: 22216

Embassy of Denmark Commercial Section
3200 Whitehaven Street, NW.
Washington, DC 20008
Tel: (202) 234-4300
Telex: 089525 DEN EMB WSH
64444 DEN EMB WSH

Dominican Republic

American Embassy Commercial Section
Calle Cesar Nicolas Penson con Calle
  Leopoldo Navarro
Santo Domingo, Dominican Republic
APO Miami 34041-0008
Tel: 682-2171
Telex: 3460013

American Chamber of Commerce in
  the Dominican Republic
P.O. Box 1221
Santo Domingo, Dominican Republic
Tel: 565-1661
Telex: 0034 TATEM DR

Embassy of the Dominican Republic
  Commercial Section
1715 22nd Street, NW.
Washington, DC 20007
Tel: (202) 332-6280
Telex: 44-0031 DOR EMB

Ecuador

American Embassy Ecuador
120 Avenida Patria

Quito, Ecuador
APO Miami 34039
Tel: 548-000
Telex: 02-2329 USICAQ ED

American Consulate General—
  Guayaquil Commercial Section
9 de Octubre y Garcia Moreno
Guayaquil, Ecuador
APO Miami 34039
Tel: 511-570
Telex: 04-3452 USICAG ED

American Chamber of Commerce in
  Ecuador
P.O. Box 9103 Suc. Almagro
Quito, Ecuador
Tel: 523-152, 523-693

American Chamber of Commerce
  in Ecuador
Escobedo 1402 y Chile
P.O. Box 4767
Guayaquil, Ecuador
Tel: 529-855, 516-707

Embassy of Ecuador Commercial Section
2535 15th Street, NW.
Washington, DC 20009
Tel: (202) 234-7200
Telex: 440129 ECUAI

Egypt

American Embassy Commercial Section
5 Sharia Latin America
Cairo, Arab Republic of Egypt
FPO New York 09527
Tel: 28219/774666
Telex: 93773 AMEMB

American Consulate General—Alexandria
  Commercial Section
110 Avenue Horreya
Alexandria, Republic of Egypt
FPO New York 09527
Tel: 801911/25607/22861/28458

American Chamber of Commerce in Egypt
Cairo Marriott Hotel, Suite 1537
P.O. Box 33, Zamalek
Cairo, Egypt

Tel: 340-8888
Telex: 20870

Embassy of Egypt Commercial Section
2715 Connecticut Avenue, NW.
Washington, DC 20008
Tel: (202) 265-9111
Telex: 89-2481 COMRAU WSH
64-251 COMRAU WSH

France

American Embassy Commercial Section
2 Avenue Gabriel
75382 Paris Cedex 08
Paris, France
APO New York 09777
Tel: 296-1202/261-8075
Telex: 650-221

American Consulate General—Marseille
  Commercial Section
No. 9 Rue Armeny 13006
13006 Marseille, France
Tel: 54-92-00
Telex: 430597

American Consulate General—Strasbourg
  Commercial Section
15 Avenue D'Alsace
67082 Strasbourg, Cedex
Strasbourg, France
APO New York 09777
Tel: (88) 35-31-04/05/06
Telex: 870907

American Chamber of Commerce
  in France
53, Avenue Montaigne
75008 Paris, France
Tel: (1) 359-2349

Embassy of France Commercial Section
4101 Reservoir Road, NW.
Washington, DC 20007
Tel: (202) 944-6000
Telex: 248320 FRCC UR

Germany (West)

American Embassy Commercial Section
Deichmanns Ave.

5300 Bonn 2, Federal Republic
of Germany
APO New York 09080
Tel: (0228) 339-3390
Telex: 885-452

American Mission—Berlin Commercial
Section
Clayallee 170
D-1000 Berlin 33 (Dahlem),
Federal Republic of Germany
APO New York 09742
Tel: (030) 819-7561
Telex: 183-701 USBER-D

American Consulate General—
Dusseldorf Commercial Section
Cecilienalle 5
4000 Dusseldorf 30,
Federal Republic of Germany
APO New York 09711

American Consulate General—Frankfurt
am Main Commercial Section
Siesmayerstrasse 21
6000 Frankfurt
Federal Republic of Germany
APO New York 09213
Tel: (0611) 740071
Telex: 412589 USCON-D

American Consulate General—
Hamburg Commercial Section
Alsterufer 27/28
2000 Hamburg 36,
Federal Republic of Germany
APO New York 09215-0002
Tel: (040) 44-1061
Telex: 213777

American Consulate General—
Munich Commercial Section
Koeniginstrasse 5
8000 Muenchen 22
APO New York 09108,
Federal Republic of Germany
Tel: (089) 23011
Telex: 5-22697 ACGM D

American Consulate General—
Stuttgart Commercial Section
Urbanstrasse 7

7000 Stuttgart, Federal Republic
of Germany
APO New York 09154
Tel: (0711) 210221
Telex: 07-22945

American Chamber of Commerce
in Germany
Flying Tigers
Flughafen, Luftfrachtzentrum
6000 Frankfurt 75,
Federal Republic of Germany

Embassy of the Federal Republic
of Germany
4645 Reservoir Road
Washington, DC 20007
Tel: (202) 298-4000
Telex: 8 9481 DIPLOGERMA WSH

Hong Kong

American Consulate General—
Hong Kong Commercial Section
26 Garden Road
Hong Kong
FPO San Francisco 96659-0002
Tel: 239011
Telex: 63141 USDOC HX

American Chamber of Commerce
in Hong Kong
Lark International, Ltd.
15/F World Commerce Center
Harbour City, 11 Canton Road
TST Kowloon, Hong Kong
Tel: 5-26595

Hong Kong Office/British Embassy
3100 Massachusetts Avenue, NW.
Washington, DC 20008
Tel: (202) 898-4591
Telex: 440484 HK WSH UY

India

American Embassy Commercial Section
Shanti Path, Chanakyapuri
110021 New Delhi, India
Tel: 600651
Telex: USCS IN 031-4589

American Consulate General—Bombay
  Commercial Section
Lincoln House
78 Bhulabhai Desai Road
Bombay 400026, India
Tel: 822611/8
Telex: 011-6525 ACON IN

American Consulate General—
  Calcutta Commercial Section
5/1 Ho Chi Minh Sarani
Calcutta 700071, India
Tel: 44-3611/6
Telex: 021-2483

American Consulate General—
  Madras Commercial Section
Mount Road
Madras 600006, India
Tel: 8304116

Embassy of India Commercial Section
2536 Massachusetts Avenue, NW.
Washington, DC 20008
Tel: (202) 939-7000

Indonesia

American Embassy Commercial Section
Medan Merdeka Selatan 5
Jakarta, Indonesia
APO San Francisco 96356
Tel: 340001-9
Telex: 44218 AMEMB JKT

American Consulate—
  Medan Commercial Section
Jalan Imam Bonjol 13
Medan, Indonesia
APO San Francisco 96356
Tel: 322200
Telex: 51764

American Consulate—
  Surabaya Commercial Section
Jalan Raya Dr. Sutomo 33
Surabaya, Indonesia
APO San Francisco 96356
Tel: 69287/8
Telex: 031-334

American Chamber of Commerce
  in Indonesia
Citibank Building, 8th Pl.
Jalan M. H. Thamrin 55
Jakarta, Indonesia
Telex: 48116 CIBSEM IA

Embassy of Indonesia Commercial Section
2020 Massachusetts Avenue, NW.
Washington, DC 20036
Tel: (202) 293-1745

Iraq

American Interests Commercial Section
Belgian Embassy
Opp. For. Ministry Club
Masbah Quarter
P.O. Box 2447 Alwiyah
Baghdad, Iraq
Tel: 719-6138/9
Telex: 212287 USINT IK

Embassy of Iraq Commercial Section
1801 P Street, NW.
Washington, DC 20036
Tel: (202) 483-7500
Telex: 64437 IRAQI YA
64464 IRAQI YA

Ireland

American Embassy Commercial Section
42 Elgin Road
Ballsbridge
Dublin, Ireland
Tel: 688777
Telex: 25240

American Chamber of Commerce
  in Ireland
20 College Green
Dublin 2, Ireland
Tel: 712733
Telex: 31187 UCIL/EI

Embassy of Ireland Commercial Section
2234 Massachusetts Avenue, NW.
Washington, DC 20008
Tel: (202) 462-3939
Telex: 64160 HIBERNIA 64160

Israel

American Embassy Commercial Section
71 Hayarkon Street
Tel Aviv, Israel
APO New York 09672
Tel: 03-654338
Telex: 33376

American Chamber of Commerce
in Israel
35 Shaul Hamelech Blvd.
P.O. Box 33174
Tel Aviv, Israel
Tel: (03) 252341/2
Telex: 32139 BETAM IL

Embassy of Israel Commercial Section
1621 22nd Street, NW.
Washington, DC 20008
Tel: (202) 364-5400

Italy

American Embassy Commercial Section
Via Veneto 119/A
00187 Rome, Italy
APO New York 09794
Tel: (6) 46742
Telex: 610450 AMBRMA

American Consulate General—
 Milan Commercial Section
Plazza Repubblica 32
20124 Milano
c/o U.S. Embassy
Box M
APO New York 09794
Tel: 498-2241/2/3

American Chamber of Commerce
in Italy
c/o Peat, Marwick, Mitchell & Co.
Via San Paolo 15
20121 Milano, Italy

Embassy of Italy Commercial Section
1601 Fuller Street, NW.
Washington, DC 20009
Tel: (202) 328-5500
Telex: 90-4076 ITALY EMB WSH

Japan

American Embassy Commercial
 Section
10-1 Akasaka, 1-chome
Minato-ku (107)
Tokyo, Japan
APO San Francisco 96503
Tel: 583-7141
Telex: 2422118

American Consulate General—
 Osaka Commercial Section*
Sankei Building, 9th Floor
4-9, Umeda 2-chome
Kita-ku
Osaka (530), Japan
APO San Francisco 96503
Tel: (06) 341-2754/7
*Includes American merchandise display.

American Consulate—
 Fukuoka Commercial Section
5-26 Ohori 2-chome
Chuo-ku
Fukuoka (810), Japan
Box 10
FPO Seattle 98766
Tel: (092) 751-9331/4
Telex: 725679

American Chamber of Commerce
 in Japan—Tokyo
c/o Burroughs Company Ltd.
13-1, Shimomiyabicho
Shinjuku-ku
Tokyo (162), Japan
Tel: 03-235-3327
Telex: 2322378 Burtok J

American Chamber of Commerce
 in Japan—Okinawa
P.O. Box 235, Koza
Okinawa City (904), Japan
Tel: 098935-2684
Telex: J79873 NANSEI OK
Cable: AMCHAM OKINAWA

Embassy of Japan Commercial Section
2520 Massachusetts Avenue, NW.
Washington, DC 20008

Tel: (202) 234-2266
Telex: 89 540

Kuwait

American Embassy Commercial Section
P.O. Box 77 SAFAT
Kuwait
Tel: 424-151 through 9

American Chamber of Commerce
 in Kuwait
P.O. Box 77 Safat
Kuwait City, Kuwait
Tel: 2555597
Telex: 46902 SGT CNT KT

Embassy of Kuwait
 Commercial Section
2940 Tilden Street, NW.
Washington, DC 20008
Tel: (202) 966-0702
Telex: 64142 KUWAIT WSH

Malaysia

American Embassy Commercial Section
AIA Building 376 Jalan Tun Razak
P.O. Box 10035
Kuala Lumpur, 01-02, Malaysia
Tel: 489011
Telex: FCSKL MA 32956

American Chamber of Commerce
 in Malaysia
AIA Building
P.O. Box 759
Kuala Lumpur, Malaysia

Embassy of Malaysia
 Commercial Section
2401 Massachusetts Avenue, NW.
Washington, DC 20008
Tel: (202) 328-2700
Telex: 440119 MAEM UI
61435 MALAYEM 61435

Mexico

American Embassy Commercial Section
Paseo de la Reforma 305

Mexico 5 D.F., Mexico
Tel: (525) 21 1-0042
Telex: 017-73-091 or 017-75-685

American Consulate General—
 Guadalajara Commercial Section
Progreso 175
Guadalajara, Jal., Mexico
Tel: 25-29-98/25-27-00
Telex: 068-2-860

American Consulate General—
 Monterrey Commercial Section
Avenida Constitucion
411 Poniente
Monterrey, N.L., Mexico
Tel: 4306 50/59
Telex: 0382853

American Chamber of Commerce
 in Mexico—Mexico City
Embotelladora Tarahumara, S.A. de C.V.
Rio Amazonas No. 43
06500 Mexico, D.F. Mexico
Tel: 591-0066
Telex: 1775481 CCDFME

American Chamber of Commerce
 in Mexico—Guadalajara
Apartado 31-72
45070 Guadalajara, Jal., Mexico
Tel: 15-88-22

American Chamber of Commerce
 in Mexico—Monterrey
Apartado 2781
Monterrey, N.L., Mexico

Embassy of Mexico Commercial Section
2829 16th Street, NW.
Washington, DC 20009
Tel: (202) 234-6000
Telex: 90 4307 OCCMEX

Netherlands

American Embassy Commercial Section
Lange Voorhout 102
The Hague, the Netherlands
APO New York 09159
Tel: (070) 62-49-11
Telex: (044) 31016

American Consulate General—
Amsterdam Commercial Section
Museumplein 19
Amsterdam, the Netherlands
APO New York 09159
Tel: (020) 790321
Telex: 044-16176 CGUSA NL

American Consulate General—
Rotterdam Commercial Section
Baan 50
Rotterdam, the Netherlands
APO New York 09159
Tel: (010) 117560
Telex: 044-22388

The American Chamber of Commerce
in the Netherlands
2517 KJ The Hague, the Netherlands
Tel: 023-339020
Telex: 41219

Embassy of the Netherlands
Commercial Section
4200 Linnean Avenue, NW.
Washington, DC 20008
Tel: (202) 244-5300

Netherland Antilles

American Consulate General—
Netherland Antilles Commercial Section
St. Anna Blvd. 19
P.O. Box 158
Willemstad, Curacao, Netherland Antilles
Tel: (5999) 613066/613350/613441
Telex: 1062 AMCON NA

New Zealand

American Embassy Commercial Section
29 Fitzherbert Terrace, Thorndon
Wellington, New Zealand
FPO San Francisco 96690-0001
Tel: 722-068
Telex: NZ 3305

The American Chamber of Commerce
in New Zealand
P.O. Box 33-246 Takapuna
Auckland 9, New Zealand

Tel: 444-4760
Telex: NZ 2601

Embassy of New Zealand
Commercial Section
37 Observatory Circle, NW.
Washington, DC 20008
Tel: (202) 328-4800
Telex: 8 9526 TOTARA WSH

Nigeria

American Embassy Commercial Section
2 Eleke Crescent
P.O. Box 554
Lagos, Nigeria
Tel: 610097
Telex: 21670 USATO NG

American Consulate General—
Kaduna Commercial Section
2 Maska Road
P.O. Box 170
Kaduna, Nigeria
Tel: (062) 213043/213074/213175

Embassy of Nigeria Commercial Section
2201 M Street, NW.
Washington, DC 20037
Tel: (202) 822-1500
Telex: 89 2311 NIGERIAN WSH

Norway

American Embassy Commercial Section
Drammensveien 18
Oslo 2, Norway
APO New York 09085
Tel: 44-85-50
Telex: 18470

Embassy of Norway Commercial Section
2720 34th Street, NW.
Washington, DC 20008
Tel: 333-6000
Telex: 89-2374 NORAMB WSH

Pakistan

American Embassy Commercial Section
Diplomatic Enclave, Ramna 5
P.O. Box 1048

Islamabad, Pakistan
Tel: 8261-61 through 79
Telex: 825-864

American Consulate General—
 Karachi, Pakistan
8 Abdullah Haroon Road
Karachi, Pakistan
Tel: 515081
Telex: 82-02-611

American Consulate General
50 Zafar Ali Road
Gulberg 5
Lahore, Pakistan
Tel: 870221 through 5

American Chamber of Commerce
 in Pakistan
3rd Floor, Shaheen Commercial Complex
G.P.O. 1322
M.R. Kayani Road
Karachi, Pakistan
Tel: 526436
Telex: 25620 CHASE PK

Embassy of Pakistan Commercial Section
2315 Massachusetts Avenue, NW.
Washington, DC 20008
Tel: (202) 939-6200
Telex: 89-2348 PARAP WSH

Panama

American Embassy Commercial Section
Avenida Balboa y Calle 38
Apartado 6959
Panama 5, Republic of Panama
Box E
APO Miami 34002
Tel: Panama 27-1777

American Chamber of Commerce
 in Panama
Apartado 5010
Panama 5, Republic of Panama
Tel: 60-0122

Embassy of Panama Commercial Section
2862 McGill Terrace, NW.
Washington, DC 20008
Tel: (202) 483-1407

Peru

American Embassy Commercial Section
Grimaldo Del Solar 358
Miraflores, Lima 18, Peru
APO Miami 34031
Tel: 44-3921
Telex: 25028PE USCOMATT

American Chamber of Commerce in Peru
3M Peru, S.A.
P.O. Box 1897
Lima 100, Peru

Embassy of Peru Commercial Section
1700 Massachusetts Avenue, NW.
Washington, DC 20036
Tel: (202) 833-9860
Telex: 197675 LEPRU UT

Philippines

American Embassy Commercial Section
395 Buendia Avenue
Extension Makati
Manila, the Philippines
APO San Francisco 96528
Tel: 818-6674
Telex: 66887 COSEC PN

American Chamber of Commerce
 in the Philippines
P.O. Box 1578 MCC
Makati
Philippines, Manila
Tel: 819-7911
Telex: (RCA) 63637 SDTCO PN

Embassy of the Philippines
 Commercial Section
1617 Massachusetts Avenue, NW.
Washington, DC 20036
Tel: (202) 483-1414
Telex: 44 0059 AMBPHIL

Portugal

American Embassy Commercial Section
Avenida das Forcas Armadas
1600 Lisbon, Portugal
APO New York 09678-0002

Tel: 726-6600
Telex: 12528 AMEMB

American Chamber of Commerce
 in Portugal
Avenida Marcechal Gomes de Costa 33
1800 Lisbon, Portugal
Tel: 853996
Telex: 12599 AUTOREX P

Embassy of Portugal Commercial Section
2125 Kalorama Rd., NW.
Washington, DC 20008
Tel: (202) 328-8610
Telex: 64399 PORT EMB P

Saudi Arabia

American Embassy Commercial Section
Sulaimaniah District
P.O. Box 9041
Riyadh, Saudi Arabia
APO New York 09038
Tel: (01) 464-0012
Telex: 201363 USRIAD SJ

American Consulate General—
 Dhahran Commercial Section
Between Aramco Headquarters
 and Dhahran International Airport
P.O. Box 81, Dhahran Airport
Dhahran, Saudi Arabia
APO New York 09616
Tel: (03) 8913200
Telex: 601925 AMCON SJ

American Consulate General—
 Jeddah Commercial Section
Palestine Road, Ruwais
P.O. Box 149
Jeddah, Saudi Arabia
APO New York 09697
Tel: (02) 667-0080
Telex: 401459 AMEMB SJ

The American Businessmen of Jeddah,
 Saudi Arabia
P.O. Box 5019
Jeddah, Saudi Arabia
Tel: 651-7968
Telex: 401906 UCAJED SJ

American Chamber of Commerce
 in Saudi Arabia
c/o Saudi Business Systems
P.O. Box 4992
Dhahran, Saudi Arabia
Tel: 864-5838, 894-8181
Telex: 670418 SABSYS SJ

Embassy of Saudi Arabia
 Commercial Section
601 New Hampshire Ave., NW.
Washington, DC 20037
Tel: (202) 483-2100

Singapore

American Embassy
 Commercial Section
30 Hill Street
Singapore 0617
FPO San Francisco 96699-0001
Tel: 338-0251

American Chamber of Commerce
 in Singapore
11 Dhoby Ghaut
08-04 Cathay Building
Singapore 0922

Embassy of Singapore
 Commercial Section
1824 R Street, NW.
Washington, DC 20009
Tel: (202) 667-7555
Telex: 440024 SING EMB

South Africa

American Consulate General—
 Johannesburg Commercial Section
Kine Center, 11th Floor
Commissioner and Krulis Streets
P.O. Box 2155
Johannesburg, South Africa
Tel: (011) 331-1681
Telex: 48-3780-SA

American Chamber of Commerce
 in South Africa
P.O. Box 1616
Johannesburg 2000, South Africa

Embassy of South Africa Commercial
Section
4801 Massachusetts Avenue, NW.
Washington, DC 20016
Tel: 966-1650

South African Consulate General—
Commercial Section
425 Park Avenue
New York, NY 10022
Tel: (212) 838-1700
Telex: 233290

South Korea

American Embassy Commercial Section
82 Sejong-Ro; Chongro-ku
Korea
APO San Francisco 96301
Tel: 732-2601 through 18
Telex: AMEMB 23108

Embassy of Korea
2320 Massachusetts Ave., NW.
Washington, DC 20008

Spain

American Embassy Commercial Section
Serrano 75
Madrid, Spain
APO New York 09285
Tel: 276-3400/3600
Telex: 27763

American Consulate General—
Barcelona Commercial Section
Via Layetana
Barcelona, Spain
Box 5
APO New York 09285
Tel: 319-9550
Telex: 52672

American Chamber of Commerce in Spain
Paseo de Gracia 95
Barcelona 8, Spain

Embassy of Spain Commercial Section
2558 Massachusetts Avenue, NW.
Washington, DC 20008

Tel: (202) 265-8600
Telex: 89 2747 SPAIN WSH

Sweden

American Embassy Commercial Section
Strandvagen 101
Stockholm, Sweden
Tel: (08) 63.05.20
Telex: 12060 AMEMB S

Embassy of Sweden Commercial Section
600 New Hampshire Avenue, NW.
Washington, DC 20037
Tel: (202) 298-3500
Telex: 89 2724 SVENSK WSH

Switzerland

American Embassy Commercial Section
Jubilaeumstrasse 93
3005 Bern, Switzerland
Tel: (031) 437011
Telex: (845) 32128

American Chamber of Commerce
in Switzerland
Bahnhofstrasse 45
8021 Zurich, Switzerland
Tel: 211 24 54
Telex: 812747 Ipco Ch

Embassy of Switzerland
Commercial Section
2900 Cathedral Avenue, NW.
Washington, DC 20008
Tel: (202) 745-7900
Telex: 64180 AMSWIS

Taiwan

American Chamber of Commerce
in Taiwan
P.O. Box 17-277
Taipei, Taiwan, R.O.C.

American Institute in Taiwan (AIT)
1700 N. Moore Street
17th Floor
Arlington, Virginia 22209
Tel: (703) 525-8474

American Institute in Taiwan (AIT)
7 Lane 134 Hsin Yi Road
Section 3
Taipei, Taiwan
Telex: 23890 USTRADE

Coordination Council for
  North American Affairs
Economic Division
4301 Connecticut Avenue, NW.
Suite 420
Washington, DC 20008
Tel: (202) 686-6400
Telex: 440292 SINOECO

USA-ROC Economic Council
200 South Main Street
P.O. Box 517
Crystal Lake, Illinois 60014
Tel: (815) 459-5875

Thailand

American Embassy Commercial Section
Shell Building, "R" Floor
140 Wireless Road
Bangkok, Thailand
APO San Francisco 96346
Tel: 251-9260/2
Telex: 20966 FCSBKK

American Chamber of Commerce
  in Thailand
4th Floor, Wanglee Building
297 Suriwongse Road
Bangkok 10500, Thailand
Tel: 234-5173
Telex: LYMAN TH 82978

Embassy of Thailand Commercial Section
1990 M St., NW., Suite 350
Washington, DC 20036
Tel: (202) 467-6790
Telex: 248 275 TTHAI UR

Trinidad & Tobago

American Embassy Commercial Section
15 Queen's Park West
P.O. Box 752
Port-of-Spain, Trinidad and Tobago

Tel: 62-26371
Telex: 22230 AMEMB POS

Embassy of Trinidad and Tobago
  Commercial Section
1708 Massachusetts Avenue, NW.
Washington, DC 20036
Tel: (202) 467-6490
Telex: 64321 TRINOFF

Turkey

American Embassy Commercial Section
110 Ataturk Boulevard
Ankara, Turkey
APO New York 09254
Tel: 265470
Telex: 43144 USIA TR

American Consulate General—
  Istanbul Commercial Section
104-108 Mesrutiyet Caddesi
Tepebasl
Istanbul, Turkey
APO New York 09380
Tel: 1436200/09
Telex: 24306 USIC TR

Embassy of Turkey Commercial Section
2523 Massachusetts Avenue, NW.
Washington, DC 20008
Tel: (202) 483-6366
Telex: 904143 TURKFIN

Union of Soviet Socialist Republics

American Embassy Commercial
  Section
Ulitsa Chazkovskogo 19/21/23
Moscow, Union of Soviet
  Socialist Republics
APO New York 09862
Tel: (096) 252-24-51 through 59
Telex: 413160 USGSO SU

U.S. Commercial Office—Moscow
Ulitsa Chaykovskogo 15
Moscow, U.S.S.R.
APO New York 09862
Tel: 001-7-95-255-46-60
Telex: 413-205 USCO SU

U.S.S.R. Trade Representative
in the U.S.A.
2001 Connecticut Avenue, NW.
Washington, DC 20008
Tel: (202) 232-2917

United Arab Emirates

American Chamber of Commerce
in U.A.E.
P.O. Box 155
Dubai, United Arab Emirates
Tel: 971-4-442790
Telex: 45544 CALTX

American Embassy Commercial Section
United Bank Building
Flat No. 702
Corner of Liwa Street
and Corniche Road
Abu Dhabi, U.A.E.
Tel: 345545
Telex: 22229 AMEMBY EM

American Embassy Branch Office—
Dubai Commercial Section
Dubai International Trade Center
P.O. Box 9343
Dubai, U.A.E.
Tel: 471115
Telex: 98346031 BACCUS EM

Embassy of the United Arab Emirates
Commercial Section
600 New Hampshire Avenue, NW.
Suite 740
Washington, DC 20037
Tel: (202) 338-6500

United Kingdom

American Embassy Commercial Section
24/31 Grosvenor Square
London W. 1A 1AE, England
Box 40
FPO New York 09510
Tel: (01) 499-9000
Telex: 266777

American Chamber of Commerce
in the United Kingdom

c/o The Chase Manhattan Bank, NA
Woolgate HSE
Coleman Street
London EC2P 2HD, United Kingdom
Tel: 01-726-5000
Telex: 8954681 CMBG

Embassy of Great Britain
Commercial Section
3100 Massachusetts Avenue, NW.
Washington, DC 20008
Tel: (202) 462-1340
Telex: 892384 WSH
892380 WSH

Venezuela

American Embassy Commercial Section
Avenida Francisco de Miranda and
Avenida Principal de la Floresta
P.O. Box 62291
Caracas 1060 A, Venezuela
APO Miami 34037
Tel: 284-7111/6111
Telex: 25501 AMEMB VE

American Chamber of Commerce
in Venezuela
Apartado 5991
Caracas 1010-A, Venezuela
Tel: 241-0882, 241-4705
Telex: 25214

Embassy of Venezuela Commercial Section
2445 Massachusetts Avenue, NW.
Washington, DC 20015
Tel: (202) 797-3800

APPENDIX F: ORGANIZATIONS OF INTEREST

ASEAN-U.S. Business Council
(U.S. Section)
Chamber of Commerce
of the United States
International Division

1615 H Street, NW.
Washington, DC 20062
Telephone: (202) 463-5486

Academy of International Business
World Trade Education Center
Cleveland State University
Cleveland, OH 44115
Telephone: (216) 687-3733

Advisory Council on Japan-
 U.S. Economic Relations (U.S. Section)
Chamber of Commerce of the United States
International Division
1615 H Street, NW.
Washington, DC 20062
Telephone: (202) 463-5489

Affiliated Advertising Agencies
 International
World Headquarters
1393 East Iliff Avenue
Aurora, CO 80014
Telephone: (303) 750-1231

American Arbitration Association
140 West 51st Street
New York, NY 10020
Telephone: (212) 484-4000

American Association of Exporters
 and Importers
30th Floor, 11 West 42nd Street
New York, NY 10036
Telephone: (212) 944-2230

American Enterprise Institute
 for Public Policy Research
1150 17th Street, NW., Suite 1200
Washington, DC 20036
Telephone: (202) 862-5800

American Importers Association
11 West 42nd Street
New York, NY 10036
Telephone: (212) 944-2230

American Institute of Marine Underwriters
14 Wall Street, 21st Floor
New York, NY 10005
Telephone: (212) 233-0550

American Management Association
440 1st Street, NW.
Washington, DC 20001
Telephone: (202) 347-3092

American National Metric Council
1010 Vermont Avenue, NW.
Washington, DC 20005
Telephone: (202) 628-5757

American Society of
 International Executives
1777 Walton, Suite 419
Blue Bell, PA 19422
Telephone: (215) 643-3040

American Society of International Law
2223 Massachusetts Avenue, NW.
Washington, DC 20008
Telephone: (202) 265-4313

Bankers Association for Foreign Trade
1101 16th Street, NW., Suite 501
Washington, DC 20036
Telephone: (202) 833-3060

Brazil-U.S. Business Council (U.S. Section)
Chamber of Commerce of the United States
International Division
1615 H Street, NW.
Washington, DC 20062
Telephone: (202) 463-5485

Brookings Institution (The)
1775 Massachusetts Avenue, NW.
Washington, DC 20036
Telephone: (202) 797-6000

Bulgarian-U.S. Economic Council
 (U.S. Section)
Chamber of Commerce of
 the United States
International Division
1615 H Street, NW.
Washington, DC 20062
Telephone: (202) 463-5482

Caribbean Central American Action
1333 New Hampshire Avenue, NW.
Washington, DC 20036
Telephone: (202) 466-7464

Caribbean Council
2016 O Street, NW.
Washington, DC 20036
Telephone: (202) 775-1136

Chamber of Commerce
of the United States
1615 H Street, NW.
Washington, DC 20062
Telephone: (202) 659-6000

Coalition for Employment
Through Exports, Inc.
1801 K Street, NW. 9th Floor
Washington, DC 20006
Telephone: (202) 296-6107

Committee for Economic Development
1700 K Street, NW.
Washington, DC 20006
Telephone: (202) 296-5860

Committee on Canada-United States
Relations (U.S. Section)
Chamber of Commerce
of the United States
International Division
1615 H Street, NW.
Washington, DC 20062
Telephone: (202) 463-5488

Conference Board (The)
845 Third Avenue
New York, NY 10022
Telephone: (212) 759-0900

Council of the Americas
680 Park Avenue
New York, NY 10021
Telephone: (212) 628-3200

Council on Foreign Relations, Inc.
58 East 68th Street
New York, NY 10021
Telephone: (212) 734-0400

Customs and International Trade
Bar Association
c/o 40 Siegel Mandell and Davidson
1 Whitehall Street
New York, NY 10004
Telephone: (212) 425-0060

Czechoslovak-U.S. Economic Council
(U.S. Section)
Chamber of Commerce of the United States
International Division
1615 H Street, NW.
Washington, DC 20062
Telephone: (202) 463-5482

Egypt-U.S. Business Council (U.S. Section)
Chamber of Commerce
of the United States
International Division
1615 H Street, NW.
Washington, DC 20062
Telephone: (202) 463-5487

Emergency Committee for American Trade
1211 Connecticut Avenue, Suite 801
Washington, DC 20036
Telephone: (202) 659-5147

Foreign Credit Interchange
Bureau—National Assoc. of
Credit Managers
475 Park Avenue South
New York, NY 10016
Telephone: (212) 578-4410

Foreign Policy Association
205 Lexington Avenue
New York, NY 10016
Telephone: (212) 481-8450

Fund for Multi-National
Management Education (FMME)
680 Park Avenue
New York, NY 10021
Telephone: (212) 535-9386

Hungarian-U.S. Economic Council
(U.S. Section)
Chamber of Commerce
of the United States
International Division
1615 H Street, NW.
Washington, DC 20062
Telephone: (202) 463-5482

Ibero American Chamber of Commerce
2100 M Street, NW., Suite 607
Washington, DC 20037
Telephone: (202) 296-0335

India-U.S. Business Council
(U.S. Section)
Chamber of Commerce of the United States
International Division
1615 H Street, NW.
Washington, DC 20062
Telephone: (202) 463-5492

Institute for International Development
354 Maple Avenue West
Vienna, VA 22108
Telephone: (703) 281-5040

International Advertising Association
475 Fifth Avenue
New York, NY 10077
Telephone: (212) 684-1583

International Airforwarders and Agents
Association
Box 627
Rockville Center, NY 11571
Telephone: (516) 536-6229

International Bank for Reconstruction
and Development
1818 H Street, NW.
Washington, DC 20006
Telephone: (202) 477-1234

International Cargo Gear Bureau
17 Battery Place
New York, NY 10004
Telephone: (212) 425-2750

International Economic Policy Association
1625 Eye Street, NW.
Washington, DC 20006
Telephone: (202) 331-1974

International Executives Association, Inc.
114 East 32nd Street
New York, NY 10016
Telephone: (212) 683-9755

International Finance Corporation
1818 H Street, NW.
Washington, DC 20433
Telephone: (202) 477-1234

International Insurance Advisory Council
(U.S. Section)

Chamber of Commerce of the
United States
International Division
1615 H Street, NW.
Washington, DC 20062
Telephone: (202) 463-5480

International Trade Council
750 13th Street, SE.
Washington, DC 20003
Telephone: (202) 547-1727

Israel-U.S. Business Council
(U.S. Section)
Chamber of Commerce of the
United States
International Division
1615 H Street, NW.
Washington, DC 20062
Telephone: (202) 463-5478

National Association of Export
Management Companies, Inc.
200 Madison Ave.
New York, NY 10016
Telephone: (212) 561-2025

National Association of Manufacturers
1776 F Street, NW.
Washington, DC 20006
Telephone: (202) 626-3700

National Association of State
Development Agencies
Hall of State, Suite 345
444 North Capitol, NW.
Washington, DC 20001
Telephone: (202) 624-5411

National Committee on International
Trade Documentation (The)
350 Broadway
New York, NY 10013
Telephone: (212) 925-1400

National Council for U.S.
China Trade (The)
Suite 350
1050 17th Street, NW.
Washington, DC 20036
Telephone: (202) 429-0340

National Custom Brokers and
  Forwarders Association of America
One World Trade Center, Suite 1109
New York, NY 10048
Telephone: (212) 432-0050

National Export Traffic League
234 Fifth Avenue
New York, NY 10001
Telephone: (212) 697-5895

National Foreign Trade Council
11 West 42nd Street, 30th Floor
New York, NY 10036
Telephone: (212) 944-2230

National Industrial Council
1776 F Street, NW.
Washington, DC 20006
Telephone: (202) 626-3853

Nigeria-U.S. Economic Council
  (U.S. Section)
Chamber of Commerce of the
  United States
International Division
1615 H Street, NW.
Washington, DC 20062
Telephone: (202) 463-5734

Organization of American States
19th & Constitution Avenue, NW.
Washington, DC 20006
Telephone: (202) 789-3000

Overseas Development Council
1717 Massachusetts Avenue, NW.
Suite 501
Washington, DC 20036
Telephone: (202) 234-8701

Pan American Development Fund
1889 F Street, NW.
Washington, DC 20006
Telephone: (202) 789-3969

Partners of the Americas
1424 K Street, NW.
Washington, DC 20005
Telephone: (202) 628-3300

Partnership for Productivity International
2441 18th Street, NW.
Washington, DC 20009
Telephone: (202) 234-0340

Polish-U.S. Economic Council
  (U.S. Section)
Chamber of Commerce of the
  United States
International Division
1615 H Street, NW.
Washington, DC 20062
Telephone: (202) 463-5482

Private Export Funding Corporation
280 Park Avenue
New York, NY 10017
Telephone: (202) 557-3100

Romanian-U.S. Economic Council
  (U.S. Section)
Chamber of Commerce
  of the United States
International Division
1615 H Street, NW.
Washington, DC 20062
Telephone: (202) 463-5482

Sudan-U.S. Business Council
  (U.S. Section)
Chamber of Commerce of the
  United States
International Division
1615 H Street, NW.
Washington, DC 20062
Telephone: (202) 463-5487

Trade Relations Council of the United
  States, Inc.
1001 Connecticut Avenue, NW.
Room 901
Washington, DC 20036
Telephone: (202) 785-4194

The U.S.-U.S.S.R.
  Trade and Economic Council
805 3rd Avenue, 14th Floor
New York, NY 10022
Telephone: (202) 644-4550

The U.S.-Yugoslav Economic
Council, Inc.
1511 K Street, NW., Suite 431
Washington, DC 20005
Telephone: (202) 737-9652

The U.S.A.-Republic of
China Economic Council
200 Main Street
Crystal Lake, IL 60014
Telephone: (815) 459-5875

United States of America Business
and Industry Advisory Committee
1212 Avenue of the Americas
New York, NY 10036
Telephone: (212) 354-4480

Washington Agribusiness
Promotion Council
14th & Independence Avenue
Room 3120
Auditors Building
Washington, DC 20250
Telephone: (202) 382-8006

World Trade Institute
1 World Trade Center 55 West
New York, NY 10048
Telephone: (212) 466-4044

APPENDIX G: FURTHER
READING/BIBLIOGRAPHY*

1. Market identification and assessment

Addresses to AID Missions Overseas, Office of Small and Disadvantaged Business Utilization/Minority Business Center, Agency for International Development, Washington, DC 20523. Free.

AID Commodity Eligibility Listing, Office of Small and Disadvantaged Business Utilization/

Minority Resource Center, Agency for International Development, Washington, DC 20523, 1984 revised. This document lists groups of commodities, presents the Agency for International Development (AID) commodity eligibility list, gives eligibility requirements for certain commodities and describes commodities that are not eligible for financing by the agency. Free.

AID Regulation 1, Office of Small and Disadvantaged Business Utilization/Minority Resource Center, Agency for International Development, Washington, DC 20523. This tells what transactions are eligible for financing by the Agency for International Development (AID), and the responsibilities of importers, as well as the bid procedures. Free.

AID Financed Export Opportunities, Office of Small and Disadvantaged Business Utilization/Minority Resource Center, Agency for International Development, Washington, DC 20523. These are fact sheets also referred to as "Small Business Circulars." They present procurement data about proposed foreign purchases. Free.

American Bulletin of International Technology Transfer, International Advancement, P.O. Box 75537, Los Angeles, CA 90057. Bimonthly. This is a comprehensive listing of product and service opportunities offered and wanted for licensing and joint ventures agreements in the United States and overseas. $72 per year.

Annual Worldwide Industry Reviews (AWIR), Export Promotion Services, U.S. Department of Commerce, P.O. Box 14207, Washington, DC 20044; tel: (202) 377-2432. These reports provide a combination of country by country market assessments, export trends, and a 5-year statistical table of U.S. exports for a single industry integrated into one report. They quickly show an industry's performance for the most recent year in most countries.

*Source: U.S. Department of Commerce

Each report covers 8 to 18 countries. A single report is $200; two reports within the same industry are $350; and three reports within the same industry are $500.

Big Business Blunders: Mistakes in Multinational Marketing, 1982, David A. Ricks, Dow Jones-Irwin, Homewood, IL 60430. 200 pp. $13.95.

Business America, International Trade Administration, U.S. Department of Commerce. This magazine is the principal Commerce Department publication for presenting domestic and international business news and news of the application of technology to business and industrial problems. Available through the Superintendent of Documents, Government Printing Office, Washington, DC 20402. Annual subscription, $57.

Catalogo de Publicaciones de la OPS, Pan American Health Organization/World Health Organization, 525 23rd Street, NW., Washington, DC 20037. A free guide of publications, many of which are in English. This catalog is published in Spanish.

Country Market Surveys (CMS), Export Promotion Services, U.S. Department of Commerce, P.O. Box 14207, Washington, DC 20044; tel: (202) 377-2432. This report series offers short summaries of International Market Research (IMR) geared to the needs of the busy executive. They highlight market size, trends and prospects in an easy-to-read format. $10 per copy or $9 per copy for six or more.

Country Trade Statistics (CTS), Export Promotion Services, U.S. Department of Commerce, P.O. Box 14207, Washington, DC 20044; tel: (202) 377-2432. This is a set of four key tables that indicate which U.S. products are in the greatest demand, in a specific country over the most recent five-year period. They indicate which U.S. industries look best for export to a particular country and the export performance of single industries. Tables highlight the top U.S. exports, those with the largest market share, the fastest growing, and those

which are the primary U.S. market. The CTS is $25 for the first country, and $10 for each additional country up to 25.

Custom Statistical Service, Export Promotion Services, U.S. Department of Commerce, P.O. Box 14207, Washington, DC 20044; tel: (202) 377-2432. Individually tailored tables of U.S. exports or imports. The custom service provides data for specific products or countries of interest, or for ones which may not appear in the standard ESP country and product rankings for a chosen industry. With Custom Statistics one can also obtain data in other formats such as quantity, unit quantity, unit value and percentages. Custom orders are priced by the number of products, countries, or other data desired, and range from $50 to $500.

Developments in International Trade Policy, International Monetary Fund, Publications Unit, 700 19th Street, NW., Washington, DC 20431. This paper focuses on the main current issues in trade policies of the major trading nations. $5.

Direction of Trade Statistics, International Monetary Fund, Publications Unit, 700 19th Street, NW., Washington, DC 20431. This monthly publication provides data on the country and area distribution of countries' exports and imports as reported by themselves or their partners. A yearbook is published annually which gives seven years of data for 157 countries and two sets of world and area summaries. $36 for 12 monthly issues, including the yearbook. Single monthly issue is $14, the yearbook is $10.

Directory of Leading U.S. Export Management Companies, 1984, Bergamo Book Co., 15 Ketchum Street, Westport, CT 06881. $37.50.

Economic and Social Survey for Asia and the Pacific, UNIPUB, P.O. Box 1222, Ann Arbor, MI 48106; tel: (800) 521-8110. This publication analyzes recent economic and social developments in the region in the context of current trends. It examines agriculture, food, industry, transport, public finance, wages and prices, and external trade sectors. $19.

Element of Export Marketing, John Stapleton, 1984, Woodhead-Faulkner, Dover, NH, $11.25.

Entry Strategies for Foreign Markets—From Domestic to International Business, Franklin R. Root, American Management Association, 1977, 51 pp., $10.

EXIM Bank Information Kit, Public Affairs Office, Export-Import Bank of the United States, 811 Vermont Avenue, NW., Washington, DC 20571. This includes the bank's annual report, which provides information on interest rates and the Foreign Credit Insurance Association.

Export Development Strategies: U.S. Promotion Policy, Michael R. Czinkota and George Tasar, Praeger, New York, NY, 1982, $27.95.

Export Directory, Foreign Agricultural Services, Department of Agriculture, 14th & Independence Avenues, SW., Room 5918-S, Washington, DC 20230. The directory describes the principal functions of the Foreign Agricultural Service and lists agricultural attaches. Free.

Export Directory: Buying Guide, biennial, Journal of Commerce, 110 Wall Street, New York, NY 10005. $225.

Export-Import Bank: Financing for American Exports—Support for American Jobs, Export-Import Bank of the United States, 1980. Free.

Export/Import Operations: A Manager's "How to" and "Why" Guide, Robert M. Franko, 1979, Professional Business Services, Inc. $35.

Export Statistics Profiles (ESP), Export Promotion Services, U.S. Department of Commerce, P.O. Box 14207, Washington, DC 20044; tel: (202) 377-2432. These tables of U.S. exports for a specific industry help identify the best export markets and analyze the industry's exports product-by-product, country-by-country over each of the last five years to date. Data

is rank-ordered by dollar value. The price is $70.00 for each ESP.

Export Strategies: Markets and Competition, Nigel Percy, 1982, Allen & Unwin, Winchester, MA 01890, $30 (cloth), $13.95 (paper).

Exporter's Encyclopedia, annual with semi-monthly updates, Dun & Bradstreet International, One Exchange Plaza, Suite 715, Jersey City, NJ 07302. This provides a comprehensive, country-by-country coverage of 220 world markets. It contains an examination of each country's communications and transportation facilities, customs and trade regulations, documentation, key contacts, and unusual conditions that may affect operations. Financing and credit abroad are also examined. $365 per year.

Exporting: A Practical Manual for Developing Export Markets and Dealing with Foreign Customs, 2nd edition, Earnst Y. Maitland, 1982, 150 pp., Self-Counsel Press, $12.50.

Exporting from the U.S.A.: How to Develop Export Markets and Cope with Foreign Customs, A. B. Marring, 1981, 114 pp., Self-Counsel Press, $12.95.

Exporting to Japan, American Chamber of Commerce in Japan, 1982, A. M. Newman. $10.

FAS Commodity Reports, U.S. Department of Agriculture, Foreign Agriculture Service, Room 5918, Washington, DC 20250; tel: (202) 477-7937. These reports provide information on foreign agricultural production in 22 commodity areas. Reports are based on information submitted by Foreign Agricultural Service (FAS) personnel overseas. The publication frequency varies with the commodity. The price is $1–$460 depending on commodity and whether the report is mailed or picked up at USDA office.

FATUS: Foreign Agricultural Trade of the United States, U.S. Department of Agriculture, Foreign Agriculture Service, Room 5918, Washington, DC 20250; tel: (202) 477-7937.

This report of trends in U.S. agricultural trade by commodity and country and of events affecting this trade is published six times a year with two supplements. The price is $19 per year.

Findex: The Directory of Market Research Reports, Studies and Surveys, FIND/SVP, The Information Clearinghouse, 500 Fifth Avenue, New York, NY 10036; tel: (212) 354-2424. Over 10,000 listings. $245.

Foreign Agriculture, U.S. Department of Agriculture, Foreign Agriculture Service, Room 5918, Washington, DC 20250; tel: (202) 477-7937. A monthly publication containing information on overseas markets and buying trends, new competitors and products, trade policy developments and overseas promotional activities. The price is $16 per year.

Foreign Agriculture Circulars, U.S. Department of Agriculture, Foreign Agriculture Service, Room 5918, Washington, DC 20250; tel: (202) 477-7937. These individual circulars report on the supply and demand for commodities around the world. Products covered include: dairy, livestock, poultry, grains, coffee, and wood products. The frequency of publication varies with the commodity. The price is $3 to $66 depending on commodity.

Foreign Commerce Handbook, Chamber of Commerce of the United States, 1615 H Street, NW., Washington, DC 20062. A publication containing organizations of assistance to U.S. exporters, as well as up-to-date published information on all important phases of international trade and investment. $10.

Foreign Economic Trends (FET), Superintendent of Documents, U.S. Government Printing Office, Washington, DC 20402. Prepared by the U.S. and Foreign Commercial Service. This presents current business and economic developments and the latest economic indications in more than 100 countries. Annual subscription, $70; single copies are available for $1 from ITA Publications Distribution, Rm. 1617D, U.S. Department of Commerce, Washington, DC 20230.

Foreign Market Entry Strategies, Franklin R. Root, 1982, AMACOM, New York, NY 10020, 304 pp. $24.95.

General Economic Problems, OECD Publications and Information Center, Suite 1207, 1750 Pennsylvania Avenue, NW., Washington, DC 20006-4582; tel: (202) 724-1859. This contains the latest monographs on: economic policies and forecasts; growth; inflation; national accounts; international trade and payments; capital markets; interest rates; taxation; and energy, industrial and agricultural policies. $144.25.

Glossary of International Terms, International Trade Institute, Inc., 5055 N. Main Street, Dayton, OH 45415; tel: (800) 543-2453. 68 pp. $17.50.

A Guide to Export Marketing, International Trade Institute, Inc., 5055 North Main Street, Suite 270, Dayton, OH 45415; tel: (800) 453-2453. $50.

Handbook of International Statistics, UNIPUB, P.O. Box 1222, Ann Arbor, MI 48106; tel: (800) 521-8110. The handbook examines structural trends in 70 developing and developed countries, including: changes in the pattern of consumption for specific commodities; long-term patterns of growth; and the export performance of key industries. $22.

Highlights of U.S. Import and Export Trade, Superintendent of Documents, U.S. Government Printing Office, Washington, DC 20402. Statistical book of U.S. imports and exports. Compiled monthly by the Bureau of the Census. $41 per year; single copies, $4.50.

How to Build an Export Business: An International Marketing Guide for Minority-Owned Businesses, Superintendent of Documents, U.S. Government Printing Office, Washington, DC 20402. $10.

International Development, OECD Publications and Information Center, Suite 1207, 1750 Pennsylvania Avenue, NW., Washington, DC 20006-4582; tele: (202) 724-1857. This contains the latest monographs on: financial resources and aid policies, general problems of development, industrialization, transfer of technology, rural development, employment, human resources, immigration, and demography. $173.

International Financial Statistics, International Monetary Fund, Publications Unit, 700 19th Street, NW., Washington, DC 20431. This monthly publication is a standard source of international statistics on all aspects of international and domestic finance. It reports, for most countries of the world, current data needed in the analysis of problems of international payments and of inflation and deflation, i.e., data on exchange rates, international liquidity, money and banking, international transactions, prices, production, government finance, interest rates, and other items. $10 per issue, or $100 per year, including a yearbook and two supplement series.

International Market Research (IMR) Reports, Export Promotion Services, U.S. Department of Commerce, P.O. Box 14207, Washington, DC 20044; tel: (202) 377-2432. This is an in-depth industry sector analysis for those who want the complete data for one industry in one country. A report includes information such as behavior characteristics, trade barriers, market share figures, end user analysis, and trade contacts. $50 to $250.

International Market Information (IMI), Export Promotion Services, U.S. Department of Commerce, P.O. Box 14207, Washington, DC 20044; tel: (202) 377-2432. These are special "bulletins" that point out unique market situations and new opportunities to U.S. exporters in specific markets. $15.00 to $100.

International Marketing, 5th edition, 1983, Phillip R. Cateora, Irwin, Homewood, IL 60430. $29.95.

International Marketing, Raul Kahler, 1983, Southwestern Publishing Co., Cincinnati, OH 45227. 426 pp.

International Marketing, 3rd edition, Vern Terpstra, 1983, Dryden Press, Hinsdale, IL 60521. 624 pp., $32.95.

International Marketing, Revised edition, Hans Thorelli & Helmut Becker, eds., 1980, Pergamon Press, Elmsford, NY 10523. 400 pp., $14.25.

International Marketing, 2nd edition, 1981, L. S. Walsh, International Ideas, Philadelphia, PA 19103. $15.95.

International Marketing: An Annotated Bibliography, 1983, S. T. Cavusgil & John R. Nevin, eds., American Marketing Association. 139 pp., $8.

International Marketing Handbook, 1985, 3 vols., Frank S. Bair, ed., Gale Research Co., Detroit, MI 48226. 3,637 pp., $200.

International Marketing Research, 1983, Susan P. Douglas & C. Samuel Craig, Prentice-Hall, Englewood Cliffs, NJ 07632. 384 pp., $27.95.

International Monetary Fund: Publications Catalog, International Monetary Fund, Publications Unit, 700 19th Street, NW., Washington, DC 20431. Free.

International Trade Operations . . . A Managerial Approach, R. Duane Hall, Unz & Co., 190 Baldwin Ave., Jersey City, NJ 07303. $42.50.

Local Chambers of Commerce Which Maintain Foreign Trade Services, 1983. International Division, Chamber of Commerce of the United States, 1615 H Street, NW., Washington, DC 20062. This is a list of chambers of commerce that have programs to aid exporters. Free.

Market Shares Reports, National Technical Information Services, U.S. Department of Commerce, Box 1553, Springfield, VA 22161. These are reports for over 88 countries. They provide basic data needed by exporters to evaluate overall trends in the size of markets for manufacturers. They also: measure changes in the import demand for specific products; compare the competitive position of U.S. and foreign exporters; select distribution centers for U.S. products abroad; and identify existing and potential markets for U.S. components, parts, and accessories.

Marketing Aspects of International Business, 1983, Gerald M. Hampton & Aart Van Gent, Klewer-Nijhoff Publishing, Bingham, MA., $39.50.

Marketing High-Technology, William L. Shanklin & John K. Ryans, Jr., DC Heath & Co., 125 Spring Street, Lexington, MA 02173. $24.

Marketing in Europe, Economic Intelligence Unit, Ltd., 10 Rockefeller Plaza, New York, NY 10020, monthly. This journal provides detailed analysis of the European market for consumer goods. The issues are published in three subject groups: food, drink, and tobacco; clothing, furniture, and consumer goods; and chemists' goods such as pharmaceuticals and toiletries. $380 for three groups per year.

Marketing in the Third World, Erdener Kaynak, Praeger, New York, NY 10175. 302 pp., $29.95.

Metric Laws and Practices in International Trade—Handbook for U.S. Exporters, U.S. Government Printing Office, Washington, DC 20402. 1982, 113 pp., $4.75.

Monthly World Crop Production, U.S. Department of Agriculture, Foreign Agriculture Service, Room 5918, Washington, DC 20250; tel: (202) 477-7937. This report provides estimates on the projection of wheat, rice, coarse grains, oilseeds, and cotton in selected regions and countries around the world.

The Multinational Marketing and Employment Directory, 8th edition, World Trade Academy Press, Inc., 50 East 42nd Street, New York, NY 10017, 1982, two volumes. This directory lists more than 7,500 American corporations operating in the United States and overseas. The directory is recognized as an outstanding marketing source for products, skills and services in the United States and abroad. It is of particular value to manufacturers, distributors, international traders, investors, bankers, advertising agencies and libraries. It is also helpful for placement bureaus, executive recruiters, direct mail marketers, and technical and management consultants. The specialized arrangement of the information expedites sales in domestic and foreign markets. $90.

Multinational Marketing Management, 3rd edition, 1984, Warren J. Keegan, Prentice-Hall, Englewood Cliffs, NJ 07632. 720 pp., $31.95.

OECD Publications, OECD Publications and Information Center, Suite 1207, 1750 Pennsylvania Avenue, NW., Washington, DC 20006-4582; tel: (202) 724-4582. Free.

Outlook for U.S. Agricultural Exports, U.S. Department of Agriculture, Foreign Agriculture Service, Room 5918, Washington, DC 20250; tel: (202) 477-7937. This report analyzes current developments and forecasts U.S. farm exports in coming months by commodity and region. Country and regional highlights discuss the reasons why sales of major commodities are likely to rise or fall in those areas. The price is $7 per year.

Overseas Business Reports (OBR), Superintendent of Documents, U.S. Government Printing Office, Washington, DC 20402. These reports are prepared by the country specialists in the International Trade Administration (ITA). They include current marketing information, trade forecasts, statistics, regulations, and marketing profiles. Annual subscription, $26. Single copies are available from ITA Publications, Rm. 1617D, U.S. Department of Commerce, Washington, DC 20230.

Product/Country Market Profiles, Export Promotion Services, U.S. Department of Commerce, P.O. Box 14702, Washington, DC 20044; tel: (202) 377-2432. These products are tailor-made, single product/multi-country;

or single country/multi-product reports. They include trade contacts, specific opportunities, and statistical analyses. $300 to $500.

Profitable Export Marketing: A Strategy for U.S. Business, Maria Ortiz-Buonafina, Prentice-Hall, Englewood Cliffs, NJ 07632. $9.95.

Reference Book for World Traders, Annual, Croner Publications, Inc., 211 Jamaica Avenue, Queens Village, NY 11428. A loose-leaf reference book for traders. Gives information about export documentation, steamship lines and airlines, free trade zones, credit and similar matters. Supplemented monthly.

Source Book . . . The "How to" Guide for Exporters and Importers, Unz & Co., 190 Baldwin Avenue, Jersey City, NJ 07036.

Trade and Development Report, UNIPUB, P.O. Box 1222, Ann Arbor, MI 48106; tel: (800) 521-8110. This report reviews current economic issues and longer run development in international trade. $15.00.

Trade Directories of the World, Annual, Croner Publications, Inc., 211 Jamaica Avenue, Queens Village, NY 11428. $59.95 plus supplements.

Trends in World Production and Trade, UNIPUB, P.O. Box 1222, Ann Arbor, MI 48106; tel: (800) 521-8110. This report discusses the structural change in world output, industrial growth patterns since 1960, changes in the pattern of agricultural output, and changes in patterns of trade in goods and services. Product groups and commodity groups are defined according to SITC criteria. $6.

United Nations Publications, United Nations and Information Center, 1889 F Street, NW., Washington, DC 20006. Free.

U.S. Export Sales. U.S. Department of Agriculture, Foreign Agriculture Service, Room 5918, Washington, DC 20250; tel: (202) 477-7937. A weekly report of agricultural export sales based on reports provided by

private exporters. There is no cost for this publication.

U.S. Export Weekly—International Trade Reporter, Bureau of National Affairs, Inc. $352 per year.

U.S. Farmers Export Arm, U.S. Department of Agriculture, Foreign Agricultural Service, Room 5918, Washington, DC 20250, 1980. Free.

Weekly Roundup of World Production and Trade, U.S. Department of Agriculture, Foreign Agriculture Service, Room 5918, Washington, DC 20250; tel: (202) 477-7937. This publication provides a summary of the week's important events in agricultural foreign trade and world production. Free.

World Agriculture, U.S. Department of Agriculture, Foreign Agriculture Service, Room 5918, Washington, DC 20250; tel: (202) 477-7937. Provides production information, data and analyses by commodity and country, along with a review of recent economic conditions and changes in food and trade policies. Price: $9 per year.

World Agriculture Regional Supplements, U.S. Department of Agriculture, Foreign Agriculture Service, Room 5918, Washington, DC 20250; tel: (202) 477-7937. Provides a look by region at agricultural developments during the previous year and the outlook for the year ahead. Reports are published on North America/Oceania, Latin America, Eastern Europe, Western Europe, U.S.S.R., Middle East and North Africa, Subsaharan Africa, East Asia, China, South Asia, and Southeast Asia. Price: $18 per year.

The World Bank Catalog of Publications, World Bank Publications, P.O. Box 37525, Washington, DC 20013. Free.

World Economic Outlook: A Survey by the Staff of the International Monetary Fund, International Monetary Fund, Publications Unit, 700 19th Street, NW., Washington, DC 20431. This report provides a comprehensive picture of the international situation and prospects.

It highlights the imbalances that persist in the world economy and their effects on inflation, unemployment, real rates of interest and exchange rates. Published yearly. $8.

World Economic Survey, UNIPUB, P.O. Box 1222, Ann Arbor, MI 48106; tel: (800) 521-8110. This publication assesses the world economy. It provides an overview of developments in global economics for the past year and provides an outlook for the future. $12.

Yearbook of International Trade Statistics, UNIPUB, P.O. Box 1222, Ann Arbor, MI 48106; tel: (800) 521-8110. This yearbook offers international coverage of foreign trade statistics. Tables are provided for overall trade by regions and countries. Vol. I: Trade by Commodity. Vol II: Commodity Matrix Tables. Both volumes $80.

2. Selling & sales contacts

American Export Register, Thomas Publishing Co., 1 Penn Plaza, 250 34th Street, New York, NY 10010, 1984. A listing of more than 25,000 firms, this book is designed for persons searching for U.S. suppliers, for foreign manufacturers seeking U.S. buyers or representatives for their products. It contains product lists in four languages, an advertiser's index, information about and a list of U.S. Chambers of Commerce abroad, and a list of banks with international services and shipping, financing, and insurance information. $112.

Background Notes, Superintendent of Documents, U.S. Government Printing Office, Washington, DC 20402. These are four to twelve page summaries on the economy, people, history, culture, and government of about 160 countries. $42 per set; binders, $3.75.

A Business Guide to the Near East and North Africa, 1981. Superintendent of Documents, U.S. Government Printing Office, Washington, DC 20402, 28 pp. This guide is designed to provide U.S. business with information on the nature of these markets, how to do business in these areas, and how the Department of Commerce can help in penetrating these markets. $4.75.

Commercial News USA (CN), Monthly export promotion magazine circulated only overseas, listing specific products and services of U.S. firms. Applications for participation in the magazine are available from the District Office of the U.S. and Foreign Commercial Service, U.S. Department of Commerce.

Directory of American Firms Operating in Foreign Countries, 10th edition, 1984, World Trade Academy Press, 50 E. 42nd Street, New York, NY 10017, 1600 pp. This directory contains the most recent data on more than 4,200 American corporations controlling and operating more than 16,500 foreign business enterprises. It lists every American firm under the country in which it has subsidiaries or branches, together with their home office branch in the United States. It also gives the names and addresses of their subsidiaries or branches, products manufactured or distributed. $150.

Export Mailing List Service (EMLS), Export Promotion Services, U.S. Department of Commerce, P.O. Box 14207, Washington, DC 20044; tel: (202) 377-2432. These are targeted mailing lists of prospective overseas customers from the Commerce Department's automated worldwide file of foreign firms. EMLs identify manufacturers, agents, retailers, service firms, government agencies and other one-to-one contacts. Information includes name and address, cable and telephone numbers, name and title of a key official, product/service interests, and additional data. $35 and up.

How to Get the Most from Overseas Exhibitions, International Trade Administration, Publications Distribution, Room 1617D, U.S. Department of Commerce, Washington, DC 20230. This eight-page booklet outlines the steps an exporter should take to participate in an overseas exhibition sponsored by the Department of Commerce. Free.

Japan: Business Obstacles and Opportunities, 1983, McKinney & Co., John Wiley, NY. $24.95.

Management of International Advertising: A Marketing Approach, 1984, Dean M. Peeples & John K. Ryans. Allyn & Bacon, Boston, MA 02159. 600 pp., $48.

Service Industries and Economic Development: Case Studies in Technology Transfer, Praeger Publishers, New York, NY 10175, 1984. 190 pp., $24.95.

Top Bulletin, Export Promotion Services, U.S. Department of Commerce, P.O. Box 14207, Washington, DC 20044; tel: (202) 377-2432. A weekly publication of trade opportunities received each week from overseas embassies and consulates. $175 per year. Also available on computer tape.

Trade Lists, Export Promotion Services, U.S. Department of Commerce, P.O. Box 14207, Washington, DC 20044; tel: (202) 377-2432. Preprinted trade lists are comprehensive directories listing all the companies in a country across all product sectors, or all the companies in a single industry across all countries. Trade lists are priced from $12 to $40, depending on the age of the publication.

World Traders Data Reports (WTDRs), Export Promotion Services, U.S. Department of Commerce, P.O. Box 14207, Washington, DC 20044; tel: (202) 377-2432. This service provides background reports on individual foreign firms. WTDRs are designed to help U.S. firms evaluate potential foreign customers before making a business commitment. $75 per report.

3. Financing exports

Chase World Guide for Exporters, Export Credit Reports, Chase World Information Corporation, One World Trade Center, Suite 4533, New York, NY 10048. The **Guide,** covering 180 countries, contains current export financing methods, collection experiences and charges, foreign import and exchange regula-

tions and related subjects. Supplementary bulletins keep the guide up to date throughout the year. The **Reports,** issued quarterly, specify credit terms granted for shipment to all the principal world markets. The reports show the credit terms offered by the industry groups as a whole, thereby enabling the reader to determine whether his or her terms are more liberal or conservative than the average for specific commodity groups. Annual subscription for both the **Guide** and **Reports,** $345.

Commercial Export Financing: An Assist to Farm Products Sales, U.S. Department of Agriculture, Foreign Agricultural Service, Room 5918, Washington, DC 20250, 1980, brochure. Free.

Export-Import Financing—A Practical Guide, Gerhart W. Schneider, Ronald Press, 1974. This book presents details of foreign trade financing and services available for making international payments. $59.95.

FCIB International Bulletin, FCIB-NACM Corp., 475 Park Avenue South, New York, NY 10016, twice monthly. The bulletin presents export information and review of conditions and regulations in overseas markets. $175 per year.

Financing and Insuring Exports: A User's Guide to Eximbank and FCIA Programs, Export-Import Bank of the United States, User's Guide, 811 Vermont Avenue, NW., Washington, DC 20571. A 350-page guide which covers Eximbank's working capital guarantees, credit risk protection (guarantees and insurance), medium-term and long-term lending programs. Includes free updates during calendar year in which the guide is purchased. $50 (plus $5 postage and handling).

Financial Institutions and Markets in the Far East, Morgan Guarantee Trust Company of New York, 23 Wall Street, New York, NY 10015. The book discusses export letters of credit, drafts, and other methods of payment and regulations of exports and imports.

A Guide to Checking International Credit, International Trade Institute, Inc., 5055 North Main Street, Suite 270, Dayton, OH 45415.

A Guide to Financing Exports, U.S. and Foreign Commercial Service, International Trade Administration Publications Distribution, Room 1617D, U.S. Department of Commerce, Washington, DC 20230, 1985. Brochure, 40 pp. Free.

A Guide to Understanding Drafts, International Trade Institute, Inc., 5055 N. Main Street, Dayton, OH 45415; tel: (800) 543-2455, 64 pp. $17.50.

A Guide to Understanding Letters of Credit, International Trade Institute, Inc., 5055 N. Main Street, Dayton, OH 45415, 138 pp. $34.50.

A Handbook on Financing U.S. Exports, Machinery and Allied Products Institute, 1200 18th Street, NW., Washington, DC 20036. $20.

Official U.S. and International Financing Institutions: A Guide for Exporters and Investors, International Trade Administration, U.S. Department of Commerce. Available from the Superintendent of Documents, U.S. Government Printing Office, Washington, DC 20402. $2.75.

Specifics on Commercial Letters of Credit and Bankers Acceptances, James A. Harrington, 1979, UNZ & Co., Division of Scott Printing Corp., 190 Baldwin Avenue, Jersey City, NJ 07036, 1979.

4. Laws and regulations

Customs Regulations of the United States, Superintendent of Documents, Government Printing Office, Washington, DC 20402, 1971. Reprint includes amended text in revised pages nos. 1 through 130 (includes subscription to revised pages). This contains regulations for carrying out customs, navigation and other laws administered by the Bureau of Customs.

Distribution License, 1985 Office of Export Administration, Room 1620, U.S. Department of Commerce, Washington, DC 20230. Free.

Export Administration Regulations, Superintendent of Documents, Government Printing Office, Washington, DC 20402. Covers U.S. export control regulations and policies, with instructions, interpretations and explanatory material. Last revised Oct. 1, 1984. $65 plus supplements.

Export Marketing of Capital Goods to the Socialist Countries of Eastern Europe, 1978, M. R. Hill, Gower Publishing Company, 200 pp. $50.75.

Manual for the Handling of Applications for Patents, Designs and Trademarks Throughout the World, Ocrooibureau Los En Stigter B. V., Amsterdam, the Netherlands.

Summary of U.S. Export Regulations, 1985, Office of Export Administration, Room 1620, Department of Commerce, Washington, DC 20230.

Technology and East-West Trade, 1983, Summarizes the major provisions of the Export Administration Act of 1979 and its implications in East-West trade, Office of Technology Assessment, U.S. Department of Commerce, Washington, DC 20230. $4.75.

5. Shipping and logistics

Export Documentation Handbook, 1984 edition, Dun & Bradstreet International, 49 Old Bloomfield Avenue, Mt. Lakes, NJ 07046. Compiled by Ruth E. Hurd, Dun's Marketing Services, 200 pp., $60.

Export-Import Traffic Management and Forwarding, 6th edition, 1979. Alfred Murr, Cornell Maritime Press, Box 456, Centerville, MD 21617, 667 pp., $22.50. This publication presents the diverse functions and varied services concerned with the entire range of ocean traffic management.

Export Shipping Manual, Indexed, looseleaf reference binder. Detailed current information on shipping and import regulations for all areas of the world. Bureau of National Affairs, 1231 25th Street, NW., Washington, DC 20037. $186 per year.

Guide to Canadian Documentation, International Trade Institute, Inc., 5055 N. Main Street, Dayton, OH 45415, 68 pp. $24.50.

Guide to Documentary Credit Operations, ICC Publishing Corporation, New York, NY 1985, 52 pp. $10.95.

Guide to Export Documentation, International Trade Institute, Inc., 5055 N. Main Street, Dayton, OH 45415, 168 pp. $44.50.

Guide to International Air Freight Shipping, International Trade Institute, 5055 N. Main Street, Dayton, OH 45415. $17.50.

Guide to International Ocean Freight Shipping, International Trade Institute, 5055 N. Main Street, Dayton, OH 45415. $34.50.

Guide to Selecting the Freight Forwarder, International Trade Institute, Inc., 5055 N. Main Street, Suite 270, Dayton, OH 45415.

Journal of Commerce Export Bulletin, 110 Wall Street, New York, NY 10005, $200 per year. This is a weekly newspaper that reports port and shipping developments. It lists products shipped from New York and ships and cargoes departing from 25 other U.S. ports. A "trade prospects" column lists merchandise offered and merchandise wanted.

Shipping Digest, Geyer-McAllister Publications, Inc., 51 Madison Avenue, New York, NY 10010. $26 per year. This is a weekly, which contains cargo sailing schedules from every U.S. port to every foreign port, as well as international air and sea commerce news.

6. Licensing

Foreign Business Practices . . . Material on Practical Aspects of Exporting, International Licensing and Investment, 1981, International Trade Administration, U.S. Department of Commerce. Available from the Superintendent of Documents, U.S. Government Printing Office, Washington, DC 20402, 124 pp. $5.50.

American Bulletin of International Technology Transfer, International Advancement, P.O. Box 75537, Los Angeles, CA 90057, $72 per year, bimonthly. This is a comprehensive listing of product and service opportunities offered and sought for licensing and joint ventures agreements in the United States and overseas.

Forms and Agreements on Intellectual Property and International Licensing, 3rd edition, 1979, Leslie W. Melville, Clark Boardman Co., Ltd., New York, NY 10014, 800 pp., looseleaf. $210.

International Technology Licensing: Competition, Costs, and Negotiation, 1981, J. Farok Contractor, Lexington Books, Lexington, MA 02173. $23.95.

Investing, Licensing, and Trading Conditions Abroad, Business International Corporation, base volume with monthly updates. $964.

Licensing Guide for Developing Countries, 1978. UNIPUB, 345 Park Avenue South, New York, NY 10010. $25. This book by the World Intelligence Property Organization covers the legal aspects of industrial property licensing and technology transfer agreements. It includes discussion of the negotiation process, the scope of licensing agreements, technical services and assistance, production, trademarks, management, compensation, default, and the expiration of agreements.

Technology Licensing and Multinational Enterprises, 1979, Piero Telesio, Praeger Publishers, New York, NY 10175, 132 pp. $29.95.

INDEX

(Page numbers in *italics* indicate Case Study boxes.)